Energy in Motion

Evolution, Revolution
and the Human Condition

SALLY ADERTON

Susie
Thank you for the gift
of sharing life, family,
and school lunch &
honor you. I love you always,
Sally Aderton

Energy in Motion: Evolution, Revolution and the Human Condition
Copyright © 2017 by Sally Aderton

ISBN: Paperback: 978-0-9968469-0-5
          eBook: 978-0-9968469-1-2

Cover and interior page design by Jeff Brandenburg

Published by Intuitive Arts & Sciences
PO Box 2651
La Jolla, CA 92038
www.intuitiveartsandsciences.com
sally@intuitiveartsandsciences.com
510-908-7319

First printing: 2017

Printed in the United States of America

Oodles of Kudos

This book is dedicated to my parents Janice Ann and George Philip Aderton. You have taught me more about love than anyone, or anything, else. You showed me how to: respect each of your children to be authentically our own person; persevere through faith; create family and friendship as the center of existence; value community service as my duty to the world; be hospitality and welcome to everyone; commit to my dreams; know that enduring love is possible; adventure and discover something good in each day; travel out in the world just to see what is there; and, forgiveness is a path of peace. I will love you Mom and Dad forever!

Nothing is created in a vacuum and I am grateful for my collaborators of life. My deepest gratitude goes to my family, clients, and friends who walk the walk with me forward. Kudos go to my Siblings, Outlaws, and your Offspring, for sharing your family units, and being My Family. Kudos to my West Coast Clan for participating in 3 decades of creating life memories with this California Girl. Kudos to my Galpals & their Men & my Man-Friends—you make my life fun and never lonely. Kudos go to my Dream Group—you are wizards with bodies. Kudos go to the men who I have loved, and who have loved me. Kudos goes to Lance Ferguson & his Skywatch Astrology. Kudos to Brian Silva—a forever Earth Angel! Kudos to my clients who asked for my help in their healing—it is a privilege and honor to touch anyone from the inside, out! Kudos go to the people who shared their stories to help others. Kudos to Susan McKearnan and Kiki Judd, the first editors of *E-Motion* over 20 years ago. Kudos go to Susan Wolf for your editing in 2013, working as my assistant in the

90's. And, to Christina Vovas and Asabi Lee, who gave me "Soulwork with Sally Aderton"—you are both masters at your craft!

Kudos to David Colin Carr—you live your tagline! David you were the gentle nudge that moved a stream to the sea. Carol Anne and Moose you answered my call for a midwife with pure grace. Jeff Brandenburg, the last loop in the chain of creation, kudos and bravo! Kudos of the highest order last but oh so not the least—to Love, my religion!

In Memoriam to Gita Jahn, Artist

May 15, 1951 to December 4, 2005

With Love to Chris and Jimena Sharma, Barcelona, Spain

Nearly a decade after she left the earth, Gita came to me in a vision. On Sunday February 8, 2015 in a meditation during the 11 am church service at Grace Disciples United Methodist Church in La Salle, Il, Gita stood before me holding her beautiful painting of the Heart Chakra. She offered the painting and asked me to use it for the cover. Thank you Chris for making it so.

Gita and I met in 1994 when I moved to Santa Cruz, CA. We had a connection to New Zealand, common friends, and a spiritual life that we shared. We traded healing sessions and I considered her a friend. We had sporadic contact after I moved in 1997. Gita and I had talked over the years about using one of the paintings from her Chakra Mandala Series for the cover of this book, then called E-Motion. It was amazing—I'd forgotten our conversations, but Gita had not.

Godspeed Gita my friend, until we meet again!
Sally Aderton, Descanso, CA April 21, 2017

CONTENTS

Part One

Evolution—Intuition in Everyday Life

Part Two

Revolution—Perceiving Beyond the Apparent

Part Three

The Human Condition—Healing the 4th Dimension

The Invocation

Before I begin any work, whether with an individual or group, I set the stage with a prayer or invocation. My intention is always to serve the highest good for all. I ask that we, you the reader and I the writer, now bring our attention to the journey that we will take together. I invite you to open both your mind and your heart for they are not the same thing.

The following poem brings alive what I believe is the simple purpose of our earth experience. If my use of the word 'God' triggers negative feelings, use your word for the Great Mystery. I have heard it called The Light, The Most High, Divine Intelligence, Source, Allah, Spirit of All Life, Hu, Divine Love, Yahweh, Supreme Being, Elohim, Krishna, Almighty, All-Powerful, All-Wise, Incomparable on High, Grace, Helper, All-Glorious, Heavenly Father, Divine Mother, Ralph and Omniscient. Then there are all the words for God in languages in the world that I have not heard. For me, they are all the same in my awareness of the Holiest of Holy. They are names for the Great Mystery that I know as God. If the word 'men' triggers you, know that this is how I heard the words come through me. I ask you to look past the sexual bias to the soul song. I offer it here as a gift and blessing. May you open to the poetry that lives in each of us.

God Has Spoken to the Land

Promise has spoken to the land
*   call forth joy and I command*
that ye shall have and have again
*   the son of God*
*   through the hearts of men*

*   Plenty has spoken to the land*
*   call forth gifts and I command*
*   that ye shall have and have again*
*   the wealth of kings*
*   through the hands of men*

*   Beauty has spoken to the land*
*   call forth grace and I command*
*   that ye shall have and have again*
*   the love of queens*
*   through the eyes of men*

Spring has spoken to the land
*   call forth birth and I command*
that ye shall have and have again
*   life eternal*
*   through the body of men*

*   Summer has spoken to the land*
*   call forth growth and I command*
*   that ye shall have and have again*
*   strength and valor won*
*   through the intention of men*

*   Autumn has spoken to the land*
*   call forth harvest and I command*
*   that ye shall have and have again*
*   sustenance and splendor valued*
*   through the minds of men*

*   Winter has spoken to the land*
*   call forth death and I command*
*   that ye shall have and have again*
*   rest from the woes*
*   for the spirit of men*

God has spoken to the land
*   call forth I and I command*
*   that ye shall have and have again*
miracles and magic
*   through the presence of men!*

And so it is! And so it shall be done! Amen! Alleluia! Shanti!
Right-On! Shalom! Salaam! Namaste! May All Blessings Be!

*"Energy is neither created nor destroyed
it can only be changed from one form to another."*

1ST LAW OF THERMODYNAMICS

Introduction

This book addresses the hope of a world unified by a new understanding of consciousness. It is time to embrace what we know as spiritual truth and affirm that we have the power within us to create miracles. I see them everyday in my life, and I am no more or less deserving than the next human being. The difference is in my perspective, the matrix in which I view the world. I intend to illustrate here my reality, my understanding of the human condition, and the philosophical foundation of my career as a non-denominational spiritual teacher and healer. It is a privileged to do what I do. Sharing this wisdom, and many miraculous stories, can awaken even more people to their capacity to live in Love.

Energy in Motion is my experience that consciousness is a perpetual motion machine of energy manifesting in infinite ways, with infinite creative potential. Thus, life is energy in motion: E-Motion. I am really addressing our ideas about God and consciousness and not just a statement about emotion, how feelings affect our lives. However, I will talk a great deal about the fourth dimensional world of feelings and emotion.

We are in a time of psycho/spiritual/ecological/social/cultural transformation. We are participating in the birth of a new zeitgeist. These stories are shared as a labor coach, to help the new paradigm become our way of life. Much of the language of this book is now in the vernacular in advertising, corporate mission statements, on the mainstream network media sources, on every social media platform, and in everyday conversation. Many know the wisdom from the Bible, 'and the word was God'. We are writing the new paradigm story with every word that is expressed on these mediums and channels today.

The narrative of the journey of consciousness and the awakening to a new potential that is offered is more of a chorus than a solo. It is impossible for me to write about transforming the human condition on Earth, without telling my own story. This book is part academic, part memoir, part telling tales of others, part personal growth workshop, part inquiry, and part solution to the ills and challenges of life. I cannot separate and share a clinical text about my theories because I do not believe that objectivity is real. I am a modern day mystic telling the stories that have been gifted to me to tell you. These stories are shared to inspire something great, something unfathomable. They are shared to motivate a new social order based on love for us all.

The most simplistic way I can describe the new paradigm from which we will create our shared reality of earth is by a historical comparison metaphor. This quantum leap is akin to the shift when most of the cultures that inhabited the earth had a cosmological system founded in the belief that the earth was flat. Through time, exploration, and science that fundamental assumption changed. Indeed, the earth was really round. The round earth truth once adopted it became the basis of how people related their microcosm to the macrocosm. There was no going back to flat. The time has come to shift our paradigm again.

This book has been a creative process that spans decades of history. The first draft was completed in Sedona in March of 1994 and 65% of the text is original material. We are graced that now included are updated testimonials of the healing stories which occurred twenty years or more ago. These updates bring a richness to this book that only the vantage point of retrospect and the passage time can give.

At the conclusion of each chapter, I suggest taking time for personal reflection and integration. I give specific tasks or concepts to experience in conjunction with the topic of the chapter. These could be via a writing process, a meditation, or an interactive exercise to do with another or the world. Perhaps writing in the book itself, having a running Note on your digital device, or keeping a journal will help to document how your energy is moved as you journey through. We are exploring the relationship between our inner world, and the outer. Vision without action has no meaning. These are simple tasks that can make visceral what I propose as truth. My hope is that you fall deeper in love with yourself, your life story, the lives of others, and this universe of which we play an integral part or we would not exist at all.

Today there are many that live in the reality that we are all connected, not separate from anything though in separate bodies. Science proved this fact decades ago. Like in ancient civilizations, they believed the world was flat. We as a collective consciousness are moving on. *Energy in Motion* is a book to help us to make the leap to a world that is not just round, but unified by biology, ecology, spirituality, emotional states, consciousness, awareness, and most importantly, by Love. So Bon Voyage—enjoy the adventures in the stories told, ponder the concepts, and feel what ***Energy in Motion*** evokes in you!

Part One

Evolution—
Intuition in Everyday Life

Chapter 1

The One Mind

In this lifetime, I have had the privilege to know people from the inside out. I have worked as a healer and non-denominational spiritual teacher for over three decades. I have counseled thousands of people, lectured, and taught workshops on Intuitive Development, modern concepts of universal spirituality, and self-awareness. I say 'in this lifetime' for it accurately demonstrates, my perspective that my consciousness has been in the human experience before. I believe that the Universe knew about recycling long before there were aluminum cans, glass, newspaper, and plastic. The world is in a constant state of renewal in every moment. As humans, we are a part of that renewal through our soul's eternal life. We live in a perpetual state of change.

Through my work, I help people see the patterns of emotion and mental constructs that support their behavior, their perspective of truth, and their subsequent interpretation of experience. This work with me helps create a better understanding of their lives and the world around them. I deal with the "why" questions about often the negative frustration, anxiety, and fears or the positive blessings and magic in their life on Earth. I hear, again and again, the question "why?" evoking God, mystery, and the directing of their course for life's journey.

There are six questions on the path forward through life. No matter what our religious ideology, economic status, physical prowess, academic training, or even consciousness of personal power and the ability to manifest our dreams, we are all in a human experience of life on Earth.

1. Who am I?
2. What am I supposed to be doing?
3. How am I to do it?
4. Where am I to do it?
5. When am I going to get there?
6. Why is this happening to me?

The answers to these questions are simple with a generic response for us all:

1. A divine eternal light of Love is who we are.
2. Sharing Love to serve ourselves, and the world is what we are supposed to be doing.
3. By being our best Self, our unique original aspect of the Divine not expecting or pretending to be like anyone else is how we play our individualized role in the cosmic drama.
4. In every moment, all the time, knowing that Love is our source, our medium, our origin and our destination, we are to share it always wherever we are.
5. We have all already arrived, as the present moment is all we have.
6. There is nothing else to do but learn about Love.

By supporting others in trusting more in their intuition and knowing their Divine appointment expressed through unique talents and presence, I witness an awakening to a greater hope for ourselves, and for the world. What gives me the insight to assist others is a combination of my deep empathy, my strong faith in something greater than us all, and my courage to be no one else, but me.

It is ignorance and arrogance to believe that there is not a greater force of nature that holds the planets in the sky, and the same that created you and me. We can call that energy by many names. I listed many in the Invocation. They all refer to the same thing, the source of life. All animate and inanimate forms originate from what I like to call The Great Mystery. I believe that God is. My faith in The Great Mystery is not conditioned by my belief, or by the ritualizing of this belief. My faith is conditioned by experience.

Through my work, I meet people whom I have never met in this lifetime, who come to me for healing and help. In a matter of minutes, I can read their body, heart, mind, and soul like a book. This seemingly magical and mystical act is possible because I know there is a Universal Mind. We are not separate beings. I know this not as a philosophical or esoteric principle, but literally. With their permission, and trusting in my perceptions, I bridge the gap between our individualization, our apparent separateness, and the truth that we are of one mind. This skill is not mine alone. We all have this innate gift for us to evolve as a species. It is through this gift that we will not merely survive, but we will thrive.

Many of us yearn for a sense of purpose and to understand why we live in such perilous and chaotic times. There is a knowing that we have to change not just for ourselves, but also for generations to come. I have met few people that do not wonder why they are alive. Many of us are questioning how to survive as the human systems move further away from the natural environment to environments controlled by human innovation and manipulation.

All life exists with purpose and intention, from the smallest organism to the most evolved species plant or animal, rock or mineral. A purpose is inherent in everything from the microcosmic subatomic quark to the macrocosmic galaxies of this expanding universe. Everything we perceive and experience is a part of the Divine Plan. To know our individual purpose gives us the power to create life on earth, to be more harmonious on all levels—spiritual, mental, emotional, and physical.

If we are alive, we have the right to create our dreams. We do this by fulfilling our unique purpose. Nature and nurture work in harmony. Together they execute our destiny. It is not one or the other but both that create our life. My intention is to share ageless spiritual principles, personal stories of transformation, and tools for healing which will make a difference. My hope is to inspire us to love our own story, no matter what. If we do not like the one we are living now, I want us to remember we have the power to change it. Even with our cleverness, step-by-step guidance to help us help ourselves created the Personal Growth Industry of today, we still are longing for more. This book was written to assist manifesting as many a-ha's it can.

As we evolve as a species, we adapt to our changing environment to survive. The environment we presently inhabit is full of beauty, natural grace, creative genius, awe-inspiring art forms conveyed through words, music, movement, and materials, as well as technological innovation. These are the positive attributes, yet the negative is equally present. Our environment is also full of war, random violence, chemical addiction, murder, rape, poverty, homelessness, suicide, disease, and fear of our neighbors. I believe we must understand the Universal Mind and recognize our oneness not only to survive these conditions but also to transform them preserving all life on earth.

Paradoxically we are ungrateful guests here on the planet which hosts us, taking more than we need, wasting irreplaceable resources, and projecting our fears onto the faces of our brothers and sisters. Embracing disowned emotions, acknowledging our purpose, trusting our intuition, and realigning our value systems with love, is all we need to do to change our experience of life on earth to be better.

We have forgotten that we come into life from love. Each of us—

from a grain of sand to the brightest of stars, to the homeless person on the street, to the winner of the latest talent show or Nobel prize—is here to share the same gift: our individual radiant presence. With focused intention and attention, we have the power to create change in the universal field that is harmonious for us individually and for every other life form. Every consciousness is creating this field in every moment, but not all of us are aware of what we are doing—because in general, we do not know any better, to do any better.

More and more individuals are waking up to our spiritual reality of the universal oneness of mind. In no way is awareness of the eternal a new idea, the conversation around it, however, continues to grow more comfortable and public. The New Age opened not just a greater marketplace for Self-Help products and services—it also gave permission for us to admit that we indeed need help. Instead of being collectively ashamed of our fallibility, vulnerability, and sensitivity—we have become champions of changing ourselves. Are we there yet? No, but we are well on the way!

The collective consciousness will eventually reach critical mass. We are ready, educated or not, to change the destiny of life. If the destiny were certain death, why would we care about making a difference? Inherent within us is the quest for greatness. This quest is moving us toward the point of no return. I have watched this movement unfold throughout this lifetime. My nickname in Jr. High was Miss Maturity for a reason! As a working mystic, I have witnessed and facilitated healing for others. Because of these experiences, I am a believer.

When I started my healing practice in the 1980s, I was on the cusp of the New Age. If I were in a social or business situation introducing myself to someone I did not know told them I was a "Healer," they would look at me with total confusion and say, "You are a what?" Then by the 1990s when I would be in a similar situation, the response would be "Do you do Reiki?" By the decade of the double Os, the response was "Did you see Eckart Tolle on *Oprah*!?" The New Age went from being marginalized to mainstream because of those committed to bringing our light to the dark. The conversation is ready for another level of true revolution. It is time to take responsibility, for we are the ones we have been waiting for to create peace on Earth. We are alive right now in the Garden of Eden. Perhaps it is time to be respectful and responsible guests. I know I am. Are you?

What if in your business you knew you had a way of predicting the perfect time to call a client and negotiate a contract that would result in success, would you use it? Of course, you would use it! What if you knew which elevator was coming first when you are in such a hurry that every second mattered, would you stand in front of that door to save steps? Of course, you would! If you knew where you needed to be to meet the perfect mate, would you go there? Of course, you would go to that party or class or vacation or lunch date or be on that bus or that plane to meet that person!

We are all born with this resource. It is our intuition. It is our inner knowing. Our challenge though is that we have been raised in the western post-modern cultural mind that has enforced another ideal. We are indoctrinated to conform. We are conditioned to believe that what is true and right and correct is outside of ourselves. We participate from the moment we arrive in comparison to others, and that outside of ourselves is where truth lives.

The evolutionary leap of our species is simple. We need to listen with our hearts. We have the opportunity to bring this innate skill forward with new honor, respect, and reward. This means new rules, new assumptions, and a new reality-base for all people, regardless of language, color, race, historical tradition, education, ecological habitat, physical health, vitality, and technological proficiency. We are one world, one universal mind—and we each also have our individual presence in the whole. We are individuated, but we are all one.

Through translators, I have worked with people of many cultures. It does not hinder my ability to know them. Nor do I find their questions about life any different than those from my culture. I listen deeply to their presence. There is a common bond in humanity. This bond is where peace is created for us all.

So, what are the new rules? As Truth is timeless, perhaps they are not so new. They, however, need to be said again in a new way. Here are some to consider:

Do unto others as you would have them do unto you. **To be loved, be loving.**

To thine own self-be true. **Trust our awareness; do not give the power of defining experience to anyone else.**

Ask, and ye shall receive. **Participate in life. We are not victims of life, nor are we ever alone in life.**

Every cloud has a silver lining. **Everything exists, occurs, or has value to serve our learning about love.**

That which is above is also below. **Hierarchy is circular, not linear.**

This too shall pass. **Patience, for the moment of change, is inevitable—good or bad.**

It's the journey, not the destination. **The journey is the destination.**

Honesty is the best policy. **The truth will always reveal itself; start with truth to save time, energy and effort.**

The simpler the principle, the more it is in alignment with spiritual truth. Simplicity is the most direct way to awareness. Prayer and meditation are the only tools necessary to be spiritual. Asking for help and listening to the answer is the fastest, most efficient, direct way of being on a spiritual path. There is no one right way. There is only our personal relationship with our Creator. How we meditate or pray, do not matter in relationship to how others practice. What matters is that we do. What matters is that we ask and listen for the answers, and also that we consider who/what we are asking and the source from which the answer comes.

One of the most common concerns of clients is that they have somehow gotten off their spiritual path. It is impossible. A spiritual path is not a doctrine of a religious or cultural tradition. When we are alive, every living moment we are on our spiritual path. It is not our rituals that make us spiritual. It is our ability to be awake, aware, and most importantly, be loving. And, even we when we are not loving, those moments too are steps on our spiritual path for in its absence, is its presence.

There is a lot to choose from in philosophical ideologies, religious traditions, and, as my friend, Shiven said to me decades ago, "the New Age Supermarket," when looking for deeper meaning to our lives. Any and all of them serve our purpose when we touch the wisdom inherent in the experience, and we are transformed. The choice is a part of our individual empowerment. However, if the choices of others inhibit, judge, violate, shame, persecute, deny, humiliate, or condemn our choices, we must question their validity.

More than ever before the choices of our lives extend not just to what we eat, where we live, how we dress, what we do as a profession, who are our friends—**we are choosing what we believe**. Instead of adapting the traditions we are born into we are questioning and seeking more. The choices include the assumptions of what is real and true that come with those cultural mindsets and norms.

We are living a global niche and are unconsciously and consciously creating cultural norms based on external values. I believe as we focus on the internal values, the world culture becomes freer for everyone. We are the curators of our own reality, and yet there is the shared experience of earth. Sometimes it boggles my mind that anything gets done or accomplished considering the infinite variables! It is impossible from my perspective not to see that there is a greater mystery involved. Life is the miracle.

Chapter 1 Practicum

⛶ Contemplate the life questions presented and answer them for yourself:

1. Who am I?
2. What am I supposed to be doing?
3. How am I to do it?
4. Where am I to do it?
5. When am I going to get there?
6. Why is this happening to me

⛶ Start the 30-Day Simple Meditation Mantra Practice in Appendix I.

Chapter 2

The Ways of An Ultra-Sensitive

There have been Intuitives throughout western civilization history that we can identify, such as Aristotle, Nostradamus, Joan of Arc, Edgar Cayce, George Washington, Carl Jung, and Albert Einstein. Prophets, poets, politicians, artists and scientists—anyone with vision is an Intuitive. All of us have the ability within us to develop this awareness. Rather than call it a sixth sense, I prefer to use the term intuitive or ultra-sensitive that Marcy Calhoun uses in her book *Are You Really Too Sensitive*? What I, and many others, experience is a heightened state of normally accepted ways of perceiving: seeing, hearing, touching, smelling, and tasting. It is not accurate to call it an additional sense when it is only the amplification of what we already perceive through the normal human senses.

Each of us is gifted with our unique qualities that affirm our individuality. Some of us are brilliant mathematicians. Some of us have a green thumb and are attuned to plants. Some of us are skilled athletes able to execute agile feats with trust in our bodies. Some of us are inspiring with our use of words or colorful creativity or with our flare for drama, musical ability, and presence on stage. Each of us is capable of being trained, to learn the skills, to overcome our fears to perform these tasks. However, it is easier to utilize our natural talent. The same applies with our ultra-sensitivity.

The ways that ultra-sensitivity manifests are: clairvoyance, by seeing; clairaudience, by hearing; clairsentience, by feeling. Additionally, with clairsentience, there are people with psychic scent, who smell changes through aromas around people and places. There is also what I call "knowing sensitivity." These people don't see, don't hear, and don't feel—they just know. I believe this is the most evolved state of human consciousness because a knowing intuitive or knowing ultra-sensitive is not using the physical body, or their mind, to perceive truth. It is for them, the awareness—like God—is just present. I call it mainlining the Source. The challenge for a knowing sensitive is to trust what they know, for they have no proof. In actuality we all share this challenge, for how do we explain our perceptions?

I am often asked how do I know the information I perceive is real. This is a good question. The answer lies in the Great Mystery. There is a force greater than myself. We are each provided the information that is appropriate for us to have at that moment, no more, no less. The information I was receiving through my work when I started my practice was not less helpful than what I receive today. I am not more accurate, or intuitive, now than I was then. I am no more or less powerful than I was when I started. The difference is that I am more comfortable with the process, myself, and my faith in All-That-Is. I have experience. Confidence has been created by the repetition of these experiences over and over again. I have lived the unity of consciousness. How do I know it's real? I trust myself.

Trust is produced when we surrender our fear to embrace our faith. Trust is the turning of our will over to God's will. Trusting our perceptions is what creates the self-validation that we need as the basis of our self-esteem. Trusting our intuition, our heightened perceptions, and our knowing sensitivity can allow us to have more information to make authentic choices for our lives. We are all capable of developing these skills. When I ask audiences "How do you know what's real?" the answer is consistent, "I feel it." The answer is never "I think it." The reality is a perceptual concept, not a rational process. Though our rational investigative intellectual abilities, we ask the questions of life. It is our intuition that answers them.

My business is named *Intuitive Arts & Sciences* because I believe that we must use both sides of our brain to evolve as individuals, and therefore, as a species. Abandoning either the intellect or the intuition is reflected in the skewed values we experience today. Creation takes both the yin-mystery-creative-art and the yang-apparent-innovative-science to manifest anything in life. Through my work, I help people come to balance with the black and white illusion to experience the wholeness in shades of gray. And, every single person has innate intuitive gifts.

Clairvoyance has been the most common form of intuition or psychic experience—to see beyond the apparent. Clairvoyance can manifest as symbolic visions, dreams, or in the physical world as auras. I have seen auras since I was a child. They have always looked like heat rising off a hot pavement, waves of shimmering energy, usually gold or silver in color. Clairvoyance was not something I was trained to do. It is just how my eyes and vision detail the world around me.

As a high school freshman, I can remember my biology teacher's aura quite easily. He was the football coach, had an intense delivery of his biology lectures, and enjoyed terrorizing freshman by intimidation. There was an incentive to pay attention not to be singled out and teased. That focus allowed me to watch his aura jump as he emphatically gave his presentations. I have also seen with my eyes the auras of trees, energy rising off of lakes, and spirits or ghosts. It is often the case when I am watching performances of theater, music, or lectures that I see auras. When people are engaged in sharing their presence and talents, I am seeing the energy that they are giving.

There is no ability to measure or standardize clairvoyance other than from the eyes of the beholder. I often see into the bodies of my clients. Once during a group channeling, I saw a blocked fallopian tube on the left side of a woman who was trying to conceive a child. After the session was over, she told the entire group that the tube was indeed, blocked. She knew because of extensive medical examinations. I "see" pain that is emotional and physical. I "see" past lives on the faces of people. I "see" psychic attachments and cords of light connecting people. I see auras of individuals and groups. I "see" spirit guides, angels, and extra-terrestrials. Visual sensitivity is given a lot of creditability in our world because of our value of sight: "I'll believe it when I see it!"

Think of the spectrum of light that you learned about in science class. The diagram in the book was a gauge 3 inches long from infrared to ultraviolet light what we have been able to measure so far. If you remember, the human eye could only see a small portion, a sliver of the range. It makes sense that there is more to "see." The gauge is only an average range, so again it makes common sense to think ultra-sensitives just do not fit into the normal range. Ask any ultra-sensitive if they ever felt average, normal, or like they "fit in": they say "no."

So seeing is believing, as much as believing is seeing. We cannot have one without the other. To trust what we see is the first step on the road to enlightened consciousness. The next step is to interpret accurately what we see. Needless to say, the second step is more than a little trickier than the first step. When we open up to our awareness of our clairvoyance, we must also be willing to open to all levels of our consciousness: hearing, speaking, feeling, and knowing.

Often we equate psychic vision with auras. There have been books written on the color of auras and the stereotyping of personality based on these colors. Like astrology, it is another system to help people understand the nature of their own, intimate personal reality as they relate to others. The sight used to see these auras most often is not actually by our eyes at all, but clairvoyance or knowing sensitivity.

Since no two people are identical, even identical twins, no two ultra-sensitives are the same either. There is a common assumption for many individuals in the New Age movement when developing awareness, that guided meditations are one of the best ways. But what if you are clairsentient and don't know it? A guided visualization could be frustrating and perhaps even affirm that you are wrong or unaware. Your receiver is a different channel. It is your body, not your imagination.

Often the receiver of intuitive information is our body. The hair stands up on the back of our neck, we get goose bumps, a chill, or a warm rush, or tears spontaneously fall when someone is talking. There is the gut reaction. Our hands turn cold, we feel sick, nauseous, or have a headache. We walk into a room and are aware of the "vibes." All of these experiences are ways that we are receiving information. The key is to bring our awareness to the experience, to be present, to be mindful, to be awake. When we are paying attention, we can be good investigators.

When teaching clients to develop their intuitive gifts, there is one tool and technique that is necessary. We must be willing to ask questions, then listen to the answers. Ask it, the sensation or pain or body sense, "What do I need to know?" "Why are you present in my awareness?" "Who is the source of this communication?" "Where do I need to pay attention?" As we ask, and if we listen, we all can get the answers.

Many times the feeling or sensation we have in our bodies is not our own. Admittedly, I am a wide open ultra-sensitive. I can't tell you how many times what I feel is not mine. I am an empath. It is how I do my work. However, even though it is the talent that helps me help others, it still can be challenging. When we feel compassion in moments of deep relating to another, we are empathetic. This is the recognition of the oneness of consciousness. Intuition via empathy is the bridge of separation between someone else's body, and our own, which then allows us to feel the connection.

In my sessions with people if I am feeling something in my body it will mirror what is happening in their body. This is true even when we are in times zones that span across the globe. Though it may be the night for them, and for me day, I can feel an energy in their body. I can feel their positive and negative emotions—fear, grief, joy, guilt, relief, and anger. I can feel their pain—headaches, fatigue, stomach upset and illness. I use this information to help them with their lives. The sensation may not be identical, yet it always acts as a guide for me to serve my client more effectively. We all can pick up a lot of my information about people through our clairsentience. However we need to ask ourselves where is the sensation coming from, then listen for the answer.

Claire-audience is the ability to hear more than the apparent. We commonly refer to our intuition as 'that little voice.' Immediately if someone refers to their conscience in this manner, we know what they are referring to. Voices, words, sounds, music, lectures—come to all of us. How often do the music and lyrics of a song play in your head when there is no stereo or iPod around? When you write a note, or email, or business plan, do you hear the words being read in your consciousness as you write them? When you read a book, do you hear the voices of the characters differentiated by gender or age or ethnic, cultural identity? Think of Ludwig van Beethoven hearing complete symphonies in his head, yet he was deaf. Imagine if he had kept his claire-audience to himself?

The evolution of humanity is not just a physical adaptation to the world around us. For human beings, it is physical, emotional, mental and spiritual. To give value to the capacities of our bodies to be attuned to more that what we see, hear, touch, smell, or taste, is what is required for our growth. As change is the constant, this is a change for the good of not just one, all. In order for us to have a more compassionate world, we need to know that we all have the ability to get insight and information that can help us be more aware of what is happening.

All of us are far more sensitive than we give ourselves or others credit for being. Becoming more aware of our ultra-sensitivity is a skill that can give us a creative edge for it opens more channels of information and insight for our success. The outcome is more personal fulfillment, a deeper knowing of our self, and an opportunity for deeper intimacy with others. As we learn to listen to our intuition and acknowledge the varied expanded methods of perception, we can become more skilled at understanding to relate to the world around us.

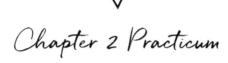

Chapter 2 Practicum

⌑ What kind of ultra-sensitivity comes naturally to you? How do you trust what you know to be true?

⌑ Share with another person an experience you have had which invited a possibility that there is something more than just your mind and five senses to perceive the world.

⌑ Ask ten people how they know what is real?

Chapter 3

Channeling as a Tool

We begin to reframe and understand our definitions of metaphysical phenomenon when we are willing to acknowledge that we can perceive beyond the apparent. Channeling is another way of learning popularized by the New Age that I must address. We are all channels. Our soul is being channeled from the infinite or universal consciousness through our physical bodies.

The bodies and minds are like radios more than most of us realize. It is possible to use our will and attention, to pick up whatever station we can with a good signal. I am one of those people who has learned to disassociate myself from my mind so that it can be a vehicle for other energies. Channeling as a medium is a practiced skill. Ester Hicks, with her relationship to her spirit guide Abraham, has made an industry out of this phenomenon. Abraham's wisdom, though, cannot come through Ester without having the use of her vocabulary and intelligence. Seth, Ramtha, Kevin McPherson, there are multiple examples over the last decades of this phenomenon. Edgar Cayce too was a channel for higher consciousness and information to serve human awareness, health, and wholeness and his information is still used today for wellness.

Often we are "channeling" and don't even realize that we are doing it. Have you ever heard yourself saying just the right thing to a friend in need? You were receiving higher guidance. Later when they come back to you thanking you for what you said, you have no recollection at all of those words most often we just dismiss it to being forgetful. That is not always the case. Where it comes from is not as important as their healing that comes from the wisdom. "Out of the blue" examples used to prove points are the same as channeling also. Always when I am giving examples in my lectures and my private sessions, or in casual conversation, I "happen" to pick visual stories that trigger emotions, ah-ha experiences, and open the awareness of others.

There is a deeper meaning of "out of the blue." This statement means the express comes out of the fifth chakra, the center of communication for our soul. I will talk more about the chakra system later in the book. No examples used to articulate a point are given without symbolic relationship to those who hear it. Begin to notice the metaphors or scenarios we use to articulate or instruct each other in communication. There will always be a deeper meaning, for there is no randomness in the Universe.

People have heard the vibrations of spirit guides in my voice during casual conversation. It is a little unnerving for them and can bring the idea of multiple personalities to mind. We all are multidimensional beings, and often we speak from the place of disassociated or split fragments of self, as in our "inner child" or our "critic" or our "Jewish mother." When this happens, however, it happens a purpose.

There is a debate whether spirit guides are other entities or just an aspect of the personality of the person channeling. The possibility that a channeler is acting out an archetype, and I mean acting as in drama as performance, is one layer of truth. However, the content of what is being said unscripted that is significant to the listener is what matters most. In my experience, I feel, see, hear, and know of another energy coming through my whole universe. When there is spontaneous channeling that happens in casual conversation, I am still aware of another energy.

Technically, if we believe we are all one consciousness, then these energies are still a part of me, so there is no debate. This idea becomes the fuel for strengthening our self-concept to know the sources of our thoughts and impressions. I questioned for a while any validity in copyrights. When you become aware of the direct communication from other levels of consciousness, the line between inspiration and genius is suspect.

The poem at the beginning of this book without a doubt was channeled. I awoke about 1:30 PM one night and grabbed a sketchpad that I kept handy. The poem came through with no editing on my part. The tone, word usage, and classical verse style are not the ways that I usually write. I have learned, however, that if it comes through our body, we have a right to own the creation. This book is coming out of my conscious teaching, the memory of experiences, intuitive knowing of what will serve you, and what I am being directed by my guidance to share. I can ethically put my name on the book, including the poem because it was my time, my insight to life, my clever crafting of words, and my effort that brought it into physical life. However, it is evident that wisdom and Truth just are. They belong to us all.

Channeling as a tool for healing and spiritual growth is effective. I have been both a witness and a participant to remarkable transformations. From 1985 until 1995, I used my body like a radio tuning into stations of other consciousnesses to be in service. I have brought through wisdom, expressions of relatives and friends of my clients who have died, other life forms like trees and dogs, highly evolved spiritual teachers, group consciousness as in the collective mind of a room full of people, and belief systems of the individual mind. We are virtually unlimited in what can be channeled. I have channeled the elements of earth, water, air, and fire within a person or the environment. I have channeled aspects of personality, past life memories, and future selves. It is only limited thinking that creates the boundaries of this human potential.

In *Seat of the Soul* by Gary Zukov, he talks about consciousness for other species and negates that they have their individual personality. I agree with him on much of his perspective on consciousness but not this point. There is the universal mind, which is fundamental in my worldview. However, I experience over and over, the individuation of animal, plant, and mineral consciousness. In my opinion, a redwood tree that lives in a California landscape for 2000 years, when the average is between 500–700 years, knows something I do not know about survival, longevity, patience, and presence. This book is meant to stimulate another perspective on the eternity of life. We do not know, nor can we, everything. A dog incarnate can be a highly evolved soul that wants to bring a gift of love to a child. A tree could be the same. We can only know though if we listen with our hearts and channeling opens up more for us to hear.

This is not anthropomorphism, the projection of human conditions or characteristics onto anything not human. This is the infinite capability of consciousness to manifest. Some of my greatest spiritual teachers have been animals with whom I have had telepathic communication. Within the form that they have chosen—horse, butterfly, or redwood tree—the soul's perspective is unique to the conditions it was born into and can be heard regardless of language. Channeling can be the medium between life on earth and off the earth, as well as between life forms.

Asking questions always brings answers. A question, even if it is not spoken, will be answered as the Universe is always listening. My job as a healer is to answer the questions that are asked and to not sensor or think I know what the answer means. Clients Gigi and Tom were pregnant when they came for a healing session. I share more of the regression in a later chapter, but when it was over, Gigi asked if there was anything the baby wanted … and I said *"Orange Juice!"* About two weeks later is when the craving started and did not stop.

Gigi shared this when I asked if she remembered the experiences of that healing and what had come through during our session:

> "It was orange juice SO much orange juice. My oldest, high school buddy became an OB/GYN Doctor, and she delivered both of my kids. She was visiting us at home and saw me downing SO much orange juice that she became alarmed and wanted to test me for maternal diabetes. She let it go. All was fine."

Now as that the soul of the baby that answered the question? Yes, absolutely When I learned to channel in 1985 from Marcy Calhoun, I learned her technique of bringing through an individual's higher mind to learn their soul's life priorities. This simple tool has supported thousands of my clients, and those that Marcy and her students have served. Each of us come with a life agenda. This reason is then supported by all of the other "-ologies" that we pre-determine: our biology by our ancestral heritage, our astrology by the time of our birth, our numerology that in divine orchestration create our personality and character as the unique human being we are. Starting my relationship to my healing clients with this information allows me to assist them to the deepest level, that of their soul, to become who they came to earth to be. It is an honor and deep privilege, I will say this over and over, to touch a heart and soul.

In 1995 I stopped allowing other Spirit Guides and consciousnesses to come fully into my body. An Actor can embody a character so deeply you believe they are their role. I could do the same with Spirit Guides so well, I was invited to travel around the United States and abroad, interviewed on network television, and had a thriving practice. I allowed not just the information to come through me but their physical energy as well. This is the process of trance mediumship. A Vedic Astrologer told me in 1991 that my real work would come to the planet that year.

After a few experiences when the clients talked negatively to the Spirit Guide about me, I was done. Like I said before unless I understood the wisdom, had the intuitive skills for the other consciousness to use, they would not be in my form. These negative experiences made me pause. I decided it was time for me to practice using more of my other tools and stop the trance mediumship. I still teach individuals to "channel" but I no longer allow the embodiment of spirit guides into my body form. It is still a team effort, and healing is always the motive. And, I will always channel the priorities of a lifetime, a year in someone's life, marriage for even they are a life, and the soul of a business.

The importance of developing our channels for the survival of humanity goes directly to the issues of the time. "Information Age" over-load keeps us always looking for the right solutions, directives, and the path to take for our daily survival. Building on the inquiry of the last chapter—how do we really know where information comes from via our intuition? Channeling is immediate, consistent dialogue with the world around us. The greater effort is the ability to trust and act on the information provided, not to get the answers to our questions. When there has been constant support from our guidance systems repetition has a benefit, it is simply easier to believe. Experience is the best teacher we have.

Chapter 3 Practicum

- ⌘ Go for a walk and have a conversation with an animal, a mineral, and a plant. Write down your experience.

- ⌘ Wait a week and go for another walk along the same route. If you see the same forms, speak again. Find out if you made a strong enough impression they remembered you.

Chapter 4

Who's Talking Now?

Continuing our discussion of channeling as an evolutionary concept, brings the need to discuss the continuity of life. All of us have spirit guides, and they are not just Ascended Masters or Angels. On a regular basis, our guides are departed friends, family and loved ones that we have shared life experience. However, when a soul leaves the body it also leaves the personality of that lifetime. So understanding who is talking to us, the source of the wisdom or guidance is relevant to our discussion.

In each lifetime, we are not born under the same conditions as energy is moving and evolving in every single instance. We choose different cultures, storylines, and casts for our soul's play. Time cannot be repeated, nor the conditions—and neither can we as people. We are born under different astrology. Our numerology is different because the name of our vibration is different. For example, you might be named after your husband's great aunt Anne who died when he was in high school. Great Aunt Anne is now being born as his daughter

Anne. Though her name is the same and her soul is the same, she is not the same. These are all ways that we set the stage to learn the lessons that correspond to the priorities that we came here to address. When the lifetime is over, we shed the part we played, retaining the wisdom as well as the unresolved emotional energy.

That a soul retains the details of their life story is unimportant. I see more often there are three main things a departed loved one will communicate. First, they love the person inquiring and appreciate the gifts, lessons, and time that were spent together in body. Second, they want to help those in body trust their life process, lessons, and unique gift for the world. Third, it is often necessary to tell those left behind that their death was timely and perfect. For me, it is the ultimate in grief counseling, and it is real. The only way the family or friends know that who they are talking to is really the being they had a relationship with in the physical, is their knowing. The meter for this knowing is the heart.

One of the greatest gifts is to help people in their bereavement. It is a privilege to be a vehicle that can help people find peace with the loss of a loved one. To channel the spirit of departed friends and relatives without fear takes strong faith—for me, and for them too. The individual's expectations of the experience are very high because they knew the departed loved one. My intention is always to help with pain, not to create more. Grief is the most complex of all human emotions. It is the ultimate realization that there is no going back to what was. We can only move forward to what possibility could be—with the only certainty being our demise. Again, the journey is the destination, and peace can come to us by living in the now.

The emotion when communicating with a departed child for their parent is the most intense I have witnessed. I have never worked with a parent who has recovered from the loss of their child. I believe that someday science will discover a gene that says, "not to expire before the parent" in our DNA. If there is any disbelief of the parents, my channel will also bring this through, confirming their disbelief. Strong faith and spiritual connection help to create a strong atmosphere of trust. I would not do this work if it evoked loss, deprivation, grief, and pain without resolution. The intention for the spirits, and for me, is to help affirm that we do have eternal life. The souls come to support our understanding that there is life after death and to resolve any karma that might still be operating.

This is evident in trance experience over and over whether it is a known or unknown spirit. When I bring in a soul that is familiar, and the feeling of that soul is what is related to more than the recollection of their previous existence. Often particular words spoken by the Spirit, indicative of their attitudes toward life or interests or events will help the friend in body trust the reading. Souls more recently departed from the body will hold more personality to help assure that it is really them communicating. When perceived via clairvoyance, they come in the form that they were so that we can recognize them. I have noticed that with the more evolved spirit guides, the greater the absence of personality. All of the souls, regardless of who they are, emanate amazing amounts of unconditional love and acceptance.

One of my most profound experiences of channeling a departed loved one was on the ABC affiliate station in Tampa, Florida on the Kathy Fountain show. Kathy was a morning talk show host that came on after Regis and Kathy Lee. I can hear you smiling as this statement dates the story back into the '90s. My practice was in rock and roll form. I was traveling and teaching, expanding the places I worked. It was an exciting time for me. A client was hosting me in Tampa, and she had been bugging the producers of the show to have me on as a guest. When the call came, I felt like I had won the lottery, I finally was stepping into the limelight with my gifts of healing and service.

When the limo picked me up that morning, I was naive to what awaited me in the studio. Before the show, I was introduced to the show's host in front of the live audience. The format of my interview was first to channel a spirit guide, then I was to channel a departed loved one, and the last segment was to be a Q & A with the audience. Before the live show, Kathy and I were asking audience members to volunteer and telling me who they wanted to be channeled. However,

I was not performing as the producers nor the host anticipated. Many of the loved ones were already back on the planet living their next life. The energy in the studio was shifting with shock and awe. Almost immediately, the producers grabbed six people from the audience and put me in a corner.

While deciding which person to help, I could hear the producers continue talking to the rest of the audience. I heard a question that made my heart stop, "Where are the Skeptics in the audience? I need to know where the Skeptics are!" It was a cosmic setup! Thank God right at that time I was doing the Workbook of *A Course in Miracles*. My daily affirmation lesson that day was "There are no enemies." How perfect that the Universe had conspired for me to live my spiritual truth, on TV, with not just a studio audience, but the local Tampa Bay Area viewing audience! As I was working nearly every day, I had lost track of which day of the week it was. Immediately, I realized that it was Friday the 13th and therefore I had not been asked to do the show because I was a skilled healer, helping many people on their life path. I had been asked to be the pawn in the media game of sensationalism. Bummer!

In the studio corner, one by one, I eliminated participants because the souls they wanted me to channel were no longer in spirit form but had reincarnated. It was down to a small Puerto Rican woman and another. There was something about this petite Latino woman that was so fragile and seemed uncomplicated. I knew in my heart she was the one I was to serve. She had lost her son and wanted to know that he was all right.

The show began with the phenomenon of Wu Lon my alchemist guide who had been most present in my sessions and public teaching at the time. Though I could channel whoever was available and appropriate for the situation, Wu Lon was my primary guide at the time. As always he was quite funny, entertaining, and had charmed the audience. However, I was acutely aware of the fact I had been set up for an attack in the last segment of the show. Regardless, I was resolved to do the best I could to help and do my part to serve God.

During the commercial break, I grabbed the hand of the mother in grief. I looked deeply into her eyes and promised that I was there for her. I was adamant pointing to the audience. "They Do Not Matter. I am here for you and your son. That is what I care about." She nodded her head and held my hand tight. This was *her* moment and more important than publicly demonstrating my talents as a healer. I had unconsciously agreed to be a part of a television show that valued drama, not spiritual service. I knew that this channeling experience for this bereaved mother had the potential to change the rest of her life. And, perhaps the dance of the coming attack would open a few more hearts and minds. The only thing that mattered in the greater truth was this grieving Mom.

Very quickly I connected to the soul of her son. I could feel his energy enter my body. He spoke to his mother about his regret that he did not kiss her goodbye the day that he died. He told her to tell his sister that he loved her. He also told his Mom that he would stay with her as her Angel for the rest of her life, and be there to greet her when she departed the Earth. Just like his mother, his energy was sweet. I could tell he had been a kind young man.

When I opened my eyes, she was crying softly, but her brown eyes were lit up like they candles in a cathedral. Immediately, Kathy wrapped her arm around this woman's neck, shoved the handheld microphone into her face, and asked: "WAS THAT REALLY YOUR SON?!!" I was mortified and wanted to push Kathy away from this beautiful mother who had, obviously to me, just had a profound spiritual experience.

With such innocence and grace that brought tears to my eyes, she looked at Kathy taking my hand again into hers and said, "Mam, I know this woman is sitting next to me, but that was my son. Sally did not know this, but a bus hit him in the morning as he walked to work. He left the house that day without kissing me goodbye, which is what he did every day. And, he has a sister still at home." The audience took a long breath together, and there were sounds of recognition and amazement as this mother shared her truth. It was her son.

The rest of the show was spent with questions from the audience. The president of the Southern Skeptics Society had a chance to fire away at my character. I intentionally radiated love to him. When I looked at him instead of seeing a righteous adult, I saw him as the wounded child he was, steeped in fear and abused verbally by his mother. I could only have empathy with him as he projected his shame, fear, and deep sadness about life onto me. It is too bad that he was not open to the magic that is available for us all. I do not proselytize. I have compassion for those who are unwilling to open their hearts to know that we are eternal, divine, and blessed beings of love. I also have the courage to proclaim it so regardless of what other people think.

Sadly, my copy of the video of this was lost over the years. I called the studio to see if I could get another copy. I thought it would be fun to have it on my website. It is a part of my historical record of helping people through the years. Though this show was filmed May 13, 1995, the possibility that it was in the studio's archives had me in hope. At the same time, I searched online for Kathy and found her still in Florida. However, her career path had taken a wide turn to another road entirely. She is now the director of a fertility counseling center and a psychotherapist helping others through the pain of not having children! Amazing how her present show—the theater of her life—and of that episode of her TV Show I was a guest, matched.

We spoke on the phone after all of these years. Kathy did not remember our show. The recording was destroyed as the studio moved to digital and wanted to minimize the archived taped shows. Kathy was asked by the studio, which of her shows she wanted to keep in her archives. She had only selected those with celebrity guests as Kathy felt they were the ones that would count in the future. I question celebrity as a method of evaluating what can contribute to our collective good. Why do we think this way? Insidious is the assumptive idea that some people are more important than others. In the divine plan, it is simply not true. We are here, so we are important!

If I were to have that documentation of my past, it would be up on my YouTube channel still helping people in grief with the loss of loved ones—especially, parents losing children. Celebrity comes and goes, but this human condition has not changed—people die, and people grieve. However, I gave the tape years ago to someone who then subsequently lost it, so it was not meant-to-be. Though I do not have the recording, I do have the memory of the experience and the miracle of healing that occurred anyway. I live the conviction to serve those who I can. I know I made a difference for that mother that day so long ago. I am not a celebrity nor was she. However, because of that moment, there was one more peaceful, accepting heart on Earth. My hope by sharing this story, it can continue to help someone somewhere with their loss.

Measuring our value against another is a ridiculous concept. If we have life, we are valuable. It is not our contributions nor how we measure against another. We do not hold the balance scale. There is a list of the most spiritually influential people of the 20th century that came out several years ago. It is a skewed perspective it does not include people like Cesar Augustus, Adolph Hitler, Charles Manson, Osama Bin Ladin, Fidel Castro, Donald Trump or any of the people in our culture who have made us question what life is about. These individuals have influenced the ethics, morality, and faith more than people who have sold millions of books on spirituality. They have made significant contributions to bettering our world by problems and pain, by instigating the solutions and inventions to overcome them. Popularity is not a measuring stick in the eternal, nor do we have the capacity to measure the growth of a soul. Whether it was a loving son or an ascended master, the souls that I channel have taught me that there are other perspectives to life in the mundane. How fortunate that we can learn from them.

Humans are ill-equipped to impose conditions or standards on what makes a soul evolved or not. In my opinion, it is God's job, and not my business. I seek here only to open doors to what can be experienced and share what has been my experience. I have channeled thousands of spirits. After a while, one begins to notice trends. I'd like to share about one of my guides who can use personality convincingly to get people to pay attention. I am pleased to introduce one of my dear friends. Here is Wu Lon and his channeled message from 1994 still relevant 20+ years later:

> "Greetings and salutations, I come through now without hesitation, anxious to share with you my unique perspective for the planet earth and your experience of her. I must say that the channel is as excited to share possibility … she is not letting us talk through her as often during this time so that she might allow her own spirit evolvement to include her intellect. We do support her in sharing and guide her writing. However, the text of her book, except where annotated, is her soul's voice.
>
> Now, about my own! I love to share with my children; for I am the grandfather that takes his child upon his knee to love them only. My children need the safety of my vibration, for their world is not always kind. Through my humor and kindness, I teach my children. I put on my blue silk robes, my blue hat with tassel, don my Fu Manchu mustache and gray goatee, and sit on my meditation cushion to talk to my children through the magic of trance. I am an alchemist, a healer, and doctor of spirit. I have been born, incarnated on to the earth plane four times. This life, of Wu Lon was my favorite! I had a beautiful wife, two talented sons, a daughter who gave me great joy, and a lovely farm to the north of Tibet in China. You can visualize Shangri-la, and it is the same! I, at that time, taught many people to use their inner sight and their hands to move light energy to create healing of the body, mind, and spirit. I am actually a part of a prism, a matrix of energy systems with 44 faces. I am not a soul. I am beyond the need of the soul to teach me. I use this costume because I like to. It is fun!

Now some of you, my children, love my humor and teasing ways. You like to sit with tea and chat. Did you know some of you do not hear my humor? Though rare, you are the children who need my love most. It is the maker of miracles, that stuff of love! Take a dose every day and call me in the mornings. I love to chat as the sun rises! I want you now to do an exercise of your soul. If you are reading this book, you are quite curious, and that is good! I want you to quiet yourself. Close your eyes after you've read all of my instructions, of course—hahaha! Now take a few deep breaths and relax a bit more. When you feel ready, ask that I come to you, ask to meet Wu Lon. Remember, I can come in your vision, you can hear me, you can feel me, and some of you will just know me. Let us have tea for now. I will come again. Namaste!"

So far I have shared channeled poetry and writing, a story of channeling a departed loved one, and introduced one of my guides through your own sensitivity, consciousness, and intellect. I trust Wu Lon can keep up with the demands of tea with all of us at once. He lives without the constraints of linear time. He forgot to mention that he is a multidimensional being, living with all of the 44 dimensions at once, in all time. That to me sounds like an evolved state of consciousness likened to a universe.

All the spirits I have channeled are as unique as all of the people who come to see me. Since I didn't limit what was the appropriate source, it was a demonstration of trusting what shows up. In the past, I channeled either the highest and best source for the moment, or I let the individual ask specifically to whom they want to talk to. There are again infinite choices depending on the intention. There is the potential that the spiritual guides that come through are not necessarily working for our highest good. To know if it is right or not, we must trust our intuition. Our feelings about the experience are what matter. We are the ones with the body, after all.

The negative spirits that I have met are ultimately seeking their own transformation and healing. We choose our soul friends, whether they are in a body or out of a body. The negative spirits often act in a manipulative or demanding manner. The key to choosing whether to relate to them or not is how they are representing themselves in speech, mannerism, and vibration. Etiquette is important with these relationships as much as with any of your friends. If it is with integrity, we have no need to question their way of being.

Channeling negative spirits can be done to assist them in transformation. Remember that as we are all one, these energies on some level are a part of us. To negate the negative does not create a positive. We must embrace the negative in love. These individual souls are a part of the universe and therefore serve some purpose. Negativity is generated by our thoughts, our actions and also by our fears. When we reject these souls in distress, we are rejecting a part of ourselves. The negative spirits, like human beings, cannot hurt us unless we allow it. Empathy is the bridge to transformation.

On the first day of the 2nd World Congress of Healers for Peace in Hamilton, New Zealand in January of 1990, I gave a lecture demonstration on releasing negative belief systems. Transforming negative into positive is the basis for all healing, no matter what modality. In the lecture, I demonstrated ways of using meditation and channeling for individuals and groups to create change. Since it was a gathering of all types of healing practitioners in the name of peace, I thought we needed to look at war. War was the perfect and appropriate belief system to use for the demonstration. I asked everyone in the audience, about 65 doctors, nurses, massage therapists, psychotherapists, artists, and interested folks, to talk about their thoughts on war and peace.

The collective agreement was the fundamental belief that we must fight for peace, "that war is the only way to peace." I channeled the spirit of that thought. No one in the room liked this guy who was arrogant, unsympathetic, nasty, and brutal. Shiven, a professional clown from Germany, asked the entity where it came from. The answer was: from the fears and insecurities of the people in the room.

Addressing this collective energy as a single living entity was possible. Those in the audience dialogued with it to convince it to change. The individuals in the audience began to see the direct relationship between their fear and its manifestation as this dark and ominous character coming through my channel. It was astonishing to hear spoken back to them their fear-filled, negative inner dialogue as the basis for the energy's presentation.

Upon agreement with the energy and the audience for the transformation, I moved out the belief system's negative energy stored in everyone's chakras. We collectively gave the negative thought to the universe to transform. All of us gathered there were then showered with love and the light of wisdom. The new belief and collective entity of thought had become "there is only one way." This new thought took us all beyond duality.

The demonstration and the healing were real, and those 65 individuals, connected by the common fear and the transformation of it, produced a wave in the collective. The Berlin wall had started to come down piece-by-piece November 9, 1989, but real demolition began at the same time. February 11, 1990, Nelson Mandela was released from jail. These events are connected. It is right to acknowledge the unity though I'm not saying the workshop was the cause for worldwide change. The message here is what I have said previously—we are all one in the universal mind. Margaret Mead, my Shero and one of the reasons I studied anthropology, said, "*Never underestimate the power of a small group of people to change the world. Indeed, nothing else ever has.*"

The universal mind is the same as Jung's collective unconscious— a moving sea of thought where our individual minds connect. The universal mind is the source for stereotypes, ideologies, cultural identities, religious creeds, philosophical attitudes, fashion trends, cultural vogues, and value systems. We are influenced by it, and it is from us that it originates. These stories shared of channeling are just three of the multitude of ways that channeling of energy, spirits, and ideas can come through our mind like a radio wave. To have a clean and clear channel, I will say again; we must be free of fear.

Chapter 4 Practicum

⌘ Have a chat with Wu Lon. Keep in mind that he is a reflection of your own inner wisdom, coming to you to remind you of your own greatness. Wu Lon can be the best friend ever so treat him kindly as you would anyone who offers unconditionally their heart to you in friendship.

Chapter 5

The Power of Imagination

*I*magination is the ultimate tool of manifestation. Everything that we see in our awareness has been imagined. Stop reading and look around you. Your chair, the rug, the lamp, the Kleenex box, your jeans, your shoes, the sidewalk, the automobiles, the litter, the street signs, the uniform rows of corn, the neatly pruned rose bushes, your computer, and smartphone—all of it—not just the art on the wall was imagined by someone. This includes our bodies, our creations, our relationships, our jobs, our societies, our cultures, and our political persuasions. One way I describe imagination is "image-in-action" or "I magnetize to action."

Our thoughts create. When we spend time imaging, like a fight with our spouse, or discussion of an issue with a boss, or raging at a friend, who has hurt us, the mental and emotional energy becomes a part of our future interactions with these individuals. We are energy forms, and that energy is a matrix between them and us. The energy usually creates an energetic barrier between us. Whoever we are mentally dialoguing with is getting that charge. Therefore, when we come into the presence of the person we have been dialoguing with in our mind, the energy is a filter that we are trying to communicate through. No wonder minor altercations can take on monumental outcomes.

Creative visualization is the thought map from an inspired idea to a physical manifestation. We are taking what is esoteric and non-apparent and building a mental blueprint. The more we charge that blueprint with emotion, the more power it carries through into the world. Everything imagined is created and everything created is imagined. Though there are many things we imagine—winning the lottery, marrying a movie star, losing weight, riding a spaceship to the moon—the actual vision is not always created, but energy attached to it is always created.

The idea of a positive mental attitude, creating from positive thought is not a new idea. However, with the rise of consciousness from the New Age movement and years of pop psychology these concepts are more alive and current in our culture. The 1937 classic "Think and Grow Rich" by Napoleon Hill is still relevant today as business wisdom. There was a book that came out in 1995 by Peter McWilliams called "You Cannot Afford the Luxury of a Negative Thought!" has such a true title. We cannot afford to continue to create pain with our thoughts. Myrtle and Charles Fillmore formed the Unity Church Worldwide on the power of positive prayer. We have volumes of books and plenty of research that show our thoughts create. These thoughts are our imaging-in-action. The more positive and good we imagine, the more positive and good we get to experience.

What concerns me is the disconnect between what we are imagining and what we are creating in the industry of Entertainment. The volume of violent games, movies, and rise in crime, terrorism, and war are not mutually exclusive. We are not just allowing but celebrating and rewarding violent imagination and the creations that come from it. When do we stop the madness? Has it gone too far? Can we begin to harness the power of our imagination to create a world of peace? Until we understand that there is a direct response in the physical world from the world of our thoughts, I do not see we can turn the tide.

As I began to learn more about the active creation that comes from our imagination, I began to be sensitive to other's energy especially— sexual energy. I, like most people, fantasized about sexual liaisons with people I was attracted to. After recognizing that I was having an energetic sexual relationship with these people, I no longer allow myself to visualize in this manner. This brings the point about psychic and intuitive etiquette. Our thoughts do not stay in our head—in our consciousness. This is a grand illusion of humanity. Our thoughts do affect others.

The word psychic is not my favorite description for it creates an expectation that the future is totally predictable. My preference is to use the word intuitive. However, in this context, it is the appropriate word to describe the mental and emotional connection between people. I will reiterate, we are all intuitive and all have psychic skills. We just do not realize the power of what we have, nor always know how to use it in service to our self and the world.

Before I stopped fantasizing about sex, I was on a bus the day after attending the Congress in New Zealand, and it occurred to me, I could make someone up. I had a great fantasy about this Nordic, muscle-bound, fair-haired, blue-eyed man. I got off the bus to spend the night in Thames, and while I was standing on a street corner, deciding which of the two hotels I would stay in that night, I saw him. Out of a bar came my Nordic man, he winked at me, got in his truck, and drove away. I was shocked and astounded. I realized that we cannot make up what is already available on psychic levels. Fantasy is active creation. It is imaging from which we experience life.

When I think about our fascination with celebrity, I realized that this plays into the need for deep seclusion for people who live in the public eye. I'm sure that psychic attachment plays a part in the difficulty for these individuals to have fidelity in relationships with significant others. Famous people are available to all of us as imaginary friends. This is a vulnerability for remember; my point is that there is no absolute separation.

Before going to New Zealand, I was in a weekly meditation support group. We would have a guided meditation journey each week to support our spiritual growth, the creation of our dreams, and to do healing work for ourselves and others. In May of 1989, in one of these groups, I journeyed in my meditation or creative visualization to New Zealand to start energetically paving the way for my future trip. During the meditation, this is what I saw and experienced:

> *"As my spirit arrived on the islands down under, I was met*
> *by a tall young man with curly blonde hair, bright blue eyes*
> *took me to a beautiful seascape, to a waterfall, and swim-*
> *ming in a deep blue bay."*

When were called in the mediation to come back to the circle, he took my hand and energetically came with me to the room in California. In my psychic vision, I could see him sitting next to my chair and smiling at me and everyone else. I shared with the group that his spirit was in the room with us. He was as delighted as they were for us to all meet in Sacramento.

After my experience in Thames, I went to visit healers that I had met at the Congress who had also been speakers. I needed some healing of my own. I was trudging up a gravel road in the rain, my suitcases heavy, and exhausted and overwhelmed from an event that would change my life forever. Out of the darkness emerged Sky, one of the healers I had enjoyed the previous week and with her was her son. They carried my bags, fed me, and gave me a nice massage and tucked me in for the night. As they turned to go, I hugged them both, Sky first, then, Finn. For the first time in the hours we were together I saw him—he was the spirit from my meditation eight months previous!

The next day, Finn came to see me. My first question of him was when did you cut your hair? His long locks we were gone. He replied two months ago. Finn then proceeded to take me on a tour of the island, including swimming in a beautiful bay. When I told Sky about the meditation in California, she shared with me, that as they were walking toward me on the road in the twilight, Finn had seen me first. He said to her, "Mom, I know that woman." He was quite surprised then when Sky and I embraced in greeting.

With these two profound teachings back to back, I began to trust more the information I was receiving on whatever level: meditation, intuition, psychic sight, channeling, dreaming, or fantasy. The choice I make from the information is not always the best choice. I make mistakes like everybody, and those mistakes are ultimately there in our paths to serve us. They don't feel good at the time, but if you review your path, everything that you have experienced brought you into this moment now. It has all served in your evolution. We do not get to where we are unless we have been where we have been. Every mistake is a lesson about love.

The imagination is a level of reality. So I hear the question, "What about hallucinations?" On some level, perhaps yet to be defined or discovered, it is real. Schizophrenia is a great example of a person sensitive to the other dimensional realities with no way to effectively bridge the expanded knowing. Remember the radio quality of the mind shown to us by those who channel. The individuals described as mentally ill perhaps can be our guides into altered states of consciousness.

The terror, destructiveness and erratic behavior that comes with the person with schizophrenia is difficult to negotiate, heal, and understand. These individuals are not able to have a core and integrated personality. The psycho/spiritual wounds are so profound from previous trauma and/or due to their inherent chemistry from their genetics—their inner landscape is full of negativity and pain. As we begin to hear them not from our fear, I have greater hope that we can learn from them about other dimensions, the workings of our computer-like brains, and find ways to bring them peace.

The power of our minds is infinite. I can be talking on the phone to someone in New York from California, describe a friend of theirs in Houston in great detail, and explain past life connections between them. The focusing of energy provided by the telephone system and video conferencing on the computer is one of the miracles I am grateful exists. With or without the technology, I can access the same information. However, I do not actively seek information on other people without their permission.

Energy healing is real. The power of prayer to assist in human dramas such as war, crime, poverty, political unrest, and crisis's of health—is documented. Each of us can use our gifts as we choose. In my practice, I prefer the participation on a conscious level with those who I am helping. It is more empowering for us both. However, my prayer life is with every thought I have. During the day, when anyone comes to my mind, I send thoughts of love. It is not necessary to be a certified energy healer, a Reiki Master, or an initiate of a mystic tradition to be in service with our minds. We are much more active consciously in our mind and soul, and unconsciously, than we know.

The simple magic that allows me to work is the phenomenon called listening. Our consciousness is a vibration of light and sound. Both of these principles are waves of energy. How to know how someone is doing is as easy as listening to their vibration and by asking them directly. Through sound, we express our vibration. By words and tone, we express our perspective, our operative reality. The gauge of the listener is not just their ear. The listening with the heart opens the empathic channel to hear even deeper that the one expressing may even be aware of.

When I was a Realtor in San Francisco, I knew that parking could affect the desirability of a particular location, the timing of a property tour, and the wear and tear on my legs with high heels on. I decided that parking would not be a problem for me. It wasn't. When someone would complain about parking, I would always comment that parking was not a problem for me. I would visualize a parking space in front of whatever building I was visiting. I would pray for one when I needed one. I would ask as I drove into the area at intersections near my destination, "Right, left, or forward?" I would receive answers and be guided to my spot.

If a spot was not available, I knew to be alert. There was always a reason. Perhaps, I need to hear something on the radio; perhaps, the person I was meeting wasn't there yet. Perhaps, I would see a store or restaurant that would later be significant. Sometimes it was because the service I was to provide for whomever I was meeting was to be late! If we are saying that "parking is a problem," that is what we are affirming, therefore, creating, therefore, proving to ourselves we are right, by having that experience.

The spiritual path for the seeker is the path to awareness of consciousness. As we open our channel, we open to more possibilities of the living reality. Our assumptions about who we are can stop being limitations. When we begin to make the total conscious connection between our experience and our imagination, perhaps we will stop feeding the negativity and brutality of crime, war, and killing that is found everywhere in our mainstream media. We are creating the pain of the world.

There is no one else to blame but us. It is time for us to think that our spot in the world is waiting and create a dialogue with the divine to find it. It is making a decision, like I did with my parking, to use our imaginations to be in service. I advocate deciding as well that we are connected to the world, not separate, and using this miraculous gift of imagination to create to healing, peace, freedom, and love.

Chapter 5 Practicum

⛢ Imagine and affirm: "Where ever I go, I find a parking spot." Visualize your destination and see yourself parking right out front. If when you arrive, it is not waiting for you, ask your intuition: "What do I need to learn, see, experience, or discover before I park." Listen for the answer and act according. When you hear anyone complaining about parking, use that moment to affirm: "Parking is not my problem." "I always find parking!" I call this **Positive Parking Attitude or PPA**. Imagine the amount of stress that will be reduced from your body, and the collective unconscious, from changing this behavior.

⛢ Spend a few quiet moments each day, imagining both your loved ones and those that challenge you sending them the message: "I love you. I am grateful for you. I honor you." Pay attention if you hear from them 'out of the blue' as you begin this practice. Notice if those whom you have had conflict with beginning to feel different, look different, you hear them different, and new insight comes from the negative interaction.

Chapter 6

Dreams and Insight

onsciousness never sleeps—only the body, emotions, and mind do. In the Dreamtime, we continue the living process, the perpetual motion machine, and our learning. The more practiced I've become, the more I remember of the dream state. When I began seriously studying metaphysics, I would wake up so tired in the morning. One of my teachers explained that I was doing healing work at night and if it was too much, to tell my guides that I want the night off. What a concept! It is important in our awakening to the truth of an expanded awareness, we recognize that we have control of our speed of development. If you feel unequipped to handle the intuitive or psychic or paranormal experiences you are having, just say "No thank you!"

Two nights before I went to my first intuitive development workshop in 1985, I woke up in the middle of the night and found myself sleeping very close to the edge of the bed. There was a big purple hooded, robed figure standing right next to me! Fearfully, I threw the covers over my head and shouted: "Go Away!" So much for my readiness for the workshop! The workshop began when I decided to do it. This apparition was there to prepare me as I slept for the upcoming weekend.

The levels of intuitive and psychic energy are more clarified at night because the majority of people have shut down three of the four states of awareness: their body, emotions, and mind. This creates the space to open up spiritually without as much static. This is why many of those who meditate are awake in the early morning hours, especially 3 am. If you wake up to use the time to speak with God, talk to your spirit friends, do prayer work, or create. The nighttime stage although is in the dark, has more clarity.

When I am working with people, sessions extend before and after the actual meeting or class. As soon as someone makes an appointment for a healing, the universe creates lessons and experiences to support that healing. Many of the people I teach are not ready for it to happen in the waking dream, so it happens in the time of sleep. The husband of one of my clients ran a large corporation—though she lives and loves metaphysical truth, he keeps to a more intellectual way of interpreting the world. I have had several dreams where this corporate executive has come to me, including his briefcase, for channeling and counseling in the Dreamtime.

Laura Mc Alpine sent this story for me to share:

> "I saw Sally for the first time 5/31/95. At the time I had been
> trying to get pregnant for 1.5 years, and I was anxious to
> know if it would happen. During our session, we worked a
> lot on blocks to my fertility and Sally suggested that I could
> be pregnant by July. When July came and went with no baby,
> I was extremely distraught. A few nights after getting my
> period, Sally came to me in a dream and was urging me to
> remember what I need to work on and that the transforma-
> tion could take longer. She was encouraging and nurturing,
> yet also firm, saying, "Remember that this work is important

and necessary to bring your child into the lifetime. I woke up feeling relieved, lighter and more resolved to continue the healing work I had started. Patience is not a strength for me, and my dream with Sally gave me a strong dose of patience and self-love."

In Laura's dream, I helped bring her attention back to herself. I do not remember this nighttime session, and I was not aware of being on duty. Often we are called to the sleeping dream as a way of working through the issues of the waking dream. Introspection, personal development, spiritual practice, navel-gazing, are considered by many in our post-technological world, luxuries. The crisis of faith, illness on any level for another or our self, or interpersonal conflicts will push us into personal evolution. It is out of necessity that re-invention becomes a survival skill as our life stories change.

Life is the waking dream. Everything that happens to us during our day can be interpreted just like we would a sleeping dream. Metaphor and symbolism are the language tools we can use to understand both dream states. Being more attentive to what happens in our dream state allows us again to open up the information available to make effective choices and decisions. In the cosmology of the Aboriginal people in Australia, they flip around their perspective—the waking dream is the sleeping dream, and real life is when they are asleep.

One Sunday afternoon in July of 1995, I was helping one of my students understand that everyday life can be interpreted as a dream. I had been teaching about life as the "waking dream" since my first Intuitive Development class in San Francisco in 1987. My client had gotten a traffic ticket for speeding on the way to her healing appointment with me. We were analyzing the scenario as a way of understanding her healing process. She was obviously rushing her life. Later while discussing my teaching; and the need to bring it to a larger audience via books and video, I commented on the fact that "I sound like a broken record!"

After the session, on her way to her car within seconds, my client was back knocking on my door. Outside my house, a broken record was lying on the lawn right in front of the doorstep! The presence of the record, and the synchronicity that came with it validated her understanding of interpreting life as a waking dream. When we are awake to the theater of our lives going on all around us, symbolism is around us all the time. Paying attention to the obvious lets us hear the dialogue that we are having with the Divine. Similar to Albert Einstein's wisdom that inherent in a problem is the solution, inherent in the dream waking or sleeping is the solution to our soul's quandaries, purpose, hopes, and dreams.

We all process our waking experience at night whether we remember dreaming in the morning or not. At night the unconscious provides us clues to making healthy choices. Jeremy Taylor, the author of Dreamwork one of the premier authorities on dreaming and my graduate thesis advisor, always says, "Dreams come from the Dreammaker in service to heath and wholeness." Dreaming can help us tremendously in our work, both personal process and professionally if we pay attention to them. One of my favorite stories of my dream life is about my friends Gary and Teddi. Gary was a real estate client in San Francisco. I was representing Gary on the purchase of a house in San Francisco and his then girlfriend; now wife was doing the preliminary search for him.

Teddi and I met in person in November of 1989 to look at properties. One of the first conversations that we shared we talked about our common interest in spirituality and healing. We were soul sisters and quite comfortable with each other. Teddi shared with me that a psychic in Los Angeles had asked her who she knew with a red truck and that this person would be very important in her life. At the time Teddi knew of no one, and she was quite surprised when I picked her up for our first property tour at San Francisco Airport in my red Chevy Luv truck. We didn't find what they needed at the time, but Teddi and I were fast friends.

In March of the following year, I attended a *Dialogue House Journal Intensive Workshop* teaching the ideas of Ira Progoff. During the weekend we were told to write down our dreams. I wrote the following about my Sunday morning dream:

> "Sold two unit building, on or near Chestnut Street in San Francisco north side of the city, water views…"

The following Wednesday, Teddi called me. She said, "Sal, I'm calling for three things. Thanks for a good time for your birthday! How was your weekend workshop? Gary's ready to buy a house, let's go shopping." Friday we went on a property tour that included a house although Gary had specifically requested condominiums with a San Francisco Bay view. Teddi fell in love with the house, and by the following Friday, we were in escrow.

The next week I received a 3R report from the seller, which is the city's history of all code work done on the building. The report said it was a two unit building—*sold two unit building*—converted into a single family home. The house was in an alley between Chestnut and Lombard Streets on Telegraph Hill in San Francisco—*on or near Chestnut Street in San Francisco*—with northern bay views—*north side of the city, water views…*! Imagine my surprise when I remembered the dream and looked back at the dream journal. It was a prophetic dream two months before Gary and Teddi bought their dream home.

Gary is a working actor, and during the escrow period, he was filming a biographic movie on location. I dreamed:

> "Teddi, Gary and I were in a hotel room. I was sitting on an ottoman channeling a spirit for Gary to talk to. The spirit was instructing Gary on how to authentically act his role in the movie, especially the death scene."

Of course, I called my pal Teddi first thing the next morning to tell her about my dream. She told me that the day before Gary had gone to the grave sight of his character the movie to help him with specifically the death scene for his role. This was the landscape of our dream reality and waking state reality colliding accurately and effectively in perfect timing.

Remember now that I was Gary's Realtor, not his Healer! When we commit to service on one level, like the physical, it opens up other levels of relationship. How often do you find yourself playing the role of therapist to your co-workers or mother to your clients or big brother to your neighbor? We are connected in infinite ways consciously and unconsciously. I was devoted to being of service as Gary purchased his first house, an important step in most people's life. This extended to my spiritual, metaphysical world because of our karma, my karma with Teddi, and everyone else that brought this real-life drama into being. Even the developer that remodeled the two unit building, his Realtor, the people that introduced Gary and I were all a part of creating this story. My intention is to be in service to love. It is my task in this lifetime to teach and lead us forward to a kinder world. We are all healers. Every person that was a character in this story—including the woman who created the Progoff workshop and those gathered to attend in Santa Barbara in March—at this moment we all become a healer and spiritual teacher for you.

Every job can be reduced to the common denominator of service to each other. No matter what task, role, job, career, position in a corporate hierarchy, or duty, all fundamentally are equal. The theater of the human condition exists to teach about love and eternal creation. There is no randomness to the path we walk each day. No matter what we are alive with the power to create ease for our world and our self. This is not always how it feels and yet it is truth. As a footnote, the house that I sold to Gary did turn out to be important to Teddi for they married there.

My dreaming of Gary and Teddi continued for years after escrow closed. I spend a lot of my sleep time working. As I became more and more aware of the service I was doing at night, I began to question our compensation system. Think about how much energy we expend toward the success of our jobs outside of the office especially now that working virtual is commonplace. This brings another level to the energy exchange between my community and me if I am working while I am sleeping. The best news is I do not have to hold the balance scale to make it fair. My reward continues to be the magic in having prophetic and mystical experiences. I have magical moments every day no matter what my mood is—good or bad. These moments of magic, witnessing the dance between the sleeping and waking dreams, are available to us all when we decide to pay attention.

It is a difficult thing to know whether a dream is prophetic, or if it is symbolic, or if it is soul extension. Sometimes they are all three. As Gail Delaney, a dream analyst in San Francisco says, the problem with prophetic dreams is that you don't know until afterward that you have been forewarned about something! I think it is safe to say that symbolic to your own process of growth is always true.

One way to comprehend and understand the sleeping dream experience is to think of our soul extended beyond our body. Part of our self is out on etheric levels living in other worlds and other realities. The healing work, channeling, teaching, counseling I do at night is done in extension. This can create physical changes to the body including being tired or emotional. Have you ever awakened from a dream in tears, or panicked or with a brilliant idea or with a story about someone else's life? In truth, there are many parts of the self. We can be many places at once and not aware of the splits in consciousness at all.

Dreams provide a rich tapestry of our inner world and sensitivity, and we are the best interpreters of our own dream symbols. An ocean to me means awe and freedom. An ocean could mean fear, isolation, power, the unconscious mind, separation, fun summers, and other possible definition. This is why we must participate in our interpretation of our waking or sleeping dream. This is the path of self-exploration, which leads to self-knowledge, self-confidence, and self-esteem. By having these growing awarenesses, self-actualization comes with ease, for we know our perspective and are not so swayed by those around us.

Dreams allow us to continue to integrate what we are learning in the waking state that we may not have time to process. In the dream state, we can even help others. I call it dreaming for someone. The dreams I have that I remember when I've taught or helped someone does not mean I feel obligated to tell them. The intimacy that is required for me to share the information is dictated by our waking state relationship. Just because we have information doesn't mean we need to take action on it. We can thank the universe and let it go.

By 1989 I was lecturing on the topic of *The Waking Dream*. Everything that we experience reflects something inside of us. Reading tarot, crystal ball gazing, psychotherapy, going to a trance medium, or looking for insight from paying attention to dreams are all doorways to open and reveal the mystery. Every experience does the same thing. It gives us insight to what is happening in our inner world, our consciousness, our emotions, our relationships, our hopes and dreams, and our health and wholeness.

Take for example earthquakes in California are common. If you experience the vibrations of an earthquake, it will initiate your emotional body for change that is appropriate. We experience the external world as difficult if our internal world is in unrest. The act of being rattled by a seismic wave is what our internal world asks for to be heard if you experience an earthquake. Perhaps you have wanted to change jobs, get a divorce, move in with your lover, have a child, or move to another city. The cosmic jolt that comes with the physical one is the recognition of your mortality. Suddenly you give yourself permission to make the changes because you have faced death.

It cannot be stressed enough that the more we acknowledge and honor what we are aware of, the more empowered we feel. The more we trust what we are aware of, the more successful we become at living. We open ourselves to be in greater service for our life, to each other, and to the world. I am a dreamer who pays attention to my sleeping and waking dreams because they are how the divine is in dialogue with me. Why not use this tool when it is given freely? All we need to do is dream.

Chapter 6 Practicum

⊠ Start a dream journal for both the waking dream and sleeping dream. To look for meaning in a waking dream here is an example: if you miss the bus, get a flat tire, or hurt yourself as you are on the way to visit a friend, how does that relate to the challenges in your life right then? To discover meaning in a sleeping dream, I recommend looking at Jeremy Taylor's process on his website and invest in his book.

⊠ Consider forming a dream group so that you can benefit from the wisdom of others. Jeremy's dream group rules are free on his website www.jeremytaylor.com. When I do dream work for clients, friends, or family—my niece is a very vivid dreamer—I always suggest meanings but do not interpret dreams. It is best to let others have their own 'ah-ha' moment if what you share does inspire them.

Chapter 7

Psychic Etiquette and the Ethics of Intuition

This reality, of the awareness being connected to everything and everyone, comes with its own social etiquette. Imagine the world with no secrets, a world where anyone can read your mind, your thoughts, your body language, and your hidden agendas? How would you behave? This is what I propose as the scenario of what the future holds. Of course, the assumption here is that the reader is interpreting correctly what they perceive.

The evolution of the human animal is not just about our ability to adapt to the environment of the earth herself. Our evolution must be in every dimension of experience—physical, emotional, mental and spiritual. To bridge our cosmology from individuation with no connection, to individuation with unity, there must be new social standards. Just like the bridge at Selma became the symbol for the Civil Rights movement in the United States, we are crossing a bridge to our right to feel and perceive more than what is obvious or apparent to all. It is time for us to acknowledge that our thoughts build the bridge between us and the world.

My friend Jim Wanless at the American Bookseller's meeting in Chicago in 1995 introduced Tanner, an agent from Australia to me. I was there to sell this book and find a publisher to work with to bring more wisdom to more people via publishing. Jim had a copy of my proposal for *E-Motion,* in his hands and was quite impressed by the title of this chapter *"Psychic Etiquette and Ethics of Intuition."* Jim was selling me on the concept to do a book just on this topic alone. Tanner's immediate response in jest was to say to me, "you mean it's not o.k. for me to undress you with my eyes!" No in truth, it is not o.k. To mentally cross personal boundaries, unless there is a shared relationship to create bridges to those boundaries, we influence the soul of each other. Remember my Nordic man story? I had learned my lesson about psychic boundaries.

Permission is essential to know and shows respect when sharing what we know with each other. I do not go into those intuitive intimate places without permission. My interest is in clearing karma, not creating it. When we project ourselves into other's inner space, story, or universe, it is an invasion of their privacy. Although secrets are a part of the illusion, respect and privacy are a part of the truth.

Shock is usually the reaction I get when I tell someone that I will read their mind if they pay me. Their egos are usually surprised that I wouldn't be interested in the dramas they have in their life energy. I remind people who question about my "reading their mind" that I have my own life to think about! I'm not interested in using my non-working time on their story instead of my own. As a human, survival depends on my ability to be present in my world to stay healthy, free, and happy. Our attention is our greatest survival tool. This is true for everyone!

When an unsolicited intuitive reading, insight, advice or projection occurs, energy is put out like casting a fishing line. The hook is indicative of the karma being addressed and allows a conduit between the reader and the person being read. The question must come before the answer if the experience it to be without attachment. When someone can verbalize a question, they are emotionally prepared for the answer, even if the answer evokes negative feelings. That is how healing and karmic cleansing happen—when we are ready. When we give answers before the questions are even formulated, we influence the spiritual development of the individual or group.

Energy attachments are quite common, and the projection of insight is only one form. The more sensitive we are to perceiving subtle energies the more open we are to pick up what is not ours. These include negative thoughts of others, not just their behaviors. One of the biggest areas of spiritual development as we increase our sensitivity to the world is to shield ourselves from the negative vibrations. They will always be present, but they can have less influence on us.

With some of my clients who experience paranoia, they actually believe that someone is "out to get them." In truth, those thoughts that we have like:

"Oh, I hate that outfit she's wearing, it is soooo ugly."

"I wonder if he knows his hair looks like it's not be washed for a week."

"What a bad mother she is putting her child on a leash!"

"Why did they paint their house that hideous color?"

"Who said that you are so smart? Who made you God?"

These thoughts do not stay within our own heads. The negative energy gets directed at the person or any other life form—dog, tree, glass of water, corporation, country, religious tradition—being judged, fueling the truth that they, in fact, are indeed being attacked.

It is easy to come up with examples of how our mind judges everything. These thoughts, as we talked about in the last chapter, do not just stay in our minds. This is one of the most important concepts that as we evolve, we must embrace. My mind is not separate from your mind. So, if someone is paranoid, there is truth to their negative feelings. Most likely the sender of the negative doesn't really mean harm to the receiver ... they just don't realize that their thoughts are creating a response.

Today there are millions of books, blogs, and videos—media of all types—about how to use our minds for spiritual growth, and personal growth from business to relationships, such with Louise Hay's classic, *You Can Heal Your Life*. We have access to centuries of teachings about the power of our thoughts and therefore our words. The New Age is the recycling of ancient philosophies and ideologies Mayan, Egyptian, Greek, Pagan, African, Asian, Native American. We have not however figured out how to use this wisdom to live in peace on Earth. The creative connection between what we think, what we speak, what we write, and ultimately how we behave brings us back to the question, "Who am I?"

Recognizing that we are God, the essence of love incarnate, the power of manifestation becomes clear. We have the option, the skills, and the courage to create the world, as we want. The reflection that is now seen is the way it is because we do not act responsibly with the tools we have been given. We do have a choice. The power to create a peace filled world is found in our words. As we speak, so we are.

Knowing that our words create, knowing that our thoughts don't stand alone, knowing that everyone else is subject to the same conditions, sets the stage for new kinds of relationships. The relationships that honor the divinity within each other are the relationships of empowerment. These are the relationships of support, friendship, and respect that can eliminate the projection of 'other' as the enemy. Developing respect for each other opens us up to trusting each other. Respect is still identified in terms of dignity and ethics.

The cultural rules and standards for psychic etiquette have yet to be defined by our current world. I see it as the same ethic that defines most religious traditions. It is the "golden rule"—treat others, as you would like to be treated. We must first, however, become aware of the power we already have. We cannot assume that our minds stay in our cranium any more than it is real that our souls only stay inside of our skin. We are porous beings!

My recommendation is to be the police of our thoughts. Police take a vow to "protect and serve" us. It is not too far-fetched to think that we can become our own thought police. Not to bring fear to the mind, but to watch and monitor our mental and emotional connection and reaction to the experience. I ask my clients to not berate themselves for having the negative thoughts toward themselves or others. This just adds to the negativity in the airwaves but to forgive themselves.

The Observer is the best part of our consciousness to have the job as our Thought Security Guard. As I said before, we all have multiple dimensions and voices within our awareness and mind. The Inner Critic, The Abusive Parent, The Shaming Sibling, where ever these voices are sourced from within the mind, we must remember there is always one that observes everything. The Higher Mind is the quiet voice, the gentle and calm perspective that perceives the world through love.

In 1986 when there was a celebration to commemorate the 50th Anniversary of the opening of the Golden Gate Bridge. City and state officials decided to open the bridge to pedestrian traffic as they had 50 years ago. There were 100,000 people that went to the Bridge, a 5-mile span, in the course of 4 hours. Always one to be in the middle of the scene when history is being made if I can, I was one of the crowd.

Never before have I been a part of such mass hysteria as the human traffic jams of that day. Bridge officials did not keep the north and southbound lanes as boundaries to regulate the flow of traffic. The consequences were immediate and messy. On the bridge that day I was literally stuck, slammed up against my neighbors, unwillingly for 1.5 hours. People need guidelines because there are so many of us participating in life on earth and it too is messy. To anticipate needs of our future based on the idea that all of us have intuition can help us not get stuck in the flow. It was only after I prayed to help me out of the situation that 10 minutes later, a man I had never met before, grabbed my hand and pulled me through the crowd. My prayer was heard. Our prayers to have peace on earth are heard. We must not just pray—but fearlessly as I did—take the hand that offers a way out,

We have the ability to pull each other through this amazing time on our planet. The virtues of human dignity, compassion, and deep listening can begin to set a standard of self-respect. With self-love, we can combat the rise of greed, malicious intent, judgment, condemnation, and fear. The first social standard the world could use is to embrace for ourselves what we want to experience as social norms. This is the essence of the tenant I shared at the beginning of this section, Evolution; to be loved, be loving.

There is a book written by Judith Martin a favorite news columnist that I own and the title alone makes me smile, *Ms. Manner's Saves Western Civilization*. The concept that being polite, sensitive, and generous with each other may seem simplistic. It is a value system that we are talking about here; yet, it's a good way to begin to cross that bridge. Let us go across with kindness and knowing that we are never, ever alone.

Chapter 7 Practicum

⊠ As you go through your day, when tempted to judge anyone you encounter, ask The Observer Self to help you rewrite those thoughts to a compliment. Thoughts are prayers. As you do this, you send positive energy to that person.

⊠ The advanced version of this exercise is to speak out loud directly to the person and share your compliment.

Chapter 8

Exercising the Intuitive Muscle

For decades I have taught others to develop their intuition and ultra-sensitivity. My goal is to have people learn to trust themselves, know they are connected to more, and realize that they are powerful. We don't need to come to a workshop to practice what we already have if we lived in a culture that valued more than the apparent. We have to want to, to have an impetus, to move into the spiritual realms of possibility. For some, being the seeker is a part of their nature. For most, it takes a crisis to be that impetus. Injury, death, or life passages can intensify the drive to know who we are, what we are capable of, and what we might do with that capacity.

Intuition exercises can be as simple as guessing which elevator door will open first as you are standing "waiting" to catch one. Another exercise I used to suggest was guessing who is on the phone when it rings before you answer it. Caller ID has made this one obsolete. The actual definition of the word guess is to have a sense of knowing, not to be unsure. Our culture has negated the true meaning, affirming for us not to have confidence in what we know without evidence. Learning to trust ourselves is the willingness to take responsibility for our perspective. It seems easier to abdicate authority, but in the end, no one can live our life for us. The more we own our truth, the happier and freer our souls are.

Practicing psychometry is another good work out for exercising your intuitive muscle. Everything is energy, and the act of psychometry is "reading" an object like a piece of jewelry or a watch or a vase or a cell phone. It is a fun 'parlor game' to do during dinner parties. Once I read objects for an entire party of 20 at a restaurant in Paris. I was able to do healing work with those readings for people who could never imagine coming for a session. Later in the dinner, one of the women there challenged me that I was 'wasting' my gifts. I assured her that I knew exactly what I was doing with my talents. Playfulness is one of the most potent ways to convey a message across so it is not a threat. I was able to help people, and we were having fun too.

This is the way that Jesus actually did his teachings. He did not have a church that he preached at every Sunday, as the custom is now for Christianity. In a class in my Graduate program, Hal Tassig was teaching on the prayer life of Jesus. Hal told us that historical record shows that Jesus was the most popular dinner guest in Galilee. He was funny and engaging. Jesus used camaraderie and humor, not intimidation to get his message across. Marketing companies of today need to take a look at Jesus' methodology. His brand is still alive and well and living in the 21st Century.

How do we develop our intuition? We use it. Our ability to edit and censor our awareness is encouraged by looking outside of ourselves for validation of what is right, true, and valuable. We need to pay attention to what we are feeling, envisioning, sensing, and the ideas we are thinking. Insight comes to awareness when we are asking to get more information through our knowing. This includes information that comes which seems idiosyncratic or outrageous or insignificant.

Remember the wisdom "Ask and ye shall receive"? It is through the willingness to have inquiry and curiosity we can have a deeper and more profound experience of life.

In workshops, I partner people to do readings for each other. As they begin to share what they perceive in some fashion, the information corresponds accurately into both their lives. This exercise has awed and inspired participants for decades that they do have the magic and power of intuition. Each time I facilitate this process, the question comes up about the accuracy of the symbols written down. They are often vague images, colors, feelings, or sounds from the environment where we are sitting. The accuracy is never the problem. The difficulty is in the interpretation of what has been perceived as the symbolic answers to our intuitive and psychic questions.

We do not need to know what the definitions of the symbols are for someone else. What we need to pay attention to in this exercise is how the information came to us. Did we feel emotions or sensations in our body? See visions, colors, or written words? Hear voices? Or just know? How we got it, helps us to understand the kind of ultra-sensitivity that is our natural talent. What I find as the greatest obstacle to using our intuition is that we discount it. Far too often we do not listen to that little voice of reason, or we edit and select what we want to pay attention to.

Participation is the most effective way to learn. We all can get information. The real challenge is in the interpretation of the information. Zealousness to prove your ability to someone of can often cause more harm than good. There have been clients who came to me after receiving readings from other people that overwhelmed them. They did not know what to do with the information and needed help to integrate it into their life.

Here I must reiterate the discussion on etiquette. **Always ask if someone wants your insight before you give it!** To throw out information just because you have it is not appropriate. For any relationship, we are always picking up the subtle energies. When we ask, "Do you want to know what is coming to me?" or "Do you want to know what I think?" we give the other person the power to choose. They can say "No." This keeps us from creating karma. It is appropriate when choosing how to express what you sense, to use words that carry kindness and love. Never underestimate the impact you can have on another's well-being.

My intention I said at the beginning of the chapter is to help people learn to trust themselves. Here are some exercises that I have used over the years to encourage intuitive development. Some of the processes I created. Those that came from workshops I attended or books that I read I have annotated as such. This section of the book is about using intuition, so let's do it.

_____ ♥ _____

Chapter 8 Practicum

Invite a friend or friends to learn, develop, and play about Intuition. Commit to a 30-day exercise program to strengthen the trust you have in yourself. Have a journal or keep a digital record of the answers, insights, and experiences. During the month meet periodically with each other to discuss the progress on your intuitive exercise program. Though the exercises are numbered, do them in the order that feels right or comfortable. Before each exercise, make sure to take a few deep breaths, have no distractions for time or attention. Specifically, turn off the mobile phone, the television, do not drive a vehicle and have at least 30 minutes to devote to yourself. Create an invocation prayer to set the intention when beginning and gratitude prayer to close. Agree with your partner to have respect, confidentiality, and to honor each other's personal journey. This is not a competition but a co-creation of empowerment.

Exercise 1—Assign odd number days to one person to be a Sender, even numbered days for the other to be a Receiver. Each day choose a color, object, or physical landscape—like a beach or forest or playground or theater—for the Sender to communicate through thoughts to the Receiver. Communicate feelings regarding the physical image too. Document the process and compare notes during meetings.

Exercise 2—Invite at night a dream regarding your partner. If you do not remember your dreams, tell yourself each night: "Tonight I will remember a dream about my partner." Expect a dream and do not allow yourself to say or believe that you cannot remember one. Write down the dream that comes. Share it and look for metaphors or symbolism that relate to your daily lives.

Exercise 3—Write down on a piece of paper a significant memory that holds a lot of positive or negative emotional charge. Put it in a sealed envelope. Give it to your partner. If you are not in the same city, mail it to them so that they can hold it. Write down any and all impressions that you receive while holding the envelope. Make sure to say a prayer, create an intention for good, and not edit whatever insight you receive physically, emotionally, mentally, or spiritually. Share your insights with your partner before reading what either of you had channeled after holding the envelope.

Exercise 4—Invite someone who is dear to you to help you with an intuitive development exercise which is not your on-going partner. Ask for them to give you something that they have or now belongs to someone close to them preferably made of metal. Psychometry is easiest with metals. Have a conversation with the object asking these questions:

1. Who owned you last?
2. How did they feel about you?
3. Is there any message for the person who it belongs to from spirit?
4. Why is this the object that is being used to teach about intuitive development?
5. Is there any message from you for us, another, or the world?

Make sure to give thanks and gratitude to the object and the owner.

Exercise 5—During the month, occasionally send a message to your partner to call, text or email you. This is being done without creating karma as you have already agreed to support each other's development. If you send a message, and they respond, make sure to tell them "You heard me!" or some other way, make sure you celebrate their successful transmission.

Exercise 6—This exercise is from a workshop with Marcy Calhoun in 1988. You must be in the same physical space as your partner so invite another friend if your study buddy is not close. Each of you chooses something that you carry with you or on you all the time—jewelry, wallet, mobile phone, or car keys. Blindfold the owner of the object. Hide the object somewhere in an open, easily accessible, safe to reach the place. Once it is there, send the picture visually of its placement to the owner. Guide them with the words "hot" or "cold" to help them find the object blindfolded. Give the receiver time and do not rush your cues. It is not a race or competition. Take turns for as long as it is fun. Make sure to be supportive, congratulatory and appreciative of your partner.

Exercise 7—Watch the video meditation "Meet Your Four Primary Spirit Guides" on https://www.intuitiveartsandsciences.com/meet-your-spirit-guides-video.html. Meet your four primary Spirit Guides for each dimension of being: physical—your totem, emotional—your warrior protector, mental—your alchemist, and spiritual—your primary cosmological teacher. Guides evolve over time, have often mysterious or revelatory agendas to support your growth, and could be in any form. For instance, guides can be mythical figures, historical figures, religious leaders, departed family members, or energy forms that have no relevance to the earth and what you have experienced before. If you do not have access to the Internet, ask a friend who does to have time on their computer. If you do not have internet access, sit quietly and ask that one by one, your Spirit Guides come and introduce themselves to you.

Exercise 8—Work with your partner to have a dialogue with each of the dimensions of being to see what messages or insight they want to share: their body or earth, their feelings or water, their mind or air, and their fire or soul.

Exercise 9—Go for a walk to a favorite place that makes you feel connected to nature. Nature is everywhere. Do not assume you must be in a rural or undeveloped landscape. Invite a conversation with the elements—earth, water, air, and fire—to share with you any wisdom they have that will help you in your life.

Exercise 10—Using your imagination in meditation, invite your Totem Spirit Guide, your earth protector, to come to you. Feel your body merging inside of their form. Travel through the world as they do. Allow them to give you lessons about survival from their perspective. Honor the gift that they give and wisdom of this experience with gratitude.

Exercise 11—This exercise is designed to help bridge the relationship between thought and the Universe. Any question we ask, The Divine will answer. We just need to be open to listening. Think of a question you have regarding something in your life. Examples: *Do I look for a new job? Is it time to commit to this relationship? How do I deal with my conflicts with my father? Where do I move to find more happiness?* Tell the Universe: *The next song or dialog or conversation I hear will have the answer or a clue toward discovering the answer.* Then either access a radio, or Pandora, or shuffle your iTunes for this fun dialog, or pay attention to any music which comes into your awareness next.

Exercise 12—Open a book, newspaper, magazine, or brochure—anything printed that is in your direct environment with the thought: What message does the Universe have for me right now? Take a breath and put your finger down. Read what is written and think about how it relates to your life. If you need more clarity, do it again with another page or document.

Part Two

Revolution-Perceiving Beyond the Apparent

Chapter 9

The Spiritual Revolution

The Merriam-Webster Dictionary defines the word revolution in four ways: "rotation; progress around an orbit; cycle; and a sudden, radical or complete change." We are living a revolution to bring collective human consciousness into the Fourth Dimensional world. As the microcosm is symbolic of the macrocosm, the DNA helix is symbolic of the sacred spiral of life. We rotate through the lessons of life similar to the way that information is encoded into the structure that supports all physical creation. We are turning on the sacred spiral to open not just another dogma but to take humanity to another level of our creative potential.

The progress that I am addressing, using the second definition, is the movement of consciousness. As I described in the introduction, the perpetual motion machine that is consciousness follows established patterns until the system can no longer support these patterns. Revolution is the awareness of this movement, the circular definition of the movement, and the capability within the movement for re-definition.

The revolution or change that we are seeing, living, and responding to on a conscious and an unconscious level is the revolution of our basic assumptions of reality. It is on the level of what anthropologists call the cosmological. "All roads lead to Rome," as the saying goes, and all cosmologies lead to a divine intelligence. What we name this intelligence is not to be debated, you say 'toemato,' and I say 'tamato,' however, the recognition of it will give us as individuals an accurate understanding of our power. The revolution of our beliefs will create the unity necessary for peace.

Revolution occurs when it is time to go to an another level of wisdom, a rotation on the sacred spiral. We now on the planet have both metaphysical/spiritual and physical/technological knowledge that can turn our pain and conflict into prosperity and acceptance. It is a matter of choice. There are many prophecies that predict great earth changes, massive devastation, and destruction to societies due to earthquakes, weather and climate changes, and nuclear warfare. We are living and witnessing these extremes producing and generating more fear. It also is producing more need for antidotes to the suffering.

Faith in something greater and the willingness for humanity to humble itself to a higher power will give us the antidote that we seek. There is more going on than we can measure, manipulate, or control. I advocate choosing expanding our perceptions instead of blind faith and assumption. It is the co-creative relationship between the dark and light, mystery, and revelation that give meaning to experience. The revolution that I believe will create a better world is not just adapting to my perceptions. It is the willingness for each of us to realize we are a part of a greater cosmos and not to be afraid because we cannot name it nor keep it from changing.

The Universe, God, or the divine wisdom of our experience is the most efficient recycling program one could conceive. Everything that you see, feel, know, and sense in your awareness transforms. Transformation is the completion of cycles of change. With every breath, a part of our body changes as those oxygen molecules join with our blood to keep the body alive. The state of homeostasis is change. We as a collective whole, have no idea where real that change is leading us other than to be gone.

The best example I can think of is coal into diamonds. The building blocks are the same, carbon and minerals but you cannot reverse the process. With time and pressure, the elements progress from coal to diamonds. Once it becomes a diamond, it does not go back to being coal. The transformation is not reversible. Think of the plant and animal life that became the coal. Think of the water, soil, and sunlight that transformed into the plants and animals. To have construction, there must be destruction, and this is the wisdom of balance. We cannot, and do not, live with just one. Here is the magic of eternal life and consciousness fuels it all.

The power of this knowledge gives us the opportunity to change everything in our awareness for the highest good. When we are attached to the outcome, we inhibit the divine wisdom of life to guide the revolutions necessary in the process of evolution. Remember, evolution is the ability to adapt, to respond to have success. As the true Darwinian theory is that the survival of the fittest is not based on domination but cooperation with the environment and conditions that a species is found in. This ability to respond is the key for humans when they understand their power of choice. Pain is an indication that there is a lesson. Rejecting it, sublimating it, hiding it are not the ways to relieve the pain. Embracing pain is how we heal it.

Pain is the indication of where to put our attention. When we focus with the intention to embrace the wisdom of the pain, we are given the freedom, and the power to transform it. Our reaction is usually to recoil from pain, bring our energy back from it. Putting our heads collectively into the sand, will not make life easier for any of us. The problems of humanity on earth are for all of us to solve. Giving our power to governments, corporations, or others does not create a peace-filled world. We are a part of the problems when we abdicate responsibility. It is this complacency that I see as the actual ill of humanity. The revolution is for us to realize that we possess the power to change the world. It is not outside, but inside of every one of us.

The ultimate test of faith is not about taking our spiritual purity somewhere else but to bring it here to the earth. I believe the revolution is about descending not ascending. The mantra "Be Here Now" as Ram Dass taught us nearly half a century ago, is the mantra of the revolution. As the destination is already known, that we die, then why do we live? We live to see what can be created in the eternal stream of constant reinvention of everything.

There are so many stories of all time, about what is good, what is right. In Joseph Campbell's book, *Hero With A Thousand Faces*, we are taken across the mythologies of history that each in their essence is the same journey—one toward self-realization, self-awareness and the nature of truth. What it means to be spiritual does not mean how we practice or promote our faith. I meet people all the time who tell me they are not spiritual. It makes me laugh. They are a soul with a body. How could they not be spiritual? Being spiritual does not mean that we wear our faith on our sleeve. We are all 'more than earth,' which is the literal definition of extra-terrestrial! We have all come from the light of love with inherent truth. Love is the essence of our spirit light.

It is time to recognize our oneness as consciousness. I'll agree that there are levels of awareness within consciousness. But what are the criteria used to measure the value of one life form over any other life? We evolve in our perspective as we gain wisdom and insight. Spiritual hierarchy though cannot be real. There is no way to know, and we do not have the power to know. We just are. Everyone else just is. Measuring gets us nowhere, except to fear each other.

There is no way to measure anyone's spiritual truth either. I am unwilling to say that if I am a student of *A Course in Miracles* that I am more spiritual than an Orthodox Jew raised in Israel and studying the Torah, or a Catholic who goes to confession and lights candles, or an Aborigine who worships the land, or a little old lady in the back pew of the Presbyterian Church, or any other way ritual supports spirituality. We are not equipped to judge another's relationship with God or universal consciousness. It is between the individual and God.

If we ask for guidance, it is given no matter what our level of spiritual knowledge and training. Guidance comes in many forms. We are spoken to symbolically, a sunset, a beggar on the street, a baby's laughter, or a tree leaning against the wind. All of what we conceive and perceive can have a meaning in relationship to the universe. Often the words of a friend can bring us back into connection with ourselves, which is why we call them our friend. Ritual is designed to do the same. The problem comes when we standardize ritual as the appropriate path to the desired outcome.

The spiritual path is the journey, not the destination. I know you have heard that one before and it is true. This is why we can be distracted by stories of other worlds and realities as being better than earth. By projecting happiness and perfection out to those other planets, or when I lose 10 pounds, or find a better job, or can do 1000 yogic prostrations, have more money, we only create a grass-is-greener mentality. Our job is to be here now! To recognize the perfection at the moment, act from virtuous intentions, and to detach from the outcomes of our actions. If we are living divine law, which is simple, we do not need others to measure our standard. It comes from within.

When we are living for a future moment, we are living what I call—**Destination Orientation Thinking**. To be in the revolution of consciousness, it means to not project our happiness until later. I championed in the Evolution section to not let others define what is real and true for us. In the Revolution section, I am encouraging us to not put off our destiny until sometime in the future. The future is going to happen, later. Now is now and it is when we have the ability to create peace.

Our personal choices, behaviors, and attitudes can either create heaven or hell, right here, right now. It is not how we celebrate our connection to God that is important. Even what path we take—and whether we do it alone or with others—is not as important as recognizing universal love and divine perfection. Being grateful and giving thanks for life is important for it is the gift we give back to the universe out of respect and acknowledgment for what is.

How then do we accept the perfect imperfection if it doesn't feel good, like being fired from a job, or our wife saying she doesn't love us anymore, or our body is filled with cancer, or if our teenage son is into gang activity or drugs? These examples scream to us about control. "If I had been more diligent, I wouldn't have been fired." "If I had been more considerate, more affectionate, or more attentive, she would not have left me." "I am sick, damaged, goods!" "If I had more money and we lived in a better neighborhood my son wouldn't be doing those things." We are in a co-creative process, so it is impossible to control events, but we can be more aware of how we are doing our part.

The variables that condition our choices are more complex than the obvious. The lesson is not to recreate what we just experienced. Own what was learned, forgive yourself, forgive the others involved, then let go. We chose the play we are performing as humans to learn, to create or destroy karma, and to experience divine love. As we are the co-creators, we must now move beyond our victimization of self.

It is so much easier to blame our life situations on others than to recognize we are 100% responsible for everything in our lives. I know that this becomes hard to believe when there are atrocities such as the vast array of illnesses—AIDS, cancer, addictions, and diseases. Then there are the ways humans are inhuman to each other—female circumcision, incest, rape, murder—all of the ways we dishonor life. Responsibility and blame are both states of mind and emotion. One is a state of power, the ability to respond. The other is a state of victimization, of being out of power. Loving action is always an option and the most powerful.

We call to us experiences in our waking dream, our life, to teach us about ourselves, and the world, through love. This in no way justifies cruel behavior, but it helps to provide clarity for what has gone on for centuries as humankind turned against his brothers and sisters. We are the only species on earth that seeks and destroys its kind through massive annihilation. Why is that so, when we consider ourselves to be the most evolved species of life on the planet?

The Internet has sped up the intensity of the revolution. We are now able to witness the pain and horror of the world in real time. Not only are we witnesses, but we are also participants. The revolt in Egypt stimulated by social media in 2011 is a perfect example of how the illusion of separation cannot persist when it is being broadcast right into our home and right into our hand that holds our electronic devices. These conflicts become our conflicts when it comes to our awareness via the media channels of today. It is not just a metaphor that 'we are one world.' It is literal and figurative and economic and environmental. The spiritual revolutionaries can be anyone and include every one of us.

Chapter 9 Practicum

¤ Write your creation myth about how and why the Universe exists. Make sure to include yourself in the story. The myth could be represented by a poem, prose, play, or some visual art. If music is a way to connect to the Divine, compose a song to tell of Life coming to form.

¤ Find someone who has been a revolutionary that you respect in any way. Write them a letter, email, blog post, social media posting thanking them for their service to our world.

Chapter 10

Black and White in a Gray World

The construction of the universe has both electric and magnetic energy in its most fundamental form. In the revolution of spiritual awareness, the dance of positive and negative forces become a pivot for the new paradigm shift. As I said in the introduction, the new paradigm is shifting our polarized, separatist thinking to perceiving through wholeness. For that to happen, we must unite the extremes. Why do we relegate dark to evil and light to good?

As a poet, I am often unable to speak to the specifics of meaning in a literal fashion. Though I consider myself both the scientist and the artist, it is often only in the clever crafting of words that I can try to explain subtle precepts.

Beyond the impossible
just near the ideal
close to the probable
next being real

There is a space
Between you and me

Infinite and yet
limited by choice
Finite and yet
opened by design

For what is ebb
without flow?
What is stop
without go?
What is yes
without no?
What is find
without seek?
What is strong
without weak?

There is a space
between us all

One without sides
It just is.

Black and white thinking stops creative potential. Relating to the world through belief systems, value systems, and cosmological systems that divide and delineate limits the shades of gray in between. In our soul bodies, we have the same construction. Our shadow side, the dark side, the intuition, the magnetic part of our nature is the inner female. The waking side, the light side, the intellect, the electric part of our nature is the inner male. One is not right or wrong, good or bad. I am saying regardless of our body type; we are influenced by these energies, both women, and men, the same. We choose which gender, body type, and sex role that will support our soul's life purpose.

We are living in remarkable times when it comes to the revolution of what is possible for the recreation of consciousness within the body of a human being. It is the first time in evolution where I can be born either male or female, and with the help of hormones, surgery, and gender identification, switch. It is possible to live either, or, or both without having to die! This is a remarkable statement about revolutionizing the experience of souls on earth. A soul is an eternal energy in continual transformation moving forward to destinations of possibility. As our creative capacities imagine more varied possibilities, they become probable because an action is taken toward them.

Although I am female in this lifetime, I still experience karma with my inner male. The issues have been profound in my experience with men—abandonment, abuse, and rejection—all of it indicative of my relationship with myself. I cannot blame them though it is easier than taking responsibility for my karma. The more I have learned about my inner male, created over lifetimes, the more I have seen the perfect imperfection in my story. This does not make my path less painful. It deepens my compassion for others. Spiritual consciousness helps me understand and accept my experiences better. I know I am here to learn about love like everyone else. The drama stories with men are my workshops of deep forgiveness and the growth opportunities for my soul.

The inner male and inner female are affected by the actions and free will choices regardless of whatever sex body we inhabit during an incarnation. They are eternal principles, electric and magnetic, within us. This is why gender and biological, physical embodiment do not always correspond. It is one reason why relationships can get so confusing. We operate using both the contiguous male and female aspects of our eternal souls bringing energetic content and relationships from previous incarnations. When we see it from this perspective, the inner male and female have more influence than just the body we chose in our current incarnation.

Imagine that your inner woman is also relating to your partner's inner woman and inner man and vice verse. Your partner is a symbol of one face or another in any given moment. For instance, two men are in a homosexual relationship, although they are both men, their inner women are a part of the equation. This is true even if one of them has a more developed female, behaves in an effeminate manner, and expresses stereotypic feminine qualities in mannerisms and behavior. He is symbolically reflecting his partner's inner female, as well as, acting out his story. Just as the more masculine partner is reflecting his inner male, they both are not just acting out socially conditioned roles.

The inner male/female is even more complex. If there are unresolved issues from the past of this life or other incarnations our partner can reflect those issues. The partner we chose, and I emphasize, chose, comes into our life to help us resolve the past, create the future, and learn in the present about who we are … and you thought it was about love! Well, it is about love—loving our Self to be free.

The ability to reach divine love comes through this incredible opportunity for growth. When we recognize the mirror, we can heal if the reflection is one that is unpleasant to us. As Thich Nhat Hanh says, *"What we notice in others, we are strengthening in ourselves."* Truly we cannot change another person. However, what we notice in them that is disturbing to us, we must then look inside ourselves to find the match. The match is always there.

If our neighbor is hostile, check inside to find your own hostility. If your husband is a hypocrite, saying one thing but doing another, see where in your life you are not walking your talk. If you notice that someone has more opportunity, clothing, or choices than you do, take an inventory of what you do have and compare it to someone living in a third world country with no electricity. If you are upset about the baseball strike, see where your play is being interrupted. To include this line of thinking within a marriage or partnership gives the people the signs for self-growth without trying to change each other. We do not have the ability to truly change another unless they have given us that power.

To continue with the example from above, what if the effeminate partner begins to act in a more assertive manner, releases some of his behaviors, and begins to redefine himself? What happens to their relationship? It will trigger the need for growth within the relationship for the mirror will not reflect the same image to the partner's unconscious mind. The answer to this growth, are numerous possibilities that always have a common factor—change—and it is always inevitably for the best.

We are in a relationship, in connection, with everything that we experience and witness. The intimacy in partnership creates a unique arena to learn about our inner strengths and vulnerabilities. To be able to see our in a partner, and into our self, we have the necessary tools for our transformation. It is also the key to a greater fulfillment of our connection. When breaking down a word, we can perceive layers of meaning. My friend Shiven in 1990 told me the meaning of intimacy. As he said, "in-to-me-see." This is an invitation to a deeper level of relationship, love, and willingness to be present with each other.

The invitation aspect of this is very important to the balancing of our male/female selves. We are welcoming to us the value of our partner and affirming our trust in them. It is a part of the inner courtship or integration, which leads to the creation of divine love. The union of heaven-male and earth-female is how we perpetuate the sacred marriage of spirit and our bodies.

To have harmony with the intellect and intuitive parts of our nature they both must have expression. The active principle, male, asks the questions of life. The intuitive principle, female, answers them. This is why we must have both prayer and meditation in spiritual discipline for balance. One or the other is not more important in the creative process as they do not exist without each other.

This mirroring effect can be expanded to include everything in our lives that we see, feel, know and experience. It is all, positive and negative, reflective of us. You might say: *"Well, I am spiritual, I love everyone! I'm not like my country that has to protect itself from the enemy!"* or *"I have a good job and a home, that homeless beggar is not me!"* or *"I am not like my mother, she and I are so different!"* I suggest we look a little closer.

How is the warring country like the religious man? Perhaps in his need to defend his religion. How is the homeless man like the content woman? The comparisons as we get to know more about each side, lead us to see that there are no real separations. We are all symbols to each other in some way, or we would not even come into each other's orbit. Everything is God, so everything that we perceive comes to serve our relationship to that Divine force of all.

A very good example of this phenomenon is our relationship. My voice in this book is reflective of your inner teacher. I am no more or less powerful than you. From a karmic standpoint, you have asked me to awaken in you what you already know. You agree to that awakening by buying the book or reading the text, regardless if you like what you read or not. This book is about, then, you, not me.

Conversely, you are a reflection of me. You reflect my curious, questing, and truth seeking self. I am a multifaceted being that wants to experience the divine in all. We had chosen these roles before we got here, and if we don't like what we chose, we can choose again. You are my teachers reflecting what I need to address inside of myself, so profoundly I must write it down. You are the desire within me to be heard, acknowledged, and witnessed.

Each class I teach or session I give is the same—I never tell people what they don't already know on some level. Acknowledgment is what we all are seeking. To be told, "I see you. I hear you. I feel you. I recognize you. I know who you are." These statements are the most powerful gifts we can give each other. This witnessing bridges the space between us so that we are reminded that we are not alone.

From the Christian creation story Eve coerced Adam to taste of the forbidden fruit—knowledge—so the material distracted us from the eternal. The original sin is not the material world or our innate perfect, imperfection. The original sin is that we forgot we were part of God and that we were separate from our eternal source. We in truth are born blessed with infinite potential. When we acknowledge each other, we help heal that deep aloneness that comes from this original sin, separation. We are here to help each other, not to make life any more difficult than it already is.

It is by seeing everything in our experience as a part of ourselves or as a reflection of ourselves that we will solidify the revolution of consciousness on the planet. When we see that behaviors toward each other which are coming from attack are attacking the self, then this energy will begin to dissipate and eventually disappear from human consciousness.

I know that my words sound hopeful, if not even idealistic. It is coming from a deeper knowing. I believe inherent with everything is the quest for greatness. From the smallest subspace particle to a single cell, to a living organism, to a nuclear family, to a community, to an ecosystem, to cosmology, to God itself, there is a desire for balance, service, and love. It is the way of truth.

Even a bank robber, computer hack, spy, or murderer wants success at what they do. These behaviors perpetuate the illusion of scarcity, betrayal, secrets, and power over another human life. The universe is a vast and ultimately fair system of energy. Until we recognize that our thoughts create, we will keep creating more and more powerful enemies. The universe creates according to our intentions and always sees to the balancing of karma. If our intention is less than virtuous, we may succeed in our action or creation, and when the time is right, we'll get the universal kick in the behind … this can go on for lifetimes. What we put out, we will get back.

So what is a virtuous intention? It is one that comes from your heart and seeks balance, service, and communication with divine love. Our souls are eternal. The choice to be free is our own. The more we are in alignment with our virtuous essence, the more we radiate light and love. Virtues are the mechanics of love. When we operate out of the light and love, we show others and ourselves the possible human.

The Earth that we inhabit is dark. The light that is here is borrowed from the sun during the day. Even the moon does not have its light but borrows the light too from the sun. However, inside the earth, there is a ball of fire. There is no difference between the human body and the soul. Our duty is to bring our soul and creative fire into the world of darkness. It is our cleverness and ingenuity that invented the ability to have light by electricity and the taming of the fire. The human experience is to experience the dark and the light. We are always moving from what we know, to what we don't, from the unseen to the known. When we move from the past, to the future it is the same. The gift of faith is the willingness to discover the mystery that is in the dark.

Early in my metaphysical studies, I read Brugh Joy's book *Joy's Way*. Reading his book was one of the most defining moments of my spiritual development and personal evolution as a Being. I was thrilled at 24-years-old to read about my reality and my perceptions. I had very little affirmation or support for my beliefs from people or books then. To read about what I knew gave me a profound courage that I'd not had before. In the book, the teaching that stood out the most was from his teacher Eunice when she said to him there were only three tenants on a spiritual path that one must live: **make no judgments, make no comparisons, and delete the need to understand**.

The first principle I had no trouble understanding the Christian ideology and values I was raised. Though it is a habit of humanity as we are all taught to stereotype, categorize, and label as a part of our social conditioning, we never have all the information, so judgments are limited thinking from their origin. The second principle made perfect sense for in a comparative anthropology class in college we had studied the theory and managed to rebut it completely from the wisdom that there are too many variables to truly compare anything, let alone people. For me, the third principle was where my growth and learning took place. *Delete the need to understand* did not make sense to such a hungry student. Isn't understanding what we are seeking on the spiritual path?

As I meditated on this principle, I began to see that what had to be changed in my perception and interpretation of the world was not **understanding,** but the **need** for it! When we are in trust, the need transforms into faith. Need creates attachment and slows the freedom of spirit. I still use this teaching from Brugh Joy often, though it is decades later. The need to know, and to understand, still trumps faith. This I believe is still one of the greatest deterrents to peace.

Daniel was not coming to hear me speak in Carmel, CA, and he wasn't interested in seeing another channeling session. Daniel was on his spiritual path, meditating, and developing his intuition. About 7:15 PM he received a clear message to attend my channeling demonstration at 7:30 PM that night at The Thunderbird bookstore. Daniel was at a point in his life that he describes as "going through the eye of the needle." Though intellectually he did not see the value, intuitively he knew he needed to go.

After my talk, he came up to me and said he felt connected to a project I was working on at the time. By listening to his guidance, it put Daniel on a path; which led him to a new love in his life, Lee. Daniel and Lee met as she later became involved in the project, fell in love, and married. We are only aware of part of our motivation to action. There are outcomes that are a part of the Divine plan that the path to the outcome is very clear when we look back. Going forward on the path is the workshop. We don't need to go to intuitive development workshops, for we live them.

Trusting the information we receive and acting from it is the testament to our connection with higher guidance. I am asked a lot, "How do you know it is accurate?" The bottom line is that it depends on the level of questioning and the degree of answers that we are talking about. Sometimes, in sessions I give misinformation, and it is perfect at that moment. I must be in a trust that whatever I am sensing is in divine order. I cannot question what I am getting as insight. However, it is perfect, appropriate, and necessary that my clients ask the for information and take action on what they intuit to be correct and right for them.

During August 16th and 17th of 1987, there was the first "New Age" holiday, a celebration of the end of the Mayan calendar promoted by Jose Arguelles called the *Harmonic Convergence*. Without the Internet, it was honored and celebrated all around the world. Individuals, in tune with their intuition, were called to be at sacred sites all over the planet. Early in July of that year, I participated in a medicine wheel ceremony and a new spirit guide, Chief Eagle Eye, came into my awareness. In the days following the ceremony, I bought an Indian drum, was told to purchase specific crystals and had repeated visions of a white snow-capped mountain. My boyfriend at the time suggested we celebrate the Convergence at Mt. Shasta.

We were invited to Lake Tahoe about a month before the Convergence. One of my guides at the time was a being called Wong Chang. In meditation, Wong Chang suggested that we get fireworks in Nevada to set off at Mt. Shasta. When all of our attempts to find fireworks failed, we were disappointed. This was 1987 no GPS or internet browsers were on our cell phones. Brick sized, expensive mobile phones were just being introduced to consumers! The search itself had been a workshop for our relationship. We began an on-going debate in Tahoe that weekend which escalated to a screaming match the first day of the Convergence.

Standing under the stars, on this beautiful mountain, we had extremely strong words with each other. It became so ridiculous I started to laugh. At that moment my guide, Wong Chang, popped into my psychic vision and was he laughing too. He said, "These are the fireworks I was talking about a month ago!" From that point on, I stayed open to the possibility, that the information I was receiving perhaps was not literal but metaphorical or symbolic. Also, it was possible that my guidance could be sending me toward a lesson that might be painful, instead of just pleasurable.

We are the best judge of what our personal truth looks and feels like. Everything, positive and negative, is a mirror of the truth but not the single source of truth. It is only the trust of the process that can be the understanding of spiritual revolution. If we seek guidance, however, listen deeply to what is begin offered to us, remember we asked for it. Black and white in a gray world are only the extremes. Life is lived in every shade in between of what we do and do not know. The metaphor continues to ending every division including female and male. Creation needs the extremes but is not limited by them. Human beings have the potential to do the same by dropping our need to know and having the willingness to discover what lies between.

The Earth itself is a place of darkness. Without the sun, there would be no light. Each morning as the dawn breaks, life on Earth in that particular longitude receives the gift of the sun. Even the Moon is dark but what we see is the sun's light illuminating it for us to see that it exists. My favorite Sufi Mystic Hafiz wrote a poem speaking about this relationship, in fact, all relationships: *"Even after all these years the sun never says to the moon, you owe me. A love like that lights up the whole sky."*

The dance of Heaven and Earth are most profound during the Equinox and the Solstice times. Rituals in most cultures though-out what we know of human cultures have celebrated the peak of light and dark in the sky. Here are two poems I wrote to honor my feelings regarding the magic of the solstices when the days that define the beginning of winter and the start of summer come.

Ode to Winter Dark

Welcome wisdom eternal
Your light remains steady
Winter arrives this day
The dark is at its zenith
On this side of the Earth, I ride

Deeper may we go
Into the Mystery that is
Finding there stillness
Resting in the quiet
Where all creation waits

Time never ends nor does
The movement of Heavens
The Earth, she flows there too
They are not separate above below
Nor are me and you
Dark is not our enemy separate
From the light who is our friend
Like soul mates, they are One

For only by and with each other
Can True Love become.

Ode to Spring Light

Welcome wisdom eternal
Your light remains steady
Summer arrives this day
The light is at its zenith
On this side of the Earth, I ride

Higher may we go
Into the Mystery that is
Finding there celebration
Dancing in the song
Where all creation begins
Times never ends nor does
The movement of the Heavens,
The Earth, she flows there too
They are not separate above below
Nor are me and you
Light is not our friend separate
From the dark who is our enemy
Like soulmates, they are One

For only by and with each other
Can True Love become.

Just like we as life forms—animal, plant, mineral—have the light of our soul radiating from the inside of every cell, we become the microcosm of the Earth who has light radiating from within her. So how could it be that light is good, and dark is bad? In truth, one does not even exist without the other. Creation must have destruction to have construction. Just as light cannot be without dark, we in the human form too must have both to be. If we pay attention to the simple models of Creation, just like simple models of spirituality, peace and love become easier to obtain.

Chapter 10 Practicum

⼝ Make a list of 10 experiences or people in your life that were painful, difficult, and challenging. With each one, write at least one gift that was a product of the experience or interaction with that person.

⼝ Make a list of 10 experiences or people in your life that were pleasurable, happy, and fulfilling. With each one, write at least one challenge that was a product of the experience or interaction with that person.

Chapter 11

Forms and Teaching of Spirit Guides

A spiritual revolution, as I have defined it, means embracing a reality beyond the physical, beyond our five senses, and beyond duality. Another aspect of the revolution is that life exists in realms we cannot perceive. We are arrogant and egocentric to think otherwise. Spirit guides can be life forms from other dimensional star systems and life forms other than human here on earth. These soul friends are around us to help out. Their perspective can help us create successful lives. Spirit guides are just that—guides. We must still take responsibility for our choices and decisions. Idolizing spirit guides is giving our power to them. Emulating spirit guides brings the wisdom they offer alive on the planet.

Though there were a lot of stories shared about spirit guides in the Evolution section, the revolution is the willingness to open our minds to more levels of reality. Spirit guides easily meet that challenge to the boundaries of what people consider acceptable to believe. Having more stories than possible to share on this topic, I am bringing several more into our journey here together that I hope will inspire your desire for relationships that expand your life experience of miracles and magic. They bring assistance that can marvel any Google search on any topic when looking for answers.

One of the most accurate channelings from a spirit guide for me came through Judith Conrad. We were attending a workshop on the Monterey Bay with Marcy Calhoun, and during one of the breaks, Judith and I decided to practice our channeling. I wished to speak to the highest and best teacher for me that day. Judith channeled my alchemist/magician/healer guide, the spirit that assists me in healing myself and others. Then my healer guide was still the Being named Wong Chang.

Wong Chang felt it would be good for me to work with a soul brother named Wong Gee so quickly exited from the channel. When Judith brought into her body the spirit of Wong Gee, I had tears of recognition to his energy. I knew this soul from another lifetime. The three of us had lived before on earth. Wong Chang had been our teacher, and we were his students and dear friends. I asked Wong Gee about learning new healing tools or modalities for helping others and myself. The information Wong Gee gave was:

> "You will take training that will initiate your hands to touch others with light. It will be taught by a man. It will be given in … ah … hmm … Oakland … Berkeley … somewhere near there and soon. It is important for your karma to do this."

When I returned from the weekend in my mailbox was a flyer advertising a free Reiki lecture in Berkeley on Tuesday that very week to promoting a workshop on this hands-on healing technique the very next weekend! It was not just serendipity … it was a clear prediction and direction for me. So without hesitation, I attended the lecture to learn about Reiki as a way of channeling energy to balance and heal.

After the lecture, I went up to Joyce Morris, the Reiki master, and told her how I was instructed to come there by my spirit guide. I let her know that I was surprised though that she was not a man as my guide had said a man would teach the workshop. Joyce laughed and said, *"My son is teaching the workshop!"* I could only smile. Then I learned that the training was to be in Emeryville, a little town nestled between Berkeley and Oakland! This is a good example of how accurate channeled information from guides can be!

For Desiree, one of my clients, the accuracy of a channeling helped her understand what could have been a difficult time. I was bringing Hermes through my channel as the spiritual guide/teacher for a small group who gathered after comedy traffic school. I never know where or when I will be in service. The 70 people in comedy traffic school had teased me all day because of my profession. I had even been named the Valedictorian for providing more laughs than any other attendee in the room. The teacher asked if I would channel for anyone who wanted to stay after. So, I did for the five people who were curious, and the spirit who showed up was Hermes.

Desiree, one of the reformed traffic offenders, asked about a job she had just started that week and how it would progress. Hermes said:

> *"The job will change in 4 months, and it will be a change for the better."*

Four months later, to the day of that channeling, I got a call from a harried Desiree. She had just been fired! At that moment, the change that had been predicted wasn't looking too good for Desiree. Several months later, she called me again to say how happy she was in her new job. The employer she was now working for was the best she had ever experienced, and the working conditions were very positive for her. As Hermes had predicted, it will be a change for the better, and so it was.

Spirit guides do not have to look like mythological characters, psychological archetypes, biblical figures, or what your neighbor's guide looks like. They are unique to you. Your vibration, your traditions, your heritage, your past lives, and the origin of your soul are all factors in who you will relate to as a guide in the spirit world. Some of my students have animals, trees or a waterfall as their spirit guides. There is no limit on what is possible as we are in a constant conversation with all that is in our awareness. The journey of consciousness is to open to what is.

There are more stories I will tell with regards to appropriate information, accuracy, and spirit guides. The important thing to realize, now at this moment, is that in our revolution of awareness the infinite is possible. We do not know the boundaries of consciousness. It is fear that keeps us from finding out that it is limitless. If we begin to acknowledge what we perceive, to ourselves first, then we can share with others, exploring our collective potential.

Without knowing it, I had a spiritual guide for years that no one could explain to me. When I was a child and would wake up frightened by a dream, get then even more frightened by the shadows in my room, and I would ask Clown Face to help me think of happy thoughts. I was about 7 when this started. I would see an apparition, which looked like tear-dropped concentric circles of white, red, green, and black light. When I focused on Clown Face it would appear to grow. I would see it if my eyes were open or shut. I felt safe with this apparition, and eventually, I would fall back to sleep.

In my first guided meditation, many years later, we were told to visualize being in a house that had something for us in each room to help us on our life's path. We were to go from the study and into the hallway of the house to meet our spirit guide. There was Clown Face! I began to cry; I was deeply moved with recognition. The light mandala that I had seen for 17 years finally had a definition. No one could ever explain to me, until that moment, what I was seeing. It wasn't just a product of my active imagination. It was a real entity. I learned later that the spirit's name is Aslyn. It took me a couple of more years to be able to have an auditory connection. To this day I still see Clown Face, my spirit guide Aslyn near me, truly a guiding light helping me know my power.

All of us, whether we acknowledge them or not, have guides. There are four primary guides for everyone. We have a totem guide, which is usually an animal or some other living creature that is alive somewhere on the planet or from other dimensional worlds like a dragon or a winged horse. This level of guidance is for our physical well being, helping us to be fruitful in the world and healthy in our bodies.

The next level of a guide is our will guide. Its responsibility is to help us with our feelings and emotions, especially feeling our self-confidence. Our will is our capacity to make choices. We feel our will power, self-determination, self-esteem and our personal authority when making choices then act on them. The trend I have seen with this guide for my clients is often a mythological or historical warrior or being known for their will, sense of duty, tenacity, and endurance.

Our alchemist, healer, or magician guide helps us to know the creative ability within us to manifest our potential through our intellect and intuition and the creative power of our mind. The spiritual teacher is the soul level of guidance. It assists us in our faith, formulating our belief systems, our understanding of the current paradigm, and our connection to God. Together they are our personal growth team, assisting us in all aspects of life in the world and as well, the beyond.

We assist spirit guides in their evolution as much as they assist us. Every student/teacher relationship is reciprocal. One of my most powerful initiations came about a year after the Harmonic Convergence. My guide Wong Chang came to me in meditation with a sword. I was surprised when he placed the sword in my hands, knelt before me, and asked if I would help him in his transformation by putting the sword through his heart. I started to cry, physically shedding tears, telling him, "No way."

Wong Chang explained to me that death is a transition. He also explained that he was stuck in his form and needed my help to be set free into his next greater wisdom role. At the time in my imagination, he wore a red silk brocade robe trimmed in gold and black, had long dark hair in a braid and dark mustache, and was quite slim with incredible long fingernails. Wong Chang explained that the sword represented my mind, that he represented healing, and that to use the sword for his death meant that I was willing to change my thoughts forever to help others and myself.

After many tears had rolled down my cheeks, I plunged the sword into his heart. In my psychic sight, I could see myself, kneeling and crying by his wounded, lifeless body. The next thing I saw was a man standing where Wong Chang's body had been. He had simple white robes tied with a rope, a fuller girth, a balding head trimmed with a fringe of white hair, a white mustache, and the brightest blue eyes one could imagine. He held me with the most loving embrace.

When I asked him his name, he said, "It is I, Wong Chang, thank you for your courage, for you have set me free." He stayed with me as my guide only for a little longer, for he was now able to journey into worlds unknown to me and his calling became elsewhere. Wong Chang's great humor, love, and light ascended again. If this was just a teaching for me about letting go of forms, it worked. However, it helped me realize that there is no hierarchy, or arriving at a place of "done" even with spirit guides. They too are in the process of growth and change, perhaps forever. It really doesn't matter. What matters is we know all things change.

We do not have to create explanations, systems, rules for the re-creation of our souls after we depart the earth. Until we master living here in the now, being unconditionally loving, having the courage to live with truth, and actualizing our unique potential, then life after death remains the Great Mystery. Knowing, however, that the soul's life continues, and is interactive with this world, can give us the hope to make the changes we need to create a better world.

To know your guides only adds more friends to your social circle. I am never alone, and neither are any of us. The guides are there to help us thrive. Their presence will help us function in our waking dream if we let them. The problems and solutions can be simple and mundane or quite evolved like my vision quest. For example on a practical level, there are parking angels or fairies. Many people I know have them.

They are there answering your intuition when you are using PPA. If you did not do the Practicum exercise at the end of Chapter 4, perhaps it would be a good time to practice.

Another way my guides worked with me to problem solve was on a ski lift in Tahoe. It was a beautiful day to ski, blue skies, crisp air, fresh powder, and good friends to be with. On the chair, I was having problems with waves of fear. I went inside to see where it was coming from. I saw in my psychic vision myself at the age of 5. She was terrified to be on the chair lift going up a mountain! I talked to her about how important skiing was to the adult part of myself. However, she was not interested. I called in my good buddy, Wong Chang, and together we found a solution. He would babysit! Happily cared for, my five-year-old did not bother me with fear the rest of the day. I skied moguls well for the first time. This is another example of the multiple levels of reality that we can experience in one moment of time.

My client, Ray's guides, get his attention in ways that he must notice. At a meeting where Ray was the head of buying men's clothing for a very large department store he looked down and in his hand was a white feather. Looking around at the other people at the table he hoped to see that perhaps they too had feathers; that he wasn't freaking out or hallucinating. Frighten he dropped the feather on the floor and struggled to pay attention to the rest of the meeting. Afterward, in his office, sharing his weird experience with a co-worker, he reached for a file to discuss at the same time. When he opened the file, there was another white feather greeting him again!

Ray was a real estate client referred to me through several different sources. Our relationship was destined. Since I believe that there are no secrets, I would often share the healing and spiritual aspects of my life, with my real estate clients. I see my real estate work as doing another form of healing work—serving people by helping them get grounded, feel safe, and meet their visual/experiential desires for a home. Because he felt safe with me, Ray shared his phenomenal manifestation of spirit.

In a meditation years before Ray and I met, my Indian spirit guide,

Chief Eagle Eye, had given me the name "White Feather." Ray wanted to know my insight and opinion of the white feathers showing up in this corporate setting. My explanation to Ray as to why this happen to him had to do with who he is, a spiritual teacher. The physical manifestation was to jolt him into being who he came to the planet to be. Ray's guides were speaking to him in a way that he had to listen. It was too weird to deny something mystical was happening to him.

Ray's story doesn't end with his white feather. Approximately two years later I was in a cafe on Polk Street in San Francisco having coffee with my friend Teddi. Just as she was saying she needed to go, into the cafe walked Ray. Astonished and joyful to see me, he sat down as Teddi went on her way. Ray had been thinking about me for several months and had lost my number. He had moved back to the east coast and was in San Francisco for only a few days to pack his things. He was leaving the very next day and his prayer to talk to me had been answered. Ray had another story to tell me.

A few months before, Ray was doing a normal daily routine of taking a shower. As he leaned back to rinse shampoo from his head and then straightened, his eyes casually glanced down he noticed an Indian head nickel on one of his thumbs! Stunned he told his lover who didn't seem to react. Later, it came to mind to ask again, "Why?"! Of course, Ray wanted to know my thoughts and manifested a chance to have them.

My answer on that day of our serendipitous meeting on Polk Street was the same as several years before. Ray's guides did not want him to deny his spirituality, to know that magic was possible, and his life purpose is to teach. Sharing his story, Ray is teaching us all. His story is one voice in the chorus of all the other people in this book. Stories will continue to be told as long as the brave are willing to push the comfort zone of others and themselves. This is where faith triumphs over fear and changes the world.

Ray is not more spiritual because his guides teach him in this way. His experience is also being created by his resistance to being who he is. Therefore, his guides are taking dramatic measures to show him what is possible. Spiritual manifestation into the physical happens all of the time. Keys disappear, furniture is rearranged, noises are heard, lights are turned on or off or flicker or are dimmed or brightened, a stone shows up on the dish drainer lost from a ring days before (yes, that one happened to me!) whatever will serve to awaken the sleeping spiritual warrior within.

After my mystical stories of Mt. Shasta, one of my friends Holly Groves just had to play with the mountain. With that attitude, the mountain played with her. Hiking on the mountain, Holly found a chair made out of stone. There are many altars, creative art forms, and devotional gifts, left by spiritual pilgrims on Mt. Shasta. After meditating for awhile, she rose to hike some more. As she walked, she heard melodious mystical singing and stopped to hear which direction it was coming from. When she stopped, the music stopped. When she walked, the music began again. Holly stopped, the music stopped. This play went on for a while that day. Holly's spirit guide at Mt. Shasta was the mountain itself, a living consciousness talking to her by song.

When I was first opening my channel to communicate with spirits, I was at a workshop, and the exercise was to go outside and talk to an animal. Well, with my normal Aries enthusiasm I marched right out to a neighboring pasture to talk a horse that I had seen that morning. With child-like joy, I said "hello" and ask the horse to talk to me. He was chewing grass and simply stared at me. I attempted again to engage him in conversation, and in my head, I heard, *"Go Away!"* That was not my expectation of how I wanted this exercise to progress. I was a star student after all. I persisted with this horse repeated asking for us to chat. Finally, very ceremoniously, he said, "Leave me alone!," turned, and strolled to the other side of the pasture.

Insulted, I retreated to a nearby willow tree for shade and comfort. While regrouping from my failure, I noticed that a dragonfly had been just sitting and swinging in the breeze on a branch of the willow. Tentatively, I asked it if it wanted to talk to me. The response was, *"I was wondering when you would ask?"* The spirit of the dragonfly was feminine and told me about manners in the spirit world. She talked about the reverence for all living forms and the importance of asking permission to participate in the healing of others or entering their universe by conversation. She spoke of the teaching of the horse as having boundaries that we can create with free will. The dragonfly's most important message was never to assume someone will desire to speak with me, human or other living forms, that it is best to invite someone into a conversation or to wait for an invitation. We must respect all life.

When sharing with the group my experience of channeling animals it was pointed out to me that in Jamie Sam's book, *The Medicine Cards*, she defines the medicine of the dragonfly as "the breaker of illusions!" The symbol of this animal matched perfectly my spiritual lesson. My expectations taught me the valuable lesson that I was raised with. "Don't judge a book by its cover!" The small dragonfly had a big message that I will never forget.

To know our guides only adds more friends to our social circle. I am never alone, and neither is anyone else. The guides are here to help us thrive. They are not just available to help us with spiritual growth, the evolution of humanity, and the revolution of living a peaceful existence on earth. The problems and solutions can be simple and mundane or quite evolved like my vision quest you will read about in the next chapter. For example on a practical level, there are parking angels, shopping angels, guardian angels, pet angels—any we can imagine to meet any need. Their presence helps us function in life if we choose to let them. What do you choose?

Chapter 11 Practicum

⋈ Watch again or for the first time, the video meditation "Meet Your Four Primary Spirit Guides" on https://www.intuitiveartsandsciences.com/meet-your-spirit-guides-video.html.

⋈ Once you have met them, take time every day to get to know your Spirit Guides by inviting them to participate in your mundane life.

Chapter 12

The Destination, Death

All of us must develop a relationship with death as a part of our life. Befriending death can help us to enjoy life. By dealing with our feelings about our eventual transition, we can overcome our fear and hopefully transform it into motivation for actualizing our dreams. The fear of death can keep us from taking risks. Self-esteem is built on the success of taking risks. If we do not allow ourselves to adventure on any level, we negate a possible source of loving, and appreciating, the possibilities of our lives.

On the spiritual path, we will meet death, and our fear of it is a path to greater levels of faith. When we face our fear of death, we face our fear of change. The relationship we have to change influences our ability to forgive, let go. Change is a constant in the universe of love. Death is around us as much as life, for they are one and the same, the point of transformation. Love is not either in life or death but both.

In truth, we face death in each and every moment. No death—from a leaf falling from a tree, to an deer shot by a hunter, to a traffic fatality, to a suicide, to a man shot at the corner drug store in a robbery, or being in a building that collapses due to a plane intentionally driving into it—happens without agreement of that soul, and God. We grieve because of our gratitude. We grieve the lost life as it represents the potential of what could be. When we loved something or someone their presence influence who we are. We grieve because we have loved, and lost. Not one of us in any form of life ever gets out of life alive. Death is the destination.

No death happens without being in perfect and divine order. We determine our death as much as we determine our life. I have worked with or known many women who have had abortions who feel like murderesses. The souls who come into their bodies do so with the knowledge that they are to be spiritual teachers for these women. Almost every one of them went through a powerful spiritual transformation, but it is not without purpose and reason to teach something about love. Perhaps the soul doesn't want to have a long life. It has karma too. Maybe to be connected to a body for four or six weeks of earth time is enough to get its lesson. We do not hold the balance scale of karma, but we are subject to it. Again, we must recognize our sometimes limited view and fear-filled perspective about what is good, right, and destined.

During a period of great transition in my life when I was deciding to leave the real estate company to do my healing work full time, I was inspired to do a vision quest. The medicine wheel I had created at Mt. Shasta in 1987 was calling to me to initiate the next stage of my life. It seemed the appropriate place to contemplate my future. I created a personal workshop to help me decide if it was time to take a leap of faith. On the way there I had a friend Brian Silva gave me a rebirthing session to release some of my fear about camping alone on a mountain. Sleeping outside by myself, vulnerable to the world was something I had only done occasionally as a single woman.

In the rebirthing healing session, a new spirit guide came to join me for my weekend camping. It was the Grim Reaper, or you might know him as the Harbinger of Death. When I left San Francisco at midnight, on a full moon solstice driving the near empty freeway, sitting next to me in the car was he was my co-pilot. In my psychic vision, I could see this skeleton in his black hooded robe holding his scythe. I was struggling to understand this apparition as my guide. He gave me the heebie-jeebies! When he placed a bony hand over mine on the gearshift, I lost it. In a nervous laugh, I said out loud, "If you're coming with me then I am going to call you Doctor D!" So, Dr. D and I went to the mountain together. This was a cosmic joke I decided. I had to just go with it.

This story has many lessons to share with you about rebirth or death, spirit teachers, and our personal path to awareness. As I said before, the spirit guides, angels, and or negative spirits come to us metaphorically and literally. The definitions and interpretation of the symbolism, we create. They come from God through our imagination, from our sub-conscious and our super-conscious minds. It was not like I made a conscious decision to invite Dr. D to come with me. By this time in my life, I had been working consciously as a medium for five years. I had now years of experience, workshops, training, books, friends and this manifestation was my reality, period. It still upset me. I had to find my faith, return to love, instead of feed my fear.

In the morning after sleeping in my car once I had arrived at the mountain. I prepared to climb to the meadow that was, based on my experience before, about a 3-hour hike. I was packing in a tent, ritual tools, books, food, clothing, and my drum. As usual, I overpacked. I attempted to put my backpack on my back, but I could not pick it up. It was way too heavy. My lesson from *A Course in Miracles* was No. 76 *"I am under no laws but God's."* Taking a deep breath, I marched around my car affirming this thought. In just a few minutes I walked over and threw my heavy pack effortlessly onto my back. I put my daypack on the front, picked up my drum, and began walking up the trail at a quick pace.

Above the parking lot, the trail made Y branching in two directions. On the right fork, I could see three young adults. On the left fork, I could see a middle aged man. My intuition was to walk towards the single man. As I passed him, he asked, "Are you going to the top?" I told him, "No, only to Upper Squaw Meadow." He commented on my rapid ascent from the parking lot and asked if he could walk with me for a bit. I said sure, and he immediately asked to carry half of my things! Within 500 yards of the car, an Angel in the human form of Ron Dunlap appeared.

Ron hiked with me, helped me find my meadow, and was thrilled to meet a conscious channel. He had been praying for a channeling teacher, so we both were serving each other. And as Buddha says, *"When the student is ready, the teacher appears."* Ron had promised to visit one of the new age bookstores in town before he went home and our journey up to Squaw Meadow had taken longer than he'd planned. It was 4:00 pm and the store closed at 5:00 pm. An athlete and a mountain runner, Ron was hopeful that he would make it back to the parking lot, drive down the mountain, and still get his shopping done. I wished him well and watched as he ran like a stag through the woods.

This vision quest for my future seemed to be going better than the night before yet Dr. D was always close in my awareness. When the sun began to set, my mood too dimmed with the light. Fears, sadness, insecurity and the old *"what am I doing here?"* scripts began to play in my head and feelings. Sitting by the fire and watching the stars lifted my attitude and I began to write in my journal and pray. During my meditation I was told:

> *"You will have no visitors tonight, man, animal, or alien but you will hear many things!"*

I also heard over and over from the inner voice and my guides:

> *"Do your healing!"*

Tired from little sleep, the enormity of the decision I was there to make about my life path, my emotions, and the physical exertion,

I fell asleep at the fire only to awaken shortly to the smell of burning rubber! I was camped at snow line even though it was July and I had placed my boots close to the fire to dry. Needless to say, it was a meltdown for me and one of my boot's instep, now sporting an egg-sized hole! I wrote in my journal a prayer to God that someone came the next day to help pack me out, as Ron helped me pack in, to this workshop I had created for myself.

Since I had fallen asleep at the fire, I figured that I would just crawl in my tent and continue the workshop in the morning. Well, guess again!? As I zipped my sleeping bag, suddenly, a great wind came and was shaking my tent violently. I was terrified. Dr. D was patiently kneeling by my head, and I felt out of control. I remembered another *Course in Miracles* Lesson No. 48 *"There is nothing to fear."* I began to repeat this as an affirmation combined with *"I am under no laws but God's."* Eventually, I relaxed enough to sleep.

The sleep, however, did not last long. About an hour later, I was awoken to the sound of—silence—dead, breathless, oppressive— silence. Again, the terror rose in my heart and mind. Again, Dr. D was just there. Again, I reached for my *Course* lessons to bring me into peace, to rest, and then thank God, sleep. About an hour later though, again, I was awakened. This time it was the sound of the wind different from before.

This wind carried music and the sound of people, voices in a haunting, mournful, wail. Again, the terror. Again, the remembrance and chanting of *"There is nothing to fear,"* and *"I am under no laws but Gods."* Again, Dr. D. watched over me. Again, I found peace, comfort in God's love, and rest, then sleep. About an hour later though, it started again, the sound of silence only this time additionally there were twigs snapping near my campsite. You know the rest of the story. This pattern went on all night!

At first light, I came out of my tent to relieve myself, happy to see the birth of the new day. I was grateful that I was seeing the sun and was there to meet another day. I got back in my tent to sleep a little longer but left the tent door open. When I opened my eyes again, my very first sight was Ron Dunlap! Ron was making tea at the fire he had built and was waiting for me to wake up and have breakfast.

Ron lived over and an hour south of Mt. Shasta. He had awakened very early in the morning, before first light, worried about me. Ron had driven to Shasta, run to my campsite to ensure that I was alright and had made it through the night. God had sent my angel back! As a side note, Ron had made it to the bookstore the night before right at 5:00 PM! He was relieved and delighted that he had listened to his intuition. We laughed about the boot and continued to learn from each other that day about the magic of life.

There were so many life lessons in this workshop I could digress. It was worth the terror to face my fear and champion it by my faith. I was truly reborn as a healer that night on Mt. Shasta. The teaching was that death is always present and it can be our guide to life. I've not seen Dr. D. around me since that weekend though I have faced death many times. Dr. D. was not a figment of my imagination or a hallucination or fantasy. He was real. My guides and the light beings I perceive are as real as the keyboard I am typing on right now.

Ron Dunlap, a man of flesh and blood, was also my spirit guide and protector. By listening to his own intuition, asking for a teacher, and being open to serve the obvious, this true story illustrates the power of coincidence, the one mind, and trusting the information that comes in our dialogue with the Divine. This story has been recounted many times and always inspires those who hear it face their fears. We can never underestimate the people that cross our path. Each of us can be a catalyst for growth, transformation, and healing of others. This is how we as individuals heal the whole world.

As far as what I was told, "you will hear many things." I could in no way prepare myself for the experience even though I had the information. Guidance comes when we need it. However, it is not meant to do our dharma which means cosmic law or karma which is our fate, journey for us. It is to make the journey even more abundant; more rich, full, interesting, and complete. Dr. D was an initiation aid to deep faith but letting go of my fears. I had to listen to the world around me, and the world inside of me, to get to the answer for my vision quest.

My journey to "do my healing," my life's work, and the message I received as the answer, brought me to another workshop. I thought the guidance was to go out into the world and be a healer. I was only partially right. After this incredible initiation, I spent the next two years doing deep emotional work on myself. I thought the message at the fire that night on Mt. Shasta meant go step out onto the world stage be the world healer like I'd was in New Zealand only six months before my vision quest. Doing **my** healing was the wisdom message. Peace to my soul instead of any ideas of external success was the immediate need coming off the mountain. By 1992 though, I was traveling nationally then by 1993 internationally as a healer. As I heal myself, I heal the world. Facing my concepts of death metaphysically was only one layer my of my healer training.

Since death is the destination of life, the lessons around it are exponential. Our discussion of death is just not the fear of it. We must also look at our yearning for it. When we make decisions that do not resonate with our integrity, we are out of alignment with our beliefs. This keeps us from loving ourselves and others, and we support our death wish. Over consumption of alcohol, drug addiction, overeating, under- eating, unprotected sexual encounters, lethargy, the carelessness that leads to accidents, are some of the ways we human beings act out our death wish.

This death urge is deep seeded in the psyche. There is a sense that home is somewhere beyond the current experience. I would say that the original sin, separation, now manifests as the child desiring to return to the womb. The womb in this metaphor is the universe, God, or All-that-is. There is the need to be out of the limitations, challenges, and karma of the lifetime. For ultra-sensitives it can be difficult to negotiate the denser vibration of the world of earth. Bodies are high maintenance! This though is the whole point, to bring the spiritual principles to the earth, to make it lighter. As the saying goes, *"To be in the world but not of the world."*

In our egocentrism we do not want to admit, we are not alone. Humanity is invested in separation and the illusions that come with it. We cannot be separate from anything ever. We are on the planet with billions of people not counting all of the other life forms. Alone is a luxury but not real. We are here to serve each other through the discovery of connection. We are not meant to go at, through, or for life alone. If you take every job description, as I have said previously, and reduce it to the end point is always the same—service.

The President of the United States takes a vow to serve the people by his leadership, the newspaper boy makes a commitment to serve his route by bringing them the news, a journalist serves the people by report the news, the garbage men serves their area by taking away the old papers and on and on it goes. Retail clerks, real estate agents, doctors, lawyers, teachers, janitors, plumbers, architects, insurance salespeople, bankers, butchers, auto mechanics, the person who flips the burgers and makes pizza, we are all in service to each other. On any level, no one is more important in the cosmic plan than anyone else. We were born into this world to serve, so we are all healers no matter what we do even if what we do is negative. And, we are all here to die.

When people talk to me about being alone, I can empathize. However, the reality is that we cannot accomplish anything alone. Who picks the beans for us to have a cup of coffee that someone at Starbucks makes into a latte for us? Who paves the road for us to drive the car or ride the bike on to get to Starbucks? Who built the bike or car that we are using to get around on these roads? Who made our clothes, built our home, designed our light switch or our television? When I pray over food, I thank all the hands that planted the seed in the soil, that brought it from the field, that brought it to the market, that brought it home, and that make it into something for me to savor and enjoy. We are never alone, ever. The memories of all those hands are what I am putting into my body too.

The immediate landscape around us is full of the spirit of creation coming through all of these beings to set the stages of our life story.

Remembering this truth can help us with loneliness. In the creative cycle at each step, there is death. The seed becomes the plant. The flower dies to become the fruit. The fruit becomes the cells of our body, and we all know what happens with the fruit that is not needed in our body. The waste becomes fertilizer for the soil to be reborn for the seed absorbed the nutrients to become the plant. Is anyone hearing Elton John sing *The Circle of Life?*

This awareness of our connection and continual renewal of creation brings a whole new possibility to what we accomplish on a daily basis in our lives. In truth, there is no scarcity. Competition for resources is not the determining motive in the survival of the fittest. Something else is happening. There is enough room for every living thing on the planet, or it would not be. Just as no death happens without God, neither does any life. All lives are born with the purpose to serve love on this earth. All deaths occur for the same purpose.

Over the last 20 years, more open discussion of the afterlife. The sharing of Near Death experience stories in mainstream media including feature films is a sign that the collective is more open to receiving this reality. Many people, because they can relate to the average woman or man explaining their NDE experiences, give this credibility. They give validation to what mystics, prophets, spiritual leaders, dogma, cosmological systems and our own intuitive knowing have told us is true.

The idea of eternal life or the afterlife is popular in the collective consciousness, or it would not be on prime time. Though death is the destination, we are reborn. To what, that is the mystery, but life does continue. This awareness of the continuum serves love and the everlasting connection of all life. I celebrate this fad. I celebrate as well that reality TV has brought us the Long Island Medium. We are listening. Life does go on.

Chapter 12 Practicum

◻ Spend an entire day as if it was your last day ever on Earth. Do what you can do that is within your power to make every second count.

◻ Live this way for the rest of your life.

Chapter 13

Money = Love + Action

Money is love in action. It is the energy of our life force that we have extended to act as a medium in creating our human existence story and the cultures we continually are creating to sustain it. Giving our esteem and value to the money alone becomes sabotage of the creative potential. Remember our true power is love, not our will, but it takes both to manifest at this in time in the shared waking dream of human existence. Money is never the reason but often the excuse for us to not take responsibility to be who we are. The manifestation of money alone can get in the way of us doing, well, anything.

The process of moving our value system back from the outcome as the reward, to the action as the reward can create a new sustainable economy. Our cultural story is pride and pleasure from the building of external success measured by material acquisition and assets of wealth. However, money is not something we as souls continue to move forward through eternity, with it in our pocket … we have no body! What we can take with us are our memories. What we can take with us are our deeds. What we can take with us is our knowing. What we can take with us is freedom. What we can take with us is love.

In loving relationships, there is no need to measure the service we provide for each other. When we are all giving 100%, that means we are all receiving 100%. If in our marriages we are keeping score, or we count how many times our friends do nice things for us, or if we wait for good to come from others, we miss the point. The point is that we do not hold the balance scale. There is always a bigger energy that is involved in what we are creating including economic systems. The choice to assert our will, in harmony with our intuition and the intention to love, will create whatever we truly need in divine order which includes money or an even better method of barter.

Our souls are all given life with the same blessing, the same hope, the same light and the same love. We are all healers. We are all teachers. However, we all come with different agendas as to how to learn about that love. What goes up, we all know, must come down. The appropriate model for energy, material or spiritual, is the sacred spiral. Twisting, turning, moving, multi-leveled and without end. How does this relate, all of us being healers/teachers and money being love in action?

We can either be aware of our connection to the divine and spiritual harmony or unaware. It is our choice. God is omnipresent. Any choice we make determines our spiritual path. We cannot make errors or mistakes. We are so used to being judged and measured it is a leap in consciousness to consider another point of view. I am talking about valuing a human life based on their material wealth. If we exist, we have value for the whole. The more we know this, the more we change the way we relate to the world around us and create harmony. This includes how we collectively value money over human life. One is temporary the other eternal.

As all of us are healers and teachers, it also means we are all in need of healing and teaching. The Sanskrit word for a human has the same root as suffering. So as we see our common pain, we can then do something about it. God, the Universe, cosmic design loves us all the same. Our challenge in the fourth dimension is to do the same. This means no judgment, no comparisons, and trusting that what we really need will be there when we need it. It also means validating what we do perceive and not fearing it.

Money is synonymous with success in our now worldwide cultural value system. We affirm it in our conversations with the saying "money makes us free." It is not true. Freedom is a state of being that has nothing to do with having or not having money. Freedom is an attitude. Money is a medium of exchange for goods and services. I have seen lots of attitude about money, but I have never seen money have an attitude. It is the people who carry the attitude, not the goods or services that the money buys. Money is a vehicle in creation but not a destination for creation.

Opening our minds to the bigger picture includes our review the economic system. It is again a system that we have created to have more ease in our lives. As societies grew, it was not possible for us to trade milk for clothes, or meat for labor, or fruits for shelter, or art for bread. We began to use the money to compensate for the direct exchange of goods and services as it was too complicated to manage as the scale grew with more people in the process. The barter system was not better than the money system, it is the basis of the money system just bigger than before.

In the evolution of life on earth, diversification is an adaptation that a species takes on in times of scarce resources. Specialization is adapted in times of an abundant supply of resources. We are still animals responding to these evolutionary impulses in our behaviors. I invite you to contemplate this for a moment. Are you required to do more of a multiplicity of activities to have your basic needs met now than 20 years ago? Adding the complexity and diversity of technology has made our human ecosystem demand even more skills than less.

As Healers it becomes even more complex. The truth is I cannot be paid for what I do. In the next chapter, I tell a story about a client having three babies after she and her husband did work with me to have one child. They came to a workshop that cost them several thousand dollars, and they did several private healing sessions with me. At that time my rates were $75 per hour. Of course, there were all the other costs of her healing with doctors, test, etc., but I am trying to make a point. There is no way to equate the outcome of our work, with the action of me performing for an hourly rate. Was the dream of having a baby, which then manifested as three children, worth the money they paid? This story is told not because I want/need/nor can take credit for the manifestation of her dream of motherhood. I want you to expand your consciousness of the illusion of a balance scale of value.

Money is a vehicle to participate in the world with food, shelter, clothing, technology, entertainment and the material resources we need to show up and do the job of being ourselves that no one else can do. If all of us were really paid in cash for all of the effort to bring more care, joy, possibility, hope, and love to the planet, no one would ever be lacking cash. The true reward is the pleasure of participating, not in the holding on to the resources and money. It is this exchange that we are reminded we are not alone in this world, but a part of something greater than ourselves.

In reality, I never lack what I think I need for cash. When I left my guaranteed income from my real estate practice not once, but twice, I have lived a marginal money existence. My source of life is my relationship with God allowing me to strip away myths and ideas about the world, and myself. I have had to learn to love myself No Matter What. Always, without fail, what I need is provided. I do not just believe the money will come. I know it will, and I am willing to take action, follow my guidance, be in service and then the money does indeed come.

My job, the real job in this life is to be me. It is the truth for every living being, to be our self. To be me, the only Sally Aderton that will ever experience life on earth includes following my passion for creation, love, and healing. When I am doing the right thing, in alignment with my soul's purpose, the money will follow my actions. Some have judged my relationship to money as being a victim. Some

have pitted me and felt guilty that they have, and I do'7
Some judge that I have money management issues and ι
wealth for myself yet in this life. I too have judged myse
not performing to my expectations. I know my toils are th
most help me help others understand money is a tool, nc
This differentiation is a part of awakening a new value systen.
Fourth Dimensional world, this new paradigm of what is real a.
true for humanity.

Early in my career I once asked my guides why I was in real estate. The answer was that I needed *"to learn about the money system which would get more difficult for people in the future."* We are in the future! Money is more difficult for many people than 1985. Guaranteed jobs are not security as companies downsize, right-size, and change. Money still is being made and lost but there has been a cultural awakening to security perhaps is not in the structures that we created—economic, political, and social. Where is your real security? How do you know you are safe in the world? How do you really know that what you have now, will be enough? What is enough, and for whom?

Imagine the world where we have an affirmation that is positive about money instead of negative. How often have you heard: *"Money is the root of all evil!"* If this is what we affirm and we believe, this is what we will see in the world around us. I want bumper stickers, billboards, social media posts, and in conversations, it said: ***"Money is love in action!"*** Every time money is used to make the world a better place, let us celebrate. I want to reward the people who let go of money to do good, instead of rewarding the people who hold on to money for their satisfaction.

More and more books are written on prosperity, spiritual abundance, and right livelihood. If we remember that money is not the power, we are, then it is possible to develop a healthier attitude and a more abundant world for everyone. Money is a vehicle, a medium, and it is energy that is meant to move. Our world of human endeavor is a work in progress. We don't know where it begins or ends. Money is another manifestation of ourselves that we have created to serve us.

we put our value back to our creation, then money becomes the
not the reward. This is the key to healing our collective world-
e relationship to money. Let creativity be the true value.

Graced to know people with wealth, and to work with people with
wealth, my perspective comes from my direct, intimate experience.
Money does not buy you love, authentic friendships or happiness.
Money does not guarantee health and wellness with your body.
Money does not pacify the pain of relationships that fail, the grief
of loved ones who die, or dreams that do not manifest. Money does
not guarantee the elimination of bigotry, hypocrisy, and social ills. It
is only how that money is used, directed, influenced that can make a
difference for the change, good or bad, in this world.

We all live every day with no guarantee of anything permanent but
change and love. I have lived now for many years with no guarantee
to my cash flow. I have never been hungry or without a bed to sleep
in. The only reason is that I am loved, and I love. A way to think of
money is that it is not just mine but as a way of serving God. In my
prayers when I get some money, I ask God how it should be spent. I
could surprise you with the number of times I've spent my last dollars only to have more dollars appear when a bill needs to be paid!
The dollars have never been my last because more always come. The
nature of money is movement, so how are you moving it along?

Could you imagine the world where to be a rock star onstage, you
had to pay your fans to come to the show? We are in a co-dependent
system. A rockstar cannot exist without fans. What if we switched the
reward? What if we had to pay people to help us be who we came to
the planet to be—a CEO, or a soccer star, or a millionaire, or a football
star, or a movie star? In truth, one cannot exist without the other, but
they also include multitudes of layers of the machine of commerce to
connect the dots. The truth is it takes everyone, from the guy selling
T-shirts, to the roadies moving the equipment, to the engineers who
built the stadium, to the radio stations playing the songs or games, to
the advertising companies . . . include every single person who was a
part of creating the experience for the ticket holder to be in that seat

at that moment for that show or game. It is a complex system. Our money system will change for it is not sustainable and contrary to the laws of the Universe. Our opportunity is to be the change, and it has already begun.

For the first time, there is a new corporate structure Benefit Corporations are showing another path for money to move. Benefit Corporations are for-profit companies that are obligated to consider the impact of their decisions on society, not only shareholders. Radically, positive impact on society becomes part of a Benefit Corporation's legally defined goals. More and more companies, not just individuals are rejecting the concept that profit is more important than public responsibility, the commitment to arts and culture, the value of natural resources, and the welfare of all. As cultural trends are started with revolutions, re-evolution is happening in the ways that money is being distributed even in very successful companies. Patagonia, This American Life, and Kickstarter are all for-profit companies with Public Benefit Corporation charters. They are economic revolutionaries.

Mirco-Financing, Crowd-sourcing, and the rise of 'shared economy' are all evidence that new ways of working with money are necessary. I say necessary for if they were not needed, or welcomed, they wouldn't exist. What is wonderful about this vogue sharing of resources, is that it has brought opportunities to countries without the standards of living we take for granted in the west. The polarization of wealth in the world is not new. It is just more pronounced.

Money is not the essential value in the system that it is a part of. Money is the medium of the value system. This medium is necessary with the number of people alive, and the complexity of the cultures we have created. A peaceful world is not necessarily a more simple world. I offer a concept of a peaceful world that is when the value system of the accumulation of wealth, is equal to the value of the sharing of wealth. What would it take to create this way of sharing the earth? Is it possible because I have imaged it, it indeed could manifest? When we use the tools offered up to now in this book, the answer for me is obvious.

How the magic of this world works is a part of the mystery we are discovering, but there are some deeper, higher conceptualizations that we are beginning to perceive not just on the individual level but the cosmological, which can help us navigate it with more ease. The change though of shifting values can happen only if enough of us want it to. All we need to do is ask, but then we have to listen and take action accordingly. What can you do to make the economy different? Do you know you have the power to do so?

We can call for help, but then we need to accept when it comes. We can pray for money, but if it does not come, we must be willing to accept that it is not truly our need or it would. We can ask for more of everything, but then we have to take care of what we have, which takes time. The consciousness kicker is time is something we can NEVER get more of. We are alive, and that is the real value, the real treasure. We have the right and destiny to be here. We have the right and destiny to be free here, and so does everyone else.

Chapter 13 Practicum

For one week, every single time you spend money to do so with the attitude that it belongs to your Higher Power, not you. Ask that Source first if how you are spending their money will serve the love you are or help you love someone else. Pay attention to the answers. Act then accordingly and notice the outcome of how you feel about the exchange.

Chapter 14

The Will to Heal

Limits on our consciousness do serve to guide the lessons we come to learn in life. No and yes are both positive and negative words. Our ability to choose, to say 'yes' to heal gives us the power to do so. The revolution of consciousness requires us to perceive beyond the apparent. It requires us to face the unknown, the mystery and going into the dark to transform it to light. There can be perfect moments, perfect experiences, and perfect expressions of creation. However, these are not static states. Time takes us to the next moment, experience, or expression.

When a 'no' comes into our experience, it does so to direct the course of our river. A 'no' is a moment to get creative. When we are talking about healing our lives, the obstacles on our paths exist as opportunities for learning about love, life, others and ourselves. In sharing the story of Lynn Abraham and Mark Chance, I can only say first that their story is a gift to us all. It is a teaching for us about life eternal and death, and the knowledge that we can heal ourselves to have our dreams come true.

Lynn had been told by a psychic that she would have a child in this life but she *'must heal herself'* to do so. She came home from that reading and said to her husband, *"Honey, we're going to Jamaica!"* She took the flyer that she had received from the Chicago School of Massage off her bulletin board and called to enroll in their upcoming annual retreat there. The flyer talked about the philosophy of the facilitator, me: *"As we heal ourselves, we heal the world."* Lynn was convinced this workshop would open to heal the parts of her that were incapable of having a child.

In learning to facilitate past-life regressions at the workshop, Lynn revealed the first of several body belief systems that her subconscious, emotional wiring, physical form and eternal spirit held in regards to having a baby. Lynn's story was as follows:

> *"I remember being a pilgrim man preparing to voyage to the new world by sea. I was deeply in love with my new wife who in this incarnation is my Mom. The pilgrim community was very devout and strict with their rules regarding the upcoming long journey. Knowing that it would be a difficult crossing for all of us, we were told, not asked, to commit to not having sexual relations with our spouses. No pregnant woman would be allowed on the ship. We boarded the ship when my wife was, unknown to the community, three months pregnant. As the pregnancy was eventually difficult to hide, the strict community shunned and shamed us for disobeying the rules. When the baby was birthed, all of the women on board were gravely ill, the men would offer no help, and I was left to care for my wife alone. She began to bleed after the birth, and I was unable to stop it. Both my wife and newborn child died. The child had been born healthy, but with no suckling mothers available, it died of starvation. A grief-struck, lonely, and*

angry man became my fate in that life. My dying thought
was, **"I couldn't stop the bleeding!"**

Lynn had experienced three miscarriages due to the fact she would
begin—bleeding! A vein would appear in utero only during her
pregnancies and bleed for no apparent reason. Lynn's relationship
with her biological mother in this lifetime is one of her priorities and
to be a mother is also a priority. These were her life priorities and
themes channeled from her higher mind during a private session with
me at the workshop. Lynn was born to a woman in this life, which
was her wife in the previous life, to heal the karma between them.
Through these miscarriages, Lynn was being given an opportunity to
heal the grief, remorse, guilt, anger and pain left from that life with
her Mother.

This Jamaica retreat was May of 1995. In June a month later, I
saw Lynn and Mark at their home in Colorado. They both did more
past-life and childhood memory regression work to let go more of
their fears about becoming parents. It was not just Lynn who had
feared but Mark too. He had been adopted in this life to a family that
loved and wanted him. Mark felt that love and missed his father now
deceased.

Predicting they would conceive in July, I was surprised to get a call
from Lynn several weeks after I had seemed her and Mark. Mark was
a computer consultant and assigned to a task in Scandinavia later
that month. Without hesitation, I told Lynn, "Go have sex in a fjord!"
Lynn got a ticket, joined Mark during his assignment and true to my
intuition, came home with a baby growing in her belly. They were
pregnant again for the fourth time with the soul of Mark's adopted
father, who would now be their child.

In September, I was preparing to go to London for a month, and
a few weeks before I left I received a panicked call from Lynn. She
had begun to bleed again, and the doctors wanted to do a D/n/C to
terminate the pregnancy the same day. Lynn felt she needed to consult
me first. She put the doctors off a few days, and the procedure was

scheduled several days later. But, Lynn knew she had a choice to do deeper process work and look at the pain. So Lynn did what she knew she could to avoid terminating the pregnancy.

In our session over the phone, I told Lynn that I could not tell her what to do, she must make the decision on her own with Mark. I asked her if she wanted to do a regression and she said "yes." We uncovered more beliefs about her relationship to getting fat and still being desired and lovable. These negative beliefs were held with fear in her uterus. She did not tell me her decision until a week later when a check came in the mail. There was a note included telling me she had canceled the D/n/C and would bed rest, pray, and see what happened.

When I returned to the States, I immediately called Lynn from New York for an update. Her bleeding had completely stopped at the beginning of the second trimester, and she was doing great. It was a boy, and they were calling him Maxx Aaron Chance. I got a call in April that Maxx had arrived! They were looking forward to his blessing ceremony in June when I could come to Colorado. We blessed Maxx and included in his blessing the acknowledgment of his life priorities that I had channeled.

Babies come to the planet with the soul's agenda already programmed into their consciousness. I said this earlier, we all come here to do our soulwork to learn about love through our unique agendas. It does not come to us later in the game of life. It is inherent why we are here. Lynn and Mark wanted to raise Maxx from the beginning of their life together as a family, to be the soul he came to the planet to be.

The gift of knowing our life priorities can help us to be happy and fulfilled because we are living true to why were are here. I have channeled the life priorities for thousands of individuals. Repeatedly, I am told: *"Oh my God, you know who I am!" "You are right on target!" "That is what I knew inside but never heard someone tell me so clearly!" "I already knew those things, but you make me feel seen and understood!"* Often, regardless if the person is male or female, they are crying by the end. This information validates them to their core.

To be witnessed for the unique being we are, with our unique agenda is the greatest acknowledgment. It also gives our separation meaning and that we matter in the divine plan. Everything does happen for a reason to serve that plan. It is not random that we are here on Earth with a deep longing in our soul for this personal expression.

The story continued to unfold for the Chance family. Two months after Maxx was born, Lynn conceived again! Un-expected twin boys arrived to join their family. In 18 months, all three souls that had wanted Lynn as their mother and Mark as their father landed on earth. Once Lynn healed her womb, her mother issues, and more of loving her body, these souls helped her life priority of being a mother, come true. Mark's karmic relationship with his children and his adoption story was healing at the same time.

Eli and Ayden, fraternal twins and Maxx their older brother had all tried unsuccessfully, before I entered their parents healing spiritual journey, to be born into life. Lynn's challenge with this next pregnancy was different. She now had a one-year-old to care for too! Just because our dreams come true, it does not mean the lessons of life end. They just evolve as we do with the conditions of life we find ourselves in.

Lynn's healing still continues. New issues arise, but her self-healing tool bag is full of many choices. She also is more confident to face those challenges because of her experience. Faith is enhanced with experience. The deeper that Lynn goes into her pain, the higher she moves into trust. Maxx, Ayden and Eli, all miracle babies, who are now in college, are Lynn's daily waking dream reflection that she can, did, and will heal herself. By allowing me to tell their story, this family becomes healers for us all. These magnificent souls were raised to be true to themselves. The Chance boys are now young men, amazing, talented, and each absolutely a unique individual. Though Lynn and Mark's marriage did not last in this life, they have given one of the greatest gifts to the planet we can give, wanted children.

Another of the many amazing graces of my decades of experience with clients is working with the parents who knew from the beginning the agenda of the soul that became their child. These parents have been able to nurture their unique children to fulfill their individuated soul's purpose. Instead of projecting their parent's unfulfilled dreams or societal expectations, these kids are being celebrated and encouraged to live from inside, out. We all need to celebrate that each of us is living our individuated personal stories. Remembering that we came from the same source, the Universe of Love, and we will return to that same source. When we can act and create along the way from start to finish with love, we will have a peaceful world to share.

There is no one right way to do life. There is no one right way to do anything. There is only the way that we choose. Healing is our right and pain is our workshop. There are a plethora of tools in the workshop to get our multi-dimensional systems operating with greater ease. But how do we know what to choose that will make us well and bring balance to our lives and the world around us? My answer is to listen, then to have the courage to act accordingly.

Lynn did not know for sure, guaranteed, that going to Jamaica would be the solution to her challenge to heal herself. Something within her was connected to that flyer that came in the mail before she even went to see the Psychic in Denver. Lynn was on the Chicago School of Massage Therapy mailing list because she had gone there to attend a Baby Massage Class! Here the symbolic, the literal, the waking dream, and the spiritual all converged in her baby story healing. Her courage was to listen to the guidance and then choose to create from it.

When inspired to call this Chapter *The Will to Heal,* my intention is to share the intimate connection between what we want, and what we are willing to do to get what we want. Lynn and Mark's story is a testimonial to both of their willpower. They did what they could do. Though the outcome of their actions was unknown, they chose to be faithful to the unfolding mystery. The creative process for each of us will follow the karma that we have come into this life to learn through about love. There is nothing else to do here on Earth but learn about love in infinite ways. Each of us come into our humanity perfectly imperfect with the job of revealing that deeper truth of who we are that we have forgotten.

What motivates us to heal? What does it take to move through the darkness, depression, disease, disfigurement, broken dreams, broken hearts, terrorism, persecution, prejudice, and all the ways that pain manifest in both the individual and the collective? Courage is my answer. We must act even with the fear present. Courage does not exist without fear as in all polarity, they are partnered and together create a whole. When we do not get what we want, then too there is a greater mystery that is unfolding. Our duty to our self if to just keep keeping on.

It was essential that Lynn and Mark chose to do what they could do. Not what was expected, nor what the cultural mainstream saw as the best outcomes for healing, or what their doctors recommended. Cultural standards are only created by individual choices. We must learn to be open and creative in finding our solutions to heal. The best news possible is that our western cultural comfort zone is expanding. However, that expansion did not just 'happen.' Just like the right to vote for woman, or the freedom of the slaves, or the fall of Rome, or the discovery that the world was indeed round and not flat. These were not random leaps in human behavior and consciousness. They happened because individuals were curious, willing to question what was happening, willing to risk, and willing to challenge the status quo.

Stories of people taking complimentary, alternative, natural and the multiplicity of paths to healing ourselves become more common every day. We persevere for a way forward because within us is the quest for greatness and the purpose we have come to fulfill in the human story. How I manage is to find something every day to appreciate about my life. No matter how much darkness I am in, I look for the light. As I know my destination, I do not focus on the end. I do not allow destination-orientation thinking when my chatter mind says, "It will be better tomorrow." I know today is the day I can use my free will to make a difference for others or myself. I focus on my reason to be. I focus on love. I do what I can.

The day I called Lynn to tell her I was sending this chapter for her family's approval, she picked up the phone, a miracle in itself with our busy lives. The day before I had edited their story re-living how powerful, touching, and miraculous our experience together was. I asked if Lynn had thought of me yesterday . . . and her answer was not just 'Yes'! Not only had she thought of me the day before, but she had also told the whole story to Maxx about his arrival on earth! In our phone conversation, we talked about the importance of being honest about our experiences and how anonymity was not as powerful. Lynn was still certain that she wanted her identity to be apparent here. Just the day before she had to find the courage to tell Maxx his creation story.

My call reminded Lynn to stand in the truth of her story. It is they best way for her to be seen for who she is. Lynn wants authentic relationships, so she must be authentic. It was not just her **belief** that we are powerful creators and there is more going on than the apparent ... it was her **experience**! Lynn risked rejection, needed to be courageous, and immediately got Universal feedback by my call to stay true to herself. Again, the One Mind also revealed itself. Was this a coincidence? No, it is another affirmation of the way consciousness works. We are all connected all the time.

Lynn said 'No' to terminating the pregnancy 21 years ago and 'Yes' to her faith. Then took action on what she could do. She did not know for certain, not terminating the pregnancy the day it was recommended, that it would terminate on its own in the days ahead. Lynn had to trust the decision she made would have the outcome that she wanted. It was her and Mark's free wills, the choices they made together that allowed this outcome to unfold. Life is this mystery that just keeps revealing itself. We get to co-create with it, instead of being victims of it. Let's choose to be creatively courageous together.

Chapter 14 Practicum

◻ Think about a pain you have in your life on any level—physical, emotional, mental, and spiritual. Make a list of things you do not have the free will authority to change that influence, or seen as the cause, for the pain. Make a list of the ALL—do not edit due to judgments, belief systems, and attitudes—the things you can do to change, elevate, or transform the pain.

◻ Do the things you can.

Chapter 15

Walk the Talk— Brain Surgery Ph.D. in Healing

*E*ach of us is on our journey of discovery and healing. Having been a companion with so many people on their healing paths for 13 years was the perfect practice for me to be ready for my crisis. *"When one is truly ready for something, it puts in its appearance."* was said to me by my friend Zoya Smithton who hired me to work for her in real estate in 1986. She was reading about mysticism, and she was embellishing the principle of the relationship between a student and a master. The day before I called inquiring about a job, she told her sole saleswoman it was time to hire another. This statement became a tenant that I will live by for the rest of this lifetime. I was truly ready for a brain tumor because it put in its appearance.

In the years since the day of my brain surgery to remove an Acoustic Neuroma, a benign tumor on the auditory nerve, I have questioned many times what God gave me. The proverbial "they say God never gives us more than we can handle" has been put to the test. It sure didn't seem that I could handle my share! I have been humbled again, and again, and again. My intuition was that I would survive the surgery—but possibly not survive the recovery. My intuition was spot on.

One of my top three life priorities is to be a spiritual teacher. My lessons about faith are every day in some way. When I was ready for a revolutionary teaching about faith in my unfolding mystery story, it showed up. The way that I have moved from surviving this experience to thriving again has been love, lots of it. The mechanism to discover the love has been forgiveness. Thank God, forgiveness was in my personal and professional healing toolbox before I went into the operating room. I had everything I needed to heal. I had great doctors, a loving family, health insurance, prayers from friends and clients around the world, and a vision that I would survive. However, the greatest tool I had was my will to heal myself. It was my deepest desire, and I would do whatever it took to live.

The process of creation and the unfolding of wisdom in our lives are not linear journeys that bring us to a stable destination. I have found that wisdom or knowledge brings the awareness that there is more to discover. The movement between the dark and the light of the Taoist symbol of yin and yang, this never-ending spinning from consciousness to unconsciousness, is what I experience daily in my quest for the divine in my life. This humbling, of moving from the known to the unknown, keeps me in the state of innocence described in the Christian teachings "that I must be like the child to enter the kingdom of heaven."

For me to write on personal responsibility for our lives is to write my story. I am unable to separate myself from my beliefs, opinions, and worldview. Never is it more profound than when trying to explain my perspective on healing. It is "in my face." This colloquialism is the metaphor for my faith in God, my personal healing story and forgiveness to set us free. Writing is a confrontational experience as I must face my knowing and try to put words to what I experience—miraculous awe.

My perspective can never be completely yours, nor yours mine. We have all been given the gift of our unique point of view. However, there is a place that we can meet, and we arrive there by compassion. Witnessing my wounds and the forgiveness of them, as I witness others', shows that we all have similar challenges. Witnessing and being present to the pain ends the separation. It is enriching with inspiration and instruction. Choosing to move this inspiration to action becomes our point of empowerment. Courage is our reward. Courage is not given but earned by our willingness to face our fears and go beyond them.

In the nineteen years since my brain surgery, life continues to fill me with awe, wonder, and miracles. The first few years of my recovery period were a very arduous and mourn-filled epoch of my life. Without forgiving God and myself, I would be incapable of functioning within the parameters of a post-modern society. Without forgiving myself for the damages to my ego, my beauty, my communication, my facial function, my hearing, my short-term memory, my ability to administrate and run my business, I would not have the simple joy of living.

This joy, somehow, eventually crept into my heart no matter how difficult the days became. The light invariably would shine through the darkness, and my hope would be renewed. It is necessary for me to tell the story of my healing to be free of it. And to tell it is my service to you who read it, for your witnessing will heal our separation, for we do have a relationship. Post Traumatic Stress Disorder from this story alone kept this book from being shared with the world. It reminded me of the roads not taken and the dreams not fulfilled by my 37-year-old self.

The realizations of truth that have come to me come this way; not always in the storm of the emotions but sometimes they come later. The wisdom is accessed through the storm and waiting quietly on the other side. These moments bring me back to the center of my being.

The new center of consciousness is usually larger than the last center because it unites the wisdom of the past with the new wisdom of the lesson learned. The center of my being is my divinely connected heart. When we are in the moments of crisis consciousness is engaged at a primal level.

To be free of something, to let it go, to give it to God, is to forgive it. I must forgive my story, layer by layer so that I can begin again. As I finish this cycle of growth, there is a 'new life' emerging. Rewriting *Energy in Motion* is a part of the letting the brain surgery story go one more time. This manuscript for 19 years was both blessing and a curse. The curse was a reminder of what did not happen in my life because of my health crisis. The blessing was the fertile ground of Chapter 16 which became the basis of my Master's thesis, *Forgiveness: A Path of Peace*. Though I have been encouraged to write separate books about my brain tumor and personal story, one about my 5-Steps to Forgiveness, one about healing techniques, one with client testimonials, and another about my spiritual philosophies, it makes no sense to me. Together, they are one big love story.

There is saying in Zen Buddhism that "We must empty the vessel to fill it up again." Whenever I have needed to let something go, or taught someone else about letting go, I remind him or her of this simple Buddhist common sense. And indeed, something else always follows. I was arrogant to think I knew the bottom of my vessel of suffering. As I move forward in my life since I discovered my brain tumor, I find I am innocent to its depths. I must just keep faithful to the unfolding no matter how often I am confronted with having to let go and empty my vessel of expectations.

Coming back to my heart reminds me that I have survived something serious. These moments remind me that I have had to recover my life. I have had to establish a new level of self-confidence. I have had to rewrite my regulations, rules, and standards for what qualifies as self-esteem. I have had to learn how to walk, how to talk, how to listen, how to blink, how to smile, and more. The hardest of these was to learn how to love me again. These lessons have not come like lightning but like the tree in my yard that suddenly is taller than I remember. It was growing every day, and suddenly, I am aware that change has happened.

Consciously working for change does not make it happen at the moment that I will it to happen. Magic is much more mysterious than pronouncing it so and then witnessing it unfold. Time, I have learned, is the power that gives the most in healing. Time combined with Love is omnipotent. These qualities partnered give us the courage to endure. I will get through this BS story, or any other on my healing journey because I know these things. I know these virtues because I am a person of faith.

Often I have wondered since my brain surgery, "What do people without faith do? How do they endure?" I know the only prayer for me when I witness the struggle for others now is "Please show them the way." Again, and again, and again, and again, I have been shown a good way. If it has happened to me, it can happen for others. I tell my story to show others a good way they also could choose, for we all deserve to have peace, health, and wholeness.

My courage was profound when I walked into the surgery room at California Pacific Medical Center in the early morning of September 8, 1998. At midnight I had stopped having any foods or fluid. At 5:20 am, I walked the Labyrinth out in front of the hospital. My mother sat on the meditation bench and waited for me as I ceremoniously moved with conscious prayer toward the center of the maze chanting to myself, "I let go of my fear of dying." On the way out of the labyrinth, my prayer mantra was "Love is my way." The courage also included profound ignorance of what I would undergo. I thought I knew about healing and then I found out there was much more to learn.

The prediction that my ability to survive the recovery was going to be harder than surviving the surgery itself gave me some comfort. My intuition knew it would be tough, but I was not prepared for the events that ensued. The ignorance of what my life would become was perhaps a blessing. Obviously, this drama story was the next step on my spiritual path, or it would not have been what was happening.

I had to persevere. What healing was to come first, I did not know. My fundamental understanding is humans are integrated systems, the physical, emotional, mental, and spiritual aspects of self, are all connected. My recovery had to happen as well on all levels.

Love is what got me through, the love of my family, the love of my friends, the love of my clients, even the love of strangers. The love of life that lives within me, my eternal faith in something greater than me, and the presence of love from all of these souls supported me through such a difficult journey back to balance. The journey is not over. I think we are always in healing whether or not we have a health crisis, illness, or injury in the body. Life to me is synonymous with the ever-present quest for something greater. That quest ultimately is love, and yet, even though its where our souls originate from. Here is the paradox. We start with love. Therefore, we have already arrived where we want to be.

The brain surgery story is not where forgiveness begins in my life. As a child who also experienced sexual abuse the wounds in my life are very deep. In a regression therapy session at 27, I remembered deciding at seven years old to disassociate myself from my pain and memories. These memories began to come back to me simultaneously as my tumor symptoms began to appear. Synchronicity is not mystical. It is logical. Another perfect example of the need to expand the conceptions of the inter-relationship between the dimensions of being. There is no need to separate body, emotions, mind, and soul for they are all ultimately one.

The tumor is where I stored those memories, fears, and anger of early wounds to my body, heart, and being. It made perfect sense as a child to store them away. When they surfaced, I had to integrate their presence into my understanding of me in this world. Remembering sexual abuse was a devastation to the false self I had built around me to adapt to the world. This awakening occurred once I created a family of friends and a support system that would hold me when my internal world collapsed. The memories surfaced to conscious awareness when

I was ready, just like the presence of the tumor. The tumor presented itself when the external circumstances would support my healing.

The consciousness of the tumor came at the moment when I needed a purpose to my life. Every crisis comes in the perfect moment to serve the process of awakening our souls, healing more of the wholeness we have forgotten. The tumor was a symbol for how much I wanted to change, to heal. The physical symptoms of my tumor had been present for at least 15 years before an MRI confirmed its presence in my head. The diagnosis came in the perfect moment to receive the wisdom and healing for not only myself but also for my family, friends, and clients. Though it was physically in my body, I learned, only by going through the painful experience of the diagnosis, surgery, and long recovery, that I was not the only person who had the brain tumor. I was never alone in the process, the healing, and the transformation of the pain. Not only was God my constant companion, so were all of the people in my life. I truly learned how arrogant it is to say, "I am alone." We are never alone, ever!

By November of 1997 the dizziness, balance problems walking at night, the babbling in my sleep, the numb right bottom lip, and the deep fatigue had escalated. I had noticed maybe six months before that I no longer chewed food on the right side of my mouth. It was just an observation, but no mental light bulb or emotional warning bell had gone off with the discovery. The most common symptom of my tumor was someone saying to me, "Sally, you have food on your lip." I was on my way to Switzerland to work and visit friends. I had been traveling there since 1995 and looked forward to being with people whom I loved and admired. I stopped in Chicago on my way to see clients and family. While there I was very triggered regarding my issues with trust and left for Switzerland in a strange mood.

The trip itself was strange. When I landed at Charles de Gaulle Airport in Paris, I was to layover for 2 hours for a direct plane into Bern. Bern is the center of the Swiss government, so there is a small airport which was my preferred travel arrangement. The Bern airport this morning, however, was fogged in. I was flown on Cross Air to

Zurich and given a train pass on to Bern. The airline announced that a designated customer service agent would be at the Zurich gate waiting for all of the passengers from Paris who had been re-routed. Because I was the last off the plane, the person with a broken leg ahead of me slowed my departure; I missed the group going to the train station. Cross Air then did not know who was supposed to help me. I had to figure it out on my own. Needless to say, I was exhausted by the time I was on the train headed to Bern. I had been traveling all night. I was emotionally hungover. Still, with all the chaos, I knew something new was being born. As things fall apart in us, or around us, revelation of something divine is also present.

During that week I had a dream:

> *My soulmate was with me standing in the doorway to a blues*
> *club in Chicago. He was standing right behind me with his*
> *chin resting on the top of my head. We were looking for my*
> *sister whom we were to meet at the club.*

When I awoke, I had the sense that I would meet a man very soon. In a few days later that very week in Bern, I became involved with a client I had met by phone six months previously. Within days we were together. He proposed almost immediately, sweeping me off my feet in the most romantic tale ever … dancing me in the moonlight under a canopy of trees in the castle gardens at Lake Thun, ah! … or, so I thought at the moment. During that same time, I damaged the cornea in my right eye. It was quite painful, and it triggered some deep healing on the issues with men in my life. It all seemed a perfect and at the time in Divine Order.

When I returned to Chicago to spend Christmas with my family, I was quite in love and very ungrounded, to say the least. My sister was now concerned and insistent that my numb lip should not be ignored. I ignored it anyway and went on with my plans to move to Zurich and be with my Beloved for the rest of my life. In April I went to live with him in the apartment we had chosen together. I can still remember the light vividly in the room in California where I was when as he visually walked me through the apartment while on the phone. Email was beginning to take hold. We were both Macintosh users, and I saw it as another 'sign' that we were meant for each other. My love was a poet and would send me beautiful love notes.

As with most passionate encounters, this fire did not have adequate fuel to keep it going. By May the relationship was in a fall toward what would become a very painful crash-and-burn ending. Being the eternal optimist and the woman who bought all the lines, I was convinced that if I just kept being the good girl, he would come around. By the end of June, I left Switzerland devastated. On some level still hopeful that he would come around and we would get back on track in the fall. His childhood friend lived in Telluride, and we had tentative plans to meet there in October. I was still wearing my engagement ring, and I still had hoped his promises would still happen. We decided we just needed time.

It was now July 1998, and my sister insisted that I had to see a therapist because of my emotional state and a neurologist because of my numb lip. Thank God for my sister. Her fierce love is one of the gifts that has kept me alive. I am so happy that we chose to be together in this life. Though, admittedly, having me as a sister, well let's extend that to daughter/friend/healer/roommate/teacher/lover, comes with non-stop growth opportunities! Anyway, she referred me to a woman in Chicago who was a psychotherapist in private practice, and that also worked at Northwestern University Hospital in the spinal cord trauma center.

Cathy was impressed with my professional practice as a healer and wanted to do trade work. Her feeling was that God had sent me as her next teacher. Cathy was ready to embrace a deeper understanding of her faith and take her traditional psychotherapy practice to a more spiritual dimension. Our connection was a divine appointment miracle on my healing path. The Universe was lining up my medicine without my knowledge it was not going to be just a broken heart Cathy would help me survive.

My days began with tears. My days ended with tears. At the time, I was working on a manuscript for a book called *The 44 Faces of God*. My Chicago-land clients didn't know I was there and I could not get myself organized to tell them. My parents moved in early July, so I became their personal assistant. They lived about 2 hours from the Chicago Loop in a rural area. I was driving back and forth from the city to the country. Another miracle manifested for this to happen by my Uncle giving me a car to drive while I was home. His rental fee was that I come to visit him, which of course I obliged. We were taking care of each other in the ways that we could.

Cathy used a new trauma technique called EMDR which had come to the forefront for people recovering from trauma after the Waco bombing. Fighting with my fiancee was trauma. During the second session, Cathy used a light machine and noticed that the right eye did not track properly. With that information, the numb lip, I acquiesced to my sister's insistence to see a specialist. The neurologist was a small town doctor in the area where my parents had just bought their retirement duplex. Angela became another one of my angels. She gave me the standard tests, had me stand on one foot at a time, walk a straight line, checked to see if both eyes tracked together, and prescribed an MRI 'just to rule out' anything major.

It was the 12th of August before I could schedule the MRI. I had explained to Angela that the symptoms had come and gone for years. I was absolutely convinced they were psychosomatic. It was the trauma of my relationship, and I was going to be fine. After my appointment with Angela, over the weekend, I traveled to Dore County, Wisconsin to perform a wedding that had been scheduled the year before for Chicago clients and the reason I had left Switzerland when I did. It was an active weekend of friends and family with 120 guests. Needless to say, it was an emotional challenge to facilitate with what was happening in my personal love story. Yet I could not have imagined being anywhere else but there, as the celebrant for these dear, loyal, and loving people.

The day before the MRI I even bought a plane ticket to attend another wedding of a good friend in Cape Cod in early September. I was acting 'as if,' as they say in Alcoholic's Anonymous—that everything was going to be fine. I was just depressed and despondent with heartbreak, and I would recover. Since my heart has been broken before, my healing affirmation was: "My heart is bigger. Breaking it means my heart is now open, larger, and has, even more, space to love and be loved." My assumption was also my engagement was a period of figuring out our commitment, and we would.

The test was done in Peru, Illinois, the town next to where my parents now lived. The small town hospital had a traveling MRI unit that made the rounds of local hospitals in central Illinois. My appointment was a week after Angela had first examined me. My parents and I decided that after the test we would take a road trip to my sister's in Bettendorf, Iowa for dinner. We planned a shopping trip as well to find a dress for the black tie wedding that I was going to attend on the East Coast. We were all being brave and acting as if there was no problem. Bettendorf is just 1.5 hours away, and it seemed to be a good distraction.

When I lay down, and my body was slid into the tight tube of the MRI machine, immediately I was panicked. I had been warned it was claustrophobic, but I was not prepared for the sense of compression that went to the core of my being. Immediately I began to pray and talk to my spirit guides. I began to take controlled breaths in through my nose and out though my mouth. This focused breathing is what I use in my rebirthing work and teach in my meditation classes. I called out mentally to my alchemist guide, Wu Lon. I practiced my deep breathing to calm down. Within seconds Wu Lon came into my awareness and showed me a future vision:

> *I am wearing a green hospital gown, laying on my left side and having the hair on the right side of the back of my head shaved off. Wu Lon explained that the MRI would show a growth in my head, which I was to go back to California to have surgery, and I was going to be fine.*

Well, I was not so fine in that moment! I was clear that I would not be able to stay in this noisy, painfully loud, test for 45 more minutes if I was in a panic attack. This is the kind of news that can be disturbing at a minimum. I knew it was not just my fantasy and imagination going wild. I told Wu Lon that he had better F*&%#ing show me what happens after the surgery or I would not stay in the machine. The technicians had already told me that they would take me out of the MRI machine if I freaked out. With the next breath I was going to have them pull me out of the tube.

Within seconds, the next picture that came into my vision calmed my spirit immediately:

> *I am very pregnant on a beach in a floral dress with red, pink, and fuchsia flowers looking at the ocean with my hair being blown by the breeze. A man comes up from behind me and puts his arms around my big belly. It was the heart of all of my dreams, my family.*

After Wu Lon had presented me with these insights, I relaxed totally. The rest of the noisy, disturbing, MRI went very quickly. The first moments had seemed like hours after my chat with Wu Lon the rest of the test seemed like minutes. When I saw my Mom in the hospital waiting room, I said nothing about my visions. We went to the mall, and she bought me a lovely black beaded gown to wear at the wedding. The dinner at my sister's house was delightful but with an undercurrent of fear from all of us. The optimism was harder for me to hold on to, or actually, the denial was harder to be in, as the evening progressed.

When we returned to my parents home, Angela had left a message for me to call her in the morning regarding the results of my MRI. By the sound of Angela's voice, we all knew the results were not good. At 5:30 am on August 13, my parents already up and walking about having coffee, awakened me. My parents were supposed to travel to Madison, Wisconsin that day for their own doctors' appointments.

My mother had recovered from bladder cancer two years earlier. My father had a heart attack the year before.

They had good doctors they loved, so the 2-hour drive to have their care was their norm. I insisted that they go on to their appointments. They did not want to, but I assured them that if there were something wrong, it would not have to be solved that morning. I needed them to just go on with the day that they had planned. Their doctors' appointments were difficult to schedule. It was important to me that they took care of their needs, especially if I might need them to go to California with me soon.

At 8 am they had left the house, and I sat down to meditate. Once again Wu Lon came into my vision and repeated the information that he had shared the day before. He also instructed me not to return Angela's call till 9 am and remain in prayer and meditation until that time. Exactly at 9 am the phone rang, and it was Angela. She was not happy that I was without transportation to come into her office right away. Angela did not want to tell me the results of the MRI over the phone, but I insisted, and she obliged. "Yes," she said, "there is a growth on your auditory nerve." It was like being suspended in a dream and yet being very centered at the same time.

Angela was going to arrange for her nurse to come and pick me up so that we could review the results together. I hung up with her and immediately went into total fear. I called my sister to tell her the news and burst into tears as I relayed Angela's diagnosis. Though the emotional waves were intense, my mind seemed to be crystal clear. My sister told me she loved me and that we would get through this together. Suddenly I had to go to the bathroom. The toilet has always been a great spot for me to talk to God. There I had my first real conversation with God regarding this situation right at that moment.

It was necessary for me to take an inventory. I reviewed my life as follows:

1. I had adventured, discovered, and explored as much of the world as I have been able.

2. I had been in service to many, many, people in many places, who are seeking a better way to live, health, happiness and spiritual growth.

3. I had created poetry, art, photography, writing, and shared my gifts with the world.

4. I had loved, been loved, and participated in life with many people.

5. My presence and influence had been experienced by others.

6. I had forgiven my family, my sexual assailants, and those who scarred me in such deep and profound ways from this lifetime and others.

7. I had been a model to others and myself to trust in the Divine.

8. I taught *A Course in Miracles* to the best of my ability, understanding to always be a student keeps me humble, honest, and open to choose love over fear as often as possible.

9. I believed the *A Course in Miracles* teaching, "Love created me like Itself."

10. I had been able to let go of material wealth as my comfort and security.

11. Safety was in my relationship with God.

Then it occurred to me, remember I am still sitting on the toilet, that I had still not created my husband, children, and therefore, a family of my own. Having a balance male-female relationship was my second priority of this life. So, I let God know in prayer that there was no possible way was I done with my life as Sally Aderton. My engagement was not stable, I was not yet a mother, this book was going to published, and I had dreams to fulfill. I had to live!

Calmly, I explained to God that I was a free agent working on God's behalf in a world that was desperate for value. I explained to God that because I was an independent agent working without specific doctrines except "love is the way" that I was needed on the planet more than in spirit. Also, since my greatest dream of my family had not been realized, I intended to get through this challenge to experience my heart's desire. Now imagine, I was by myself, at my parents house, in the middle of cornfields, in the middle of Illinois, in the middle of the United States, in the middle of summer, in the mists of a crisis, however, I never once felt alone. I knew that I was going to be alright no matter what the outcome. What I did not know is how hard it was going to be to heal myself.

The phone was ringing so I finished my business in the bathroom and went to answer it. Angela was calling back to tell me she was on her way to fetch me. Her 10 am appointment was a no-show. Angela decided to pick me up herself and go to the hospital to get the MRI films and report. This is not the kind of behavior that I would expect from a neurologist; it was above the call of duty. Angela was acting out of kindness, generosity, and compassion. She was a rural doctor in the Heartland who out service to my wellness first.

Angela had called a neurosurgeon who rotated through the small towns in the area and who "happened" to be in Peru that day. He could see us after 11 am. Wow! Another miracle in the story—these were affirmations indeed a divine plan was in action. We are not victims to life; when we are in the flow, it is so obvious it is hard to not be in gratitude. I was even smiling when I got off the phone knowing the Angel Angela was on her way to carry me into the next scene of this unfolding drama.

The neurosurgeon was quite casual about the whole thing. He told me it was probably benign, it had been in my head a very long time, and I should enjoy the wedding in Cape Cod. The surgery could wait till my schedule was free. It was "elective" so I should go to California to have it done where my insurance would better cover the costs. My anxiety and fears were beginning again. I could feel the heaviness of the situation begin to grow. It was like walking through deep water with all my clothes on, but Angela was right there with me the whole time. Angela then took me to a Bagel shop for coffee and comfort, and we talked about my options for healing. She was for me returning to California but felt that it was important to get different opinions. This included my general practitioner's opinion, before making any decisions.

When Angela dropped me off at my folks, I immediately called Switzerland. My fiancee had known that I was having the MRI and wanted to know the results. I reached him at home since there was a 9-hour time difference and for him, it was nearing 10 pm. His first response to my news was "I am reminded of Stuart." It was an a-ha moment: my latest heartbreaker bringing to my attention, my first heartbreaker, Stuart. Stuart was my first love who died of a brain tumor when I was 28 years old. Wow, again! He said a part of our issues he felt were my fears around losing someone. For him, my behavior was too controlling because of my fear that every man would leave. Of course, the fear came from my direct experience of my first love Stuart who did leave, permanently.

Here forgiveness of what has been could create another way to my self-healing. I had tried for years since Stuart's death to enter healthy love relationships with men. They never worked. Now, he was pointing out one of the obvious reasons why. Though I had addressed these issues many times in therapy, never did the therapy impact me in the way his words did that day. The diagnosis of the tumor, the epiphany of having my dream-come-true vision during the MRI exam, and the wisdom of my fear, the men I love leave me, all collided together in that conversation.

This is the way consciousness evolves. It is truly the ongoing journey of experience and the narration of that flow. The destination of the consciousness is not even our death when one believes as I do in reincarnation. Our personality and body die, our story dies, but our soul does not. I believe that God knew about recycling before human beings began to figure it out. My brain tumor was already serving the purpose of creating the changes in me by showing me what I needed to forgive my fear of men leaving me to be that woman on the beach barefoot, pregnant, and partnered.

From the moment of the diagnosis, I was forced to make decisions and choices to change my life to save my life. I went back to California. My family came to California. Letters were sent to 1200 people in the United States and 200 people in Europe to pray for me during the surgery. Apple computer donated a laptop computer for me to use. Miracles happened and are still happening every day. The only way for these miracles to occur has been for me to trust, to stay in faith, and to change. I could no longer live the same life. Although I have greatly mourned my story's passing, I also know that it was the way for me to survive. Survival, however, is not enough; I want to thrive.

The deepest wound was to my confidence in my Self. I still trusted God, but I no longer trusted my body. After the surgery, I needed a reason to get up in the morning. I chose graduate school to be that reason, and it worked! The choices and healing I have done to try to weave together my life BBS and ABS—Before Brain Surgery and After Brain Surgery—required me to be reborn. My first waking thought in the Intensive Care Unit was powerful: *I have this body to teach people about God!* This first imprint into my mind, after a 14-hour operation, while violently sick from morphine and physical pain which I hope never to experience again, was about my life purpose. I have no doubt why I am alive. Additionally, I am here to love and be loved, or I would not be.

In the recovery of my smile, literally and figuratively, I have used the principles of my 5 Steps of Forgiveness—Ownership, Empathy, Release, Understanding, and Change. I began formulating this wisdom in the early '90s as the necessary logical steps to freedom from pain through forgiveness. This outlined path brought authentic forgiveness and resurrection. I had to own my shame, my hatred, my ignorance, my blame, my arrogance, my anger, my victimization, my hopelessness, my sorrow, my judgment, and mostly, my humanity. I believe that I am well because I faced myself by seeing again that innocent child of God.

The most difficult part of my forgiveness has been to myself. I came out of the brain surgery with a new face. The 7th cranial facial nerve became the major focus of trauma physically and metaphorically. The miracle of my nerve regeneration is the power of faith in action. It was the same nerve that had caused my lip to numb, as the tumor grew the nerve was stretched. When the tumor was removed, the nerve died. When I woke from the surgery the right side of my face was totally frozen, my hearing was gone, but I was alive.

One year after the surgery I still had only 2.2% of function to motivate the right side of my face. A respected doctor at Stanford told me, "Sally you will NEVER have any function on your face." Immediately I leaned toward him asking how he could say that? Without hesitation, he puffed out his chest and said, "I am a doctor at Stanford, and I have more experience with this than you do!"

What the Stanford doctor did not have though was experience with me. I was not willing to take on his proclamation as my truth. I told him I would go home and pray which is exactly what I did. My meditation that evening I heard God tell me specific things I needed to do if I wanted my face to function again. Ten months before this Stanford test, I had started giving myself daily acupuncture sessions. I was getting massages, Reiki healing, psychotherapy but there one other specific task revealed. My guidance was:

> *Keep doing your acupuncture daily. Keep doing all the other healing therapies too. Take a Model Mugging class.*

The Model Mugging program was developed in the San Francisco Bay Area by a woman, a black belt in karate, who was raped. It was a class on how to fight from a prone position. The others in the class told me that they were glad it was not them who I was fighting. In my mind, I was fighting the neurosurgeon, who I loved, but he had cracked my head open. My body remembered that though my mind did not.

Following my guidance, being courageous, and the blessing of tenacity have brought the nerve alive again. This Ph.D. in Healing taught me more about compassion than any book or spiritual workshop or sermon ever has. If I can do it, so can others.

*Smiling in Summer 1997
in Vail, CO*

*Smiling Thanksgiving 1998
in Bettendorf, IA*

*Smiling in Autumn of 2015
in Encinitas, CA*

One of the most important discoveries of my healing crisis is recovery, not a place. It just keeps evolving. My friends continue to alert me when they noticed changes in my expressions and the function of my right eye. It took years for me to have my right tear duct produce tears to keep the eye moist and I still need to use artificial drops occasionally. Around 2008 my Chiropractor Dr. Hillari Hamilton in San Diego and I were talking about how my face seemed different to her. She adjusted my neck and was holding my cranium. Hillari said something that triggered me to cry. For the first time since my surgery, tears came out of both eyes at equally at the same time! To this day, we both remember that moment as the miracle it was.

In late August 2015, I had a regression session that was one of the most amazing to date … and that says a lot! A healer held her elbow on my back like she was drilling to China. It hurt, but it awoke within me a memory of where my soul was during my brain surgery. Many people, especially clients, expected me to have soul recall from the 14-hour operation to remove the tumor. I had none until 18 years later nearly to the day. The anniversary was a week away. I had a very, very clear vision:

> I am sitting on the floor of the operating room watching the doctors. The tension in the room is very, very high. I see Brian Silva my healer friend go out the door. I am terrified that I will not get my body back. It is not going well. The surgeon has told my parents that hourly he would send someone from his team down to let them know how it was going. No one had left the room for a long time, and I saw Brian go. I could tell he was bracing himself to comfort my parents.

At some point, several years after the surgery I had found out there was about a four hour period that no one went to speak to my parents. It was evidently a critical time for the repair of my body, and my soul was afraid. Most near death experiences, afterlife recall or out of body recall are without emotions. In this regression, I was flooded with fear and sadness. I bridged time and integrated that frightened self back with love to the present moment. A reclaimed sense of my authority over my life began to unfold. The healer was a client/friend whom I had known since 1992. She shared with me that day her vivid recall of her first session with me in New York. The woman had met me when I was, in her words, 'fearless'! In the safety of her heart, facing my terror of losing my body, I found that strength again, and my life began to change again from the inside, out.

The revolution is that each one of us has brain surgery in some way. Every day there is crisis of illness, accidents, faith, betrayals in relationships, wars and experiences that rock our foundation of safety and security. These experiences remind us of how tenuous the relationship between our body and soul is. The revolution is to move from a victimization mentality about what is happening to us, to understand the spiritual lesson of what is happening through us.

My community of family, friends, clients and myself was able to navigate this BS drama chapter or personal growth workshop called Brain Surgery in the Life and Times of Sally Aderton because of our faith in something greater. The miracles were one right after another from both my angels in a body and those without form. All life is in a constant, moving, alive, dynamic co-creation with something greater than us all. We just need to listen, then act courageously to become the revolutionaries of miracles to change the human experience in the world.

Chapter 15 Practicum

- ⋈ Ask a friend to reflect back to you the times they have seen you be courageous in the times of crisis in your life. Invite them to share their perspectives of whatever revolutions occurred around you due to this crisis. Be grateful for what you discover in this exchange and their willingness to reveal what they see in you.

- ⋈ Return the favor and share with them how you have witnessed their moments of courage.

- ⋈ Make an inventory list in your journal of your most important life accomplishments.

Part Three

The Human Condition—
Living in the 4th Dimension

Chapter 16

Forgiveness, the Path of Peace for Karma in the Now

I n this last section of *Energy in Motion*, we address how we can recreate our experience of life by opening up the boundlessness of consciousness. It is fear that most often stops this adventure. By bringing love to the feelings of fear, we can transform. Emotions are the soul's response to experiences in the physical, mental, or spiritual worlds. They are the conductor system that expedites, or impedes, the progress of evolution or revolution. Feel, being sentient is the way for all living forms—plants, minerals, and animals—of which includes human beings. Yes, we are animals! Energy and life vibrates at different frequencies.

Emotion is the vehicle that can help us return to love consciousness. Love is respect for all life and reverence for truth. Loving everyone does not mean we will like everybody, be pals with everyone, and have free love, or free sex. God's will for us is happiness, joy, abundance, and the recognition of our value to others, our world, and ourselves. Pain is both the barrier and the path that we must all utilize to move through our life journey. Truth and the lessons behind those experiences are the expressions of the will of the Divine in co-creation with our soul's purpose.

When we resist change, we create pain. We hold on to the illusion of what we think is in our best interest, what we want, what we desire, or what we deem worthy. Karma is our story line and our life patterns. Karma is best discovered by personal archeology induced by the attention call from any conflict or pain we encounter along the way. The gift of any conflict is clarity. This 'call to attention' on every possible level—physical, emotional, mental, spiritual, ethical, political, environmental, social, moral—any level, is why we are alive. From the clarity of the life lesson, we learn hopefully to make better choices.

Becoming the experts of our karma, our evolution, our history, our healing—by becoming self-aware—we become empowered. This power is our right and our destiny no matter who we are. Every life forms are all aspects of the Divine Eternal Light of Love. We can give ourselves freedom and liberate ourselves from our patterns, which most often do not make us happy. This self-awareness and knowledge are the product of a spiritual path. Most people who identify themselves as 'spiritual' do not negate the negative aspects of their life. We do not victimize ourselves but understand these conflicts come to awaken us to more. And, the Love-that-Is is infinite (which is really, really big for a really, really, really long time ;-)!

Throughout the journey that we have been on together in this book, I have shared examples of how healing has manifested in the lives of my clients, and myself. In this last section I have called The Human Condition, I want to offer a more modern, and less restrictive, definition of karma. I respect the traditions of Hinduism and Buddhism from a place of honor and reverence. However, like telling me a 3000-year-old tree is a lesser life form, I cannot believe that we know the path of our soul's eternal life. I do not agree that I am here on earth just to suffer and do good, to be rewarded later.

Human Beings respond to immediate gratification. If the choices I am making in this lifetime are for good in another, why would I bother? If the choices I am making are to receive the benefits in heaven, why would I bother? If I am making amends for creating harm in the last lifetime, why would I bother? These examples are again of Destination Orientation Thinking. Additionally, humans always operate with an underlying motive: **what's in it for me?** We want the reward now but have belief systems that tell us the reward is somewhere down the road. If I never can arrive, because all I have guaranteed is this moment, wouldn't then this be the moment that counted in the bigger scheme of things? We want the ticket to heaven but do not see that is where we live.

In this section, I will continue to share stories of healing, to demonstrate how we can live in more love for everyone now, not later. My theory on the creation of peace on earth is a simple formula. First, we must embrace intuition and expanded awareness within our body and consciousness. Second, we must accept the fact that the morphic field of universal consciousness is real and we are not in this life alone. This last step then is how to get out of our own way to forgive the human legacy that has created civilization so far and be free.

The mechanism that allows us to set ourselves free is forgiveness. One of my favorite sayings is from Confucius for it incorporates both the teaching of letting go and uses symbolism significant in my waking dream and life story. The saying is *"He who cannot forgive another, breaks the bridge over which he himself must pass."* This statement teaches us about karma as well. As we are all connected, there is no guarantee that we will never cross paths again with someone we are in conflict with. Bridges show up in the landscapes of my sleeping dream whenever I am integrating parts of myself that have fragmented due to broken relationships.

To forgive means to give over, to let go, and to surrender. To forgive another, we must own what we are letting go. Forgiveness is an emotional process, not a mental one. Ownership is the ability to articulate what we feel due to conditions or situations in our lives, to take responsibility for our side of the bridge. We cannot let go of what we do not own of our feelings. They are the conduits, cords of light or energy streams, between people that connect us in the morphic field, or what Jung called the collective unconscious. We forgive to rewire the energy so that it flows and is not blocked, which is what causes emotional pain.

Karma is the reenactment of the patterns of behavior, systems of thought, or conditions of the relationship between people, events, and locations. The adage, "What comes around, goes around" describes the causation relationship. What you put out to the world in energy, the world gives back. However, sometime it will be lifetimes for the wave to return. The recycling of our energy goes into positive action, feeling, thought or belief, as well as, negative. The first law of thermal dynamics is not conditioned by time.

The laws of karma are the laws of the Universe that we have already addressed. They are the positive and negative forces that always are seeking wholeness, greatness, and balance. The universe is ultimately fair and just. As humans, forgiveness is a much more powerful act than getting even. As Gandhi said, *"An eye for an eye ends up making the whole world blind."* The universe, through the laws of karma, will always see to the debts that we carry for others and ourselves.

Retribution can sometimes take centuries and multiple lifetimes, or it can happen in an instant with grace. Regardless it is guaranteed that the energy will recapitulate. Instead of hurting each other to account for being hurt, our job is to love each other. I offer another spiritual axiom taking Gandhi's wisdom to this 21st century way of human existence. We still do not live his wisdom, so perhaps it needs to be simplified. **A heart for a heart makes the whole world shine!**

Our incentive to move away from judgment, condemnation, persecution, and fear of the diversity in human experience, is simple. We do not know exactly where we have been in the past, nor where we are going in the future. Reincarnation is the recycling of the souls. If I war against someone because they have a different religion than me, it could easily be true that I am fighting against my past or future self. I could be Christian in this life, Buddhist in the next, Muslim in the next, Pagan in the next, and then a religion that does not exist yet after that. This example continues with warring against friends, enemies, family, states and nations—any other way we can relate to each other as individuals or cultures we might have been, or could become.

Layna Chavez came to see me with her son Eli Sandoval regarding the anger she felt toward her at the time ten-year-old son. She had scheduled back-to-back appointments with me, as she wanted Eli to have his own personal time to address his own anger. That Eli provoked the feeling of rage in her seemed unfair to him. Layna was frightened that she could have such a strong reaction to behavior that was quite normal for his age. These feelings in Layna always intensified when she looked Eli directly into his eyes.

In a regression session, Layna remembered a lifetime where she was a mentally retarded, deformed woman, living in an institution, dependent totally on the hospital for her survival. She recalled a particular nurse treating her with great hostility. The nurse taunted her about "being useless," criticized her as being an "abomination of God" and was quite brutal in her hygienic care. As Layna recounted the memory, her body was very tense, and she felt immobilized while regressed into the trauma memories of that lifetime.

Although Layna in that incarnation had no language or ability to communicate using the body her soul inhabited then, she was completely aware of the wrongful acts of this nurse toward her. Layna's perceptions were limited to loving or non-loving energy, by feeling in the exchanges with others. In the regression, she had full recognition also of total fear and terror of this nurse. Latent within Layna's body and consciousness were these memories of this other time and place. The feelings mirrored and matched what she felt when angry with her young son. She felt powerless.

During the session, Layna remembers one night the nurse came into her room and strangled her to death. Looking into the eyes of the nurse, as the eyes are the windows to the eternal soul, Layna burst into tremendous amounts of tears. Without hesitation, she exclaimed that she saw the soul of her son Eli. To clear this karma, Layna, as she is in present form, used her imagination to bridge time. She was able to forgive the nurse for anger, betrayal, and powerlessness that she still was carrying in her soul from that experience. Feelings of deep love and possibility replaced the negative feelings, and Layna was healed of this karma and memory.

Eli, who waited patiently out of my office, had no knowledge of what had happened during his Mom's session. During his private time with me, he agreed to a regression to see if we could find a deeper meaning for his anger. Without my influencing to what point in time his consciousness would remember, Eli saw himself as an angry nurse. The first image he saw was of pushing someone down a flight of stairs to break their neck. He saw this nurse behaving with the same vengeance toward other patients. Eli remembered specifically strangling a woman that he identified as Layna. When Eli bridged time to forgive himself, he was able to understand what conditions of the nurse's life had created such atrocious behavior. By owning the anger, which was also grief at her own childhood traumas, Eli could then understand where some of the unexplainable rages were coming from in his relationship with his mother and sisters of this life.

After their independent healing sessions, immediately when the two saw each other they both noticed a new softness between them. Eli said to Layna, *"Wow, Mom I killed you!"* but they both felt celebration in this knowledge instead of the pain of the past. They embraced with their eyes, and arms, knowing that something had changed on a very visceral level, releasing the love to flow between them. Layna was so committed to her parenting in this life, and she was willing to dig past the apparent. This soul archeology set them both free to be more trusting, kind, and loving of each other.

Notice however that independently they forgave not just the obvious persecution of Layna, but themselves for the beliefs they carried about who they were in those life stories. Layna forgave the world for not knowing that she had awareness, herself for not being able to communicate, and Eli for his brutal actions. Eli forgave himself for the judgment he held of people who were imperfect and his belief that he was doing them a favor to end their suffering. In truth, Eli in abusing others was trying to relieve his own suffering from childhood sexual abuse of that life. The physical and mental disabilities of these mental patients mirrored his own incapacities to deal with the emotional pain of his own life.

When updating *Energy in Motion*, I contacted both Layna and Eli to insure that now decades later they still wanted their stories shared and if they had any additional wisdom to add. Their story is a perfect living example to each about past life influences. During the conversation, I said to him *"you might not remember, but I want to tell about a session you had with your Mom...."* Eli interrupted my sentence and said, *"Ohhhh, I know **Exactly** what you are talking about! Do you know how many times I have told that story over the years!"* As Eli matured into the beautiful man he is today, he holds this memory of healing with his Mom as a turning point in his own personal evolution.

Our consciousness is infinitely wise. Each will go to the memories that are important to address at that moment in time. We can see the truth when we are ready emotionally and not before. Eli had been ready at nine-years-old to address the karma with his mother. To get ready emotionally, we must feel safe in our lives that the information will bring us wisdom instead of more grief. There needs to be a level of healing and recovery already stable within us before we can go on these deep, dark, emotional paths to God. We are facing what is negative in our consciousness with love, not judgment. It is this courage that brings, even more, love into our lives. Layna is the perfect mother to have nurtured her son the way he needed to be nurtured.

When I asked Layna to share how being Eli's mother over the decades progressed, she had many stories to share. Here she tells us all how the work the three of us did together have, and still has, influence today:

"*Twenty years later ... E-motions. When I met Sally in 1989, it was absolutely one of the most pivotal times of my life. One story I want to share in particular happened years later. I moved back to Kauai with my children in 1995. Eli wanted a CD recorded, and we went to see a friend at our community radio station. She was getting ready to go on air live, her guest had canceled, and she spontaneously asked us if she could interview us instead. Why, or what she would interview us about we had no idea at the time. But the universe had its own agenda.*

As much as I can talk up a story, I am personally not comfortable with talking on a microphone even without a live audience. Of course, this is just more past life stuff to clear. So Eli just bursts out, "Let's talk our about the time that Sally did our first session together!" He was about nine years old when we did the healing session with Sally, and at this time he was about 17. We did on that day about a 40-minute live interview. Eli and I both shared our story about our work with Sally. We talked about how we both realized that we would still experience the intensity of our karma and so had remembered many other lifetimes since that first session. When the feelings would surface, we would both be aware we were working on both past and present emotions.

The person who interviewed us that day on the radio, by the way, was also a Healer in the community. She later shared with me that this interview helped her to understand some feelings that she felt with her own children. There were parallels in Eli and my story with one of her daughters, but not both, that also made her feel bad. She asked for Sally's number and wanted to experience sessions for herself. Also one of our local therapists, whom I did not know at the time, I later met through a mutual friend. She came up to me and said she recorded the radio interview and used it in her family practice. When she felt it could help by giving another perspective in difficult family dynamics, she would share the recording with some of her clients.

In all areas of our lives still to date, Eli and I chose not to dismiss any of our many, many, intense emotions that come up. We allow ourselves to have these experiences and observe them at the moment. And yet we always share and talk about it if not then, later. Eli and I are aware that we chose each other and no matter what—no one is to blame! We both have the insight and the Love to take responsibility for our actions. This knowing is partly because of our work with Sally but also because we continue to willingly do the process in many other ways, and forms, that are conducive to our wellbeing. We have learned to pay attention or seek comfort from within, and to trust that we are here to Heal.

My son and I both had several individual sessions after our initial experience. I know that my body both felt and sensed these experiences during the sessions as if I was there in that past moment. Upon completion of this work with a forgiving heart, I had a realization that we carry memories into this life. I was convinced that we are here to experience life, and also to clear the personal and collective energy field that holds on to us on this human journey. This memory is real, and this unseen energy affects all of us on this planet.

During that time in San Francisco, when Eli was 9, we also took an 8-week Intuitive Development Class with Sally at Fort Mason. In the late '90s, there were not many resources to help my child. The New Age was just getting visible. I had been born with a knowing of my sensitivity, but I had never been trained to work with it. I needed help and found Sally. Eli had a lot of voices in his head, was super sensitive, and I wanted to know how to teach him how to evolve these as gifts into a conscious human being. Eli wrote to me in a letter at 19 that he realized he would have been a drug addict or dead by the age of 14 if he had not had my help. I intuitively knew *as his mother it was up to me to give him tools to deal with his sensitivity and honor his gifts. There are many resources today, but then it was not as openly available. I had to seek it out. Once I found Sally, I found a teacher that could teach me how to work with Eli and help us both on our spiritual consciousness paths.*

Each week Eli would surprise all of these adult students in what he shared and could know by his intuitive gifts. During the guided meditation times, he would crawl under his chair and lay on the floor looking like he was asleep. He was a kid and acting like one. Then, when we would be sharing about our journeys, Eli would tell about the most magical and profound experiences he would have with his Spirit Guides. He taught all of us that we must never underestimate the wisdom in children. Of course, I was his Mom, so I knew from the moment he was conceived he was destined for something special. His journey has not been easy but his singing voice is one of an angel, and he continues to inspire people every day to Be Love. His voice is his conduit between Heaven and Earth, and he must share it in order for him to feel vital and connected to his passion and purpose.

The story about our sessions with Sally has been shared to date with many people. It has shed light or insight into matters with people whom just cannot get clarity on some sadness or anxiety or just a deep sense of pain or suffering that comes on. Especially, sometimes when the emotion makes no sense at all. There is something real there, and sometimes this emotion manifests physically and mentally. Just sharing my personal experiences has helped many people. I have also referred many people to Sally, and they have themselves been awakened and helped dramatically. I truly love life and embrace it all, unforeseen and seen, known and unknown, to date. We are all a WIP—work in progress—and now with

the quickening upon us, we can really progress, through a
healthy healing regress, and evolve. This is evolution."

People have come to me for past life information or to have past life regression experiences out of intellectual curiosity, just see if it is real. My attitude is that this is not a good reason to dance between the veils of time. Past life regressions are a sacred journey to resolve the unexpressed energies and heal karma. They are not for the sake of the ego; they are for the salvation of the soul. We have all been famous, rich, poor, talented, injured, greedy, geniuses, imbeciles, hopeless, men, woman, heterosexual, homosexual, asexual, red or yellow or black or white or pink skinned. If you can name it, you have probably done it. Eternal life is the truth. It is the incredible recycling program of the Universe and consciousness. Our soul energy is not being created, nor is our soul destroyed. It just moves around, forever, recreating into new forms.

My love for Layna and her family is eternal. Though she and I did not speak for over a decade, Eli and I have kept in touch with the contemporary tools for relationships today. Facebook, I call *The-Country-With-No-Borders*, is a gift for maintaining relationships in this post-technological time. I embrace technology instead of rejecting it for it allows me a platform and vehicle to stay connected to people I care about. The Internet is the physical manifestation of the collective unconscious or morphic field. With social media, I can stay more current other's personal journeys forward. My digital stomp, I went past a footprint long ago, allows me to send out love into the digital highway through my art, words of wisdom, and emojis. I love bitmojis and emojis because they are fun. The happiness I feel when I use them is conveyed too.

The people I work with the desire to move through, with understanding and knowledge, the barriers that keep them from experiencing their possible self. We all have an idealized image of the self and the actual self. Often we see the patterns of our childhood, the conditions of the moment, and yet all of our attempts to change our behavior fail. Layna and Eli still have moments of anger yet no longer does Layna fear the rage or Eli carry a sense of guilt and latent hostility towards his mother. By their re-membering, re-structuring, and re-wiring the emotional content between them, they set themselves free of one of the karmic ties that brought them together in this life.

When I talked with Eli about what he wanted to say regarding his experience with me in his life, Eli's initial commentary was similar to what he said to his Mom at 19:

> *If it wasn't for my mother's unconditional love and willingness to go outside of the box for my best interest, I might not be here today! My mom finding Sally when I was about nine and Sally teaching us meditation and guiding us into past life regressions made me who I am today. It gave me tools I needed to survive and flourish into the conscious whole and self-sustained spiritually balanced being that I am today. Sally Blessed me with the guidance that I needed and would need to deal with my extreme sensitivity, the curve balls, and even the bombs that life would drop on me in the future.*
>
> *I remember almost everything about the experience before and after with this particular regression with my Mom. It was undeniably a pivotal point in my life and my relationship with my mother. After the regression, I remember hanging out with Mom and feeling "lighter." We shared our experience and were both so amazed that we'd clearly gone to the same lifetime without sharing any information about what we experienced in the regression until after the session. That always stayed with me and totally validated the experience. The karmic energy between us was balanced and restored to a harmonious state. We did "the work" and are better for it. Although it was unbelievable and unconventional at the time, it was just what we needed and is really "real." Beyond the "new agey-ness" of it all the core of the experience is about bringing things to the conscious forefront of our aware-*

ness so that it can be identified and in turn healed! We can release these Karmic energies and patterns, to heal ourselves and each other! We have the divine capacity to FORGIVE!!! What a huge understanding for me to gain at that age!

Love is a healer, and lack of love is a killer! The lack of love experienced in that particular lifetime lead me or the "nurse" to physically kill my mother or the "patient" in that life. So painful and sad! I learned that I could forgive myself and therefore heal that lifetime's experience! It's really quite simple and now much more accepted in mainstream culture. There are many paths to healing one's own "stuff" many valid ones! This was an immensely healing experience, and I will never forget it! I am eternally grateful to my mother and my "spiritual godmother" Sally. We are all one. There is no separation. Life is a gift were all here to share."

The challenges that Eli faced were beyond what most humans experience. Those challenges will be Eli's legacy to share. **We do not get to where we are unless we have been where we have been.** Abiding in all of these traumas and dramas was Eli's willingness to persevere by the love that he is. All of us, whether we want to believe it or not, are eternal Beings. Learning about who we are beyond the apparent, can help us choose what we can do now to bring greater peace to our souls at the moment. I left all of the exclamation points in his narrative so that you can feel along with him the magnitude of those two hours carried forward over decades.

As we forgive the pain of the past which informs our ability to choose in the present, we create a different future. This is a new way of addressing the laws of karma. We do not need to be victims to what our choices were in the past. We do not need to continue to perpetuate an idea that we know who owes whom anything. If we are here, we are here to learn. The syllabus for our soul is the same for everyone. We are here to learn about love, and how to be loved. By consciously becoming aware of our karma, when the apparent life conditions do not resolve our conflicts, we are empowered from the inside out to be, as Gandhi said, ". . . *the change we wish to see in the world.*"

A married couple came to see me regarding an undercurrent of anger in their relationship. I introduced Gigi and Tom in Chapter 3 with the story about orange juice for the baby growing inside of her. They loved each other but would repeatedly hit what Tom called 'a wall' that they could not seem ever to get over. Instead of the separate sessions like Layna and Eli chose, they wanted to do a regression together. So we journeyed into their shared past to heal the source of this anger that they could not understand in the present. Laying down side by side, image Gigi also around seven months pregnant.

During the session, they both went, by their own ultra-sensitivities and present awareness senses, to the same moment in time. Together they witnessed their shared history witnessing the past betrayals, mis-communication, and individual fears that created the latent hostility in their present lives together as a married couple. We visited that day not just one, but two different incarnation stories of lifetimes they as souls had experienced life on earth together.

One of these past life experiences was Tom killing Gigi. As an Irish settler, Tom immediately felt fear when he saw his son with a Native American man. Tom's reaction was to immediately shoot the Native American man but had no comprehension of the relationship he and his son had formed. The Native man, Gigi's soul in that life, was not angry at Tom or his actions. Gigi's eternal self, her spirit, could forgive his fear. Gigi's soul was saddened by the loss of her body she inhabited in that life. By remembering together, corroborating the same story and truth of their previous connection, Gigi and Tom found forgive-ness for each other.

This example of emotions that were carried over time helps us to understand again the universal story of interconnectedness. It is the unresolved emotional energy that pulls our souls back into physical form. For Gigi and Tom, the opportunity to love each other in this life was a soul contract that they had made before entering into life on earth again. In another lifetime that we touched on in the same session, they remembered a life where the attraction to each other was not deniable but impossible to actualize. In this next life that they were now looking at to heal, Gigi and Tom remembered they did not consummate nor commit to each other with sadness for them both.

Here this karma between the souls of Gigi and Tom brought a new awareness of who they were as individuals now. It was an ideology that keeps them apart. In this lifetime Gigi and Tom are committed to their own spiritual paths and traditions. Their past lifetime desire was a positive emotion that co-existed with the negative emotion of betrayal. Gigi and Tom were both aware that the fear of being together due to cultural norms at the time left them feeling inauthentic and ashamed. They were betraying not each other but their own personal truth of who they thought they were supposed to be.

Healing from this past lifetime was one of the reasons each of them is on earth at this very time in the human revolution. They are here in service to each other to be awake, to self-actualize their authentic nature, and be aware of the eternal truth of being. The religiosity of that lifetime is being healed in this life by letting go of dogmas. Gigi and Tom came with these spiritual goals not just for themselves, but the children that were born in their union too!

Early in my practice, I began to see a very clear pattern or system of how to forgive. I witnessed five specific points of reference and perspective that individuals would move through that brought them freedom and the ability to let go of their pain. I define these steps as **ownership, empathy, release, acceptance,** and **change**. The steps are the basis to recreate the emotional energy, our system of patterns that substantiate the ideology that we carry on any level. These steps apply whether the pain came from the past or a present lifetime experience.

The first step of **ownership** is very clear. We cannot let go of something we do not own, that we do not acknowledge, that we do not perceive, that we do not take responsibility for possessing. What we name we can have a relationship to. By owning what we are forgiving we are naming our personal truth. For example, Tom had to own his fear and Gigi had to own her anger as the first step to healing the 'wall' in their marriage. Instead of focusing on what the other was doing, or nor not doing, we brought their attention back to the perceiver instead of the perceived.

Ownership is as simple as making an "I am __" statement. This names our position and reference point, where we are coming from. Once this is accomplished, we can do our own archaeology to see how we evolved to this point of view. Our perspective can be sourced to beliefs about ourselves and the world. These beliefs are held due to experience, which can either reinforce that belief or discredit it.

Once we have claimed ownership of our pain on any level, we can find out what brought us to this pain, what in our history validates our awareness, and if it is still our truth. Tom in his Irish settler past life was fearful because he was in a new land and did not understand the customs or the language of the native people. He was not encouraged by the settlers in his community to learn about the native people whom they judged as primitive to themselves. Tom dealt with his fear by consuming alcohol to numb his fear.

Gigi was angry that Tom shot her because due to his fear, Tom was incapable of forming a relationship with the Native man like his son had with him. The Native man was curious about these foreigners now sharing the land. Gigi in that life was upset not because of losing her life, for, from the Native cultural viewpoint, she knew that life was eternal. Gigi was upset for losing her fine, strong, handsome, beautiful body! Gigi liked the form she was in and was angry and disappointed to leave it when she did.

Gigi carried anger not just because of the loss of her body, but also Tom's disrespect for his own body which he numbed with alcohol. In the present, Gigi was losing her slim form with a big pregnant belly. She knew when in the process of remembering this lifetime with Tom, some of that frustration was not about her current condition. Tom got her pregnant, though willingly, it made her fat. He participated in this lifetime for her to loose her fine, beautiful body. We know that Gigi and all pregnant woman's bodies are is beautiful. However, it is common that they do not feel that way!

The next step on the path of forgiveness is **empathy**. How often do we ask someone who hurt us, "Why?" How often is it impossible to find out the answer because we no longer have a relationship with them? Empathy is one way for us to know the why. For us to understand why we must perceive from their viewpoint. We do not need to agree with their rationale, their truth, their reality. However to forgive them, when we acknowledge where they are coming from, gives the possibility of compassion to be born. When we see from their eyes, heart, experience, history, it gives us the power to be able to do something about our relationship to them. Gigi could forgive Tom when she could see the pain hidden behind the alcohol. Tom could forgive himself when he acknowledged his fear instead of justifying why he behaved as he did. From this awareness, we then can cross the bridge, or release the energy that was unexpressed from that time. The greatest gift of empathy is understanding. It is empathy that answers our desire to know why.

To be empathetic is to have the ability to feel what another feels. However, our feelings are not produced in a vacuum. Feelings are reactions to stimulation. To be able to perceive through another's point of view is the capacity to see the evolution of their perspective. What this step of empathy is about is to be able to see as another does for their perspective came from experience. In a regression, my facilitation helps someone to see literally through the perspective of whoever has hurt them. Through our ultra-sensitivity, we can and do know how others come to their viewpoint. More often than not, my clients will see fear as the driving force behind someone's actions to cause them pain.

I have called the next step of forgiveness, **release**. What I am talking about is the transformation of the energy that we are holding in our bodies. Release is the choice to let go of the fear, the anger, the shame, the guilt, the regret, and any of the pain that we owned in the first step. Re-leasing can be done in many ways. Transformation of the negative sets the energy free to be absorbed into the system in a new positive way. Writing, speaking, dancing, physical movement, any of these modes will allow the release in the present. The energy must be in motion, e-*motion*, energy in motion!

In a transformative healing, we need to have faith that the energy will recreate itself in a positive form. As I have witnessed these transformations thousands of times, I do not need faith or belief if what I propose is true—I have experience. My experience has shown me over and over again that there is an innate intelligence in every one of us that is seeking wholeness and peace. As this energy is our essence, and our essence is love, it always transforms for good to support us in becoming more of our pure potential.

The movement of the energy is done by our free will, therefore, influencing our sense of personal power and choice. In an emotional release, we can be afraid to let go of the old patterns as they are familiar and habituated. Though change is the natural order of the universe, we become stuck in the familiar thinking that is safe. To release the old ways is taking responsibility and behaving differently, or at least with the awareness as to why we behave as we do. Gigi and Tom both released the old resentments in their individual bodies in their own ways. Gigi needed to talk about the loss of her body. Tom just needed to cry and allow the grief of that life. Tears are the most powerful way to release the pain of the past.

Tears are the water in our body. Crying tears is the most powerful way to heal and transform. There is a stress-reducing hormone in tears! It is the emotional system, water, in the earth that we are. Crying releases emotional tension though it is uncertain as to exactly the karma that is healed in the process. For example, imagine we take all of Tom's anger at himself and put it into a drinking glass. Then put the anger at his son, for seeming to be vulnerable to an enemy, into another. Now pour both glasses into a pitcher. Effortlessly, the water mixes and shifts to the new container. It is the same for our emotions. Integration is one of the reasons emotions are so difficult to understand. Emotions are a woven complex system!

Sound, our breath the air of our being, is the other easy vehicle to forgive energy. Sound that we express through our voice is the soul's expression of its vibration. Both, tears and sound we can express in either positive or negative way. Tears are a response to happiness or sadness. We can speak with anger or with compassion. In a forgiveness process, it is essential to move the stuck energy as it is this energy that fuels the patterns that result in pain for others or ourselves.

Moving the emotional energy can be done consciously by writing, talking, drawing, exercising, dancing, laughing, lovemaking, drama, and any creative action. When we do not move the energy in positive ways, we are not taking responsibility for ourselves, and the creation of a more peaceful world. Internalizing the negative energy only prolongs the process. In taking steps to release the pain by forgiving another or ourselves, we are empowering ourselves as only we can. No one can give us the power to heal, nor can they take it away. We are responsible, period.

Once we have released the negative energy, we are free to take the next step on our journey. It is **acceptance.** We surrender to a greater truth of what is for we can see from both sides of the conflict, not just our own. It is impossible to recreate the events of the past. It is possible to recreate our perspective on them. This new view will set us free from expectations set by the experience, to create a different future. Until the healing session, Gigi's subconscious continually gave her the message that she must protect herself from Tom, thus producing a 'wall' that Tom kept hitting. Gigi and Tom in the present have differences in ideology. Gigi is no longer afraid to be true to herself nor Tom afraid of her spiritual beliefs. This common, almost innocent or naive, reaction to each other—resistance and judgment—created the unresolved energy block between them. Accepting what was, brings the wisdom forward to help in the creation of what will be. Just like we cannot change someone else, we cannot change the past but only our perspective, therefore our relationship, to it. The expression of this acceptance is love.

In all of the regressions I have facilitated, the bottom line is always the same for the creation of the pain—acknowledgment. Observe children for they teach us repeatedly about what is important—attention.

When we deny children our attention, they react. Attention bridges the gap of separation. Children do need to learn autonomy, but the hope is they do so without the belief they are alone in this world. When they have been emotionally conditioned through interaction, acceptance, and attention, trust becomes the natural expression of their humanity. Trust is sourced from love and is the product of faith.

Recognizing that we are loved sets us free to create the new expression of our being as we transform by forgiveness. The last step on the path to peace is the reason we go through the process to heal. **Change**, to embrace the new vitality, the product of what we have released, brings a new awareness of who we are. Our behavior then shifts toward the innate love that we are instead of the separation from it. The reinvention of ourselves, the reprogramming of the computer of our mind, giving it new software, that will, in turn, produce the new understanding of the data, gives us a new way to perceive the world.

Gigi's 'new program,' her new belief system is "I am safe with Tom." Tom's new program is "I am grateful for Gigi's presence." When they journeyed together into their past life, they consciously chose to break down the wall in their marriage that the apparent did not explain. They gained information that helped Gigi and Tom understand why they fell in love in the first place. They gained information about themselves and each of their own conceptions of who they are in this life, to accept their unique talents and expressions. They bridged the gap between themselves with more acceptance, more acknowledgment, and could then bring new attention to each other. This helped them feel even more committed to the love between them. Whatever, or whomever, we are forgiving, love is the vehicle—and the bridge—that ends separation creating wholeness.

Imagine what is possible for this world when we adopt an expanded perception of what is real. Imagine what is possible when we begin to allow ourselves to see deeper into the mystery. Imagine how your relationships would change if you could understand the depths of feeling evoked by those around you. Imagine that we no longer are victims to history nor holding on to victimization as a mantle justifying violence of the past, for retaliated violence of the present. Look at what the invention of computers and the internet did to destroy Blockbuster and Tower Records, or what a parents divorce did to the lives of their children. Mourning the past is important as it gives validity to the love and honor we had for something. However, we cannot take back what was created. We can take back negative feeling the creation evoked—the guilt, shame, anger, persecution, betrayal, regret—by owning it. Once we do, we can let it go.

How often do you think that if someone apologized for hurting your feelings, it would resolve the pain? How long are we going wait for a collective apology from the slavers, the tribal chiefs, and the merchants who together brought human bondage to the United States when they are no longer alive? Why are the decedents of only the persecuted responsible for making amends when all karma includes everyone involved? We are all a part of every action in the Universe that brought us into this moment in time. If atrocities happened, then the power to heal them also exists. Forgiveness is that power.

When will we forgive the manifest destiny that created the United States at they same time created the demise of cultures that were here before western civilization? Are we going to stay victims to the choices of our ancestors? If we do not forgive them for what they did, we are prisoners and persecutors still. Shirley MacLaine during the last season of the Oprah show said, "When we all realize reincarnation is real, we will stop killing each other." Shirley is right. Our ancestors are gone in body but not in soul. They are us reincarnated. Gigi and Tom's story gave us a small glimpse of a bigger mystery in the creation of the United States. Imagine your prejudices and then look back at your soul's evolution. I know for me, there is no more room for righteousness. I have been a slave, a master, and I have been a man who freed them.

Forgiveness is the key to creating harmony and peace on the planet. It is the journey that we all must take consciously. The norm is we wait until the pain is too great before we make changes. I suggest we begin right now. Is there anyone in our life we need to forgive? Are there any self-recriminations that we are holding onto, beating ourselves up with that can be forgiven right now? Try these five steps—**ownership, empathy, release, acceptance,** and **change** to embrace the new. Just see what happens in your vitality and every other aspect of your awareness. It indeed, I trust, will change.

In Appendix II at the end of *Energy in Motion*, is the handout, from my workshops in the 90's when I started sharing this road map to peace. Visceral experience is the most effective way to know the worth of a tool or process or belief or theory. When we do it, then we know it best. Life is an inside-out job after all. We have the ability to forgive a culture, a person, our self, a system, a cultural institution, a historical event, or whatever holds negative feelings in us. We are not prisoners of our external manifestations. Our resistance to forgive keeps us incarcerated personally and collectively. Let's unlock us from the pain of the past to emancipate our future. When we let go of that pain, we can be free. In freedom, there is peace.

Chapter 16 Practicum

Use the 5-Steps to Forgiveness provided in the Appendix in three distinct ways. First, as a writing exercise regarding your judgments about who you are from the critical voice to your eternal self. Second, as a writing exercise forgiving someone or something that has hurt you in the past. Third, speak with someone you want to heal a recent experience that affected the intimacy, friendship, or work relationship between you. Use the script to share with them the lesson about forgiveness.

Chapter 17

Defining the
Fourth Dimension

The mind contains information, but it is how we interpret and perceive information that makes the data meaningful. For over three decades I have regressed, re-birthed, facilitated soul retrieval, guided sacred journeys—however you want to label the experience— for individuals seeking to transform their lives. The outcome of these sessions is consistent. Their awareness of the events in their soul history—this life, past lives or future lives—is remarkable and magical. Always the story collaborates with the pain in their present moment. It helps to understand reactions, feelings, and the personal choices of their current lifetime.

The body holds all memories of all time and experiences of the consciousness of the soul. Our Being remembers with thoughts, visions, impressions, awareness, feelings, emotions, tensions, physical discomfort, pain, sounds, smell, sight, taste and sound, and sometimes, just plain old knowing. Not all memory is in the mind. The mind contains information, but more importantly, the mind is how we process, interpret and perceive information. The emotional system has a wisdom of its own. The emotional world is where transformation occurs.

The more unresolved the emotional energy, the more the soul must participate in the school of earth. A soul can have grace set them free, yet more common is to have the right use of will create the alignment of the soul. The Unforgiven energy must be moved from the system to open it for change. Feelings that are not acknowledged do not just disappear. They are displaced. Emotions communicate the soul's response to a physical or mental experience, which then brings insight and awareness. They are both the conductor for information as well as the barometer of how it feels.

When I am working with a client, and they are telling their drama story of what needs healing in their life, I will randomly ask them to tell me the first number that pops into their head. Every single time, the number is associated with past trauma. They do not randomly answer my innocent question. The assumptions we make is that our feelings are about the present moment, and present conditions. However, since the Fourth Dimension is timeless, we are now consciously accessing the past and future moments to be freer in the now.

Earth is a magnet, and the emotional energy is a receptor to the magnet. Our souls are light. What allows the density of body/earth to combine with our soul/fire are the mediums of emotion/water and mind/air. It is the is the sacred marriage of heaven and earth. The Fourth Dimension paradigm is the key to living in greater harmony. We have moved past the Trinity as our spiritual model. The quadripolar magnet, as Franz Bardon called it, is more accurate.

The spiritual path is the path of peace, joy, and love. This subtle shift, giving greater attention to the emotional world, we have the potential to have more of those qualities daily. I know many spiritually adept and aware people, yet we all have anger, sadness, fear, resentments, and judgments of others and ourselves. The experience

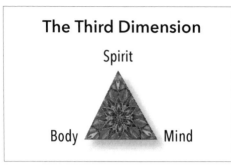

of emotion is what defines the human condition. When the emotions are given appropriate channels of expression, pain transforms. It changes into acceptance, which is the essential ingredient to peace. Even with thousands of years of billions of people all praying for a world of peace, we still do not live in one. These prayers are still not answered, yet the desire to pray for peace has not stopped. Perhaps by placing a new understanding and value on our emotional world, we can create balance for us all.

All negative emotion can be reduced to fear. Shame is the fear of not being worthy of love. Guilt is the fear that a promise or action was not honorable. Regret is the fear that one did not make a right choice when using their will and intention. Denial is the fear that the truth is too painful to endure. Anger is the fear that one is not loved and respected and, the deep grief that this produces burns in our being. Hatred is the fear that another's actions keep us from our power. Jealousy is the fear that another is more worthy of love and its reflections than we are. Of course, these are simple reductions.

I suggest that when we feel each of these negative emotions, we then ask ourselves: *"What am I really afraid of?"*

Even too much of a positive emotion can be to our detriment and create the imbalance in our Being that keeps peace elusive. The attitude of conceit is too much self-love. Idolization is the belief that someone has more worth or power than we do. The euphoria created by stimulants, chemically or naturally produced, creates addictions which are a way to sabotage our success. Laughter, though the sign of joy, often is not. It can be a response to nervous discomfort and anxiety caused by fears.

One way to describe the evolutionary shift to the Fourth Dimension is by centering of consciousness from the third to the fourth Chakra. Chakras are the communication channels between the soul body to the physical body. There are seven primary Chakras for all life forms, including animals, plants, and minerals. Each Chakra has qualities and attributes that help us understand ourselves. Here is a very fundamental teaching about this self-awareness tool that has been known for centuries in the cosmologies My goal here is not to replace or review what is known about Chakras. My intention is to give a post-technological perspective on this ancient wisdom. The charts I have created are simple, they are not in competition with other ways of understanding or seeing these wheels of life. Keeping ideas simple allows them to be embraced, and user-friendly. My goal is to create a visual framework for what is not apparent to many eyes.

In the following diagram, I detail out the significance of each colored Chakra, their relationships to the four levels of our awareness physical, emotional, mental, and spiritual—and the blending of the levels to allow the sacred marriage of heaven-spirit and earth-physical in the mediating additional three Chakras. This basic presentation is meant to give structure and a reference to what I am talking about esoterically.

Moving the center of experience from the third Chakra into the fourth Chakra or from the Third Dimension to the Fourth Dimension is the next step in evolving the human condition. We have been

Primary Chakras
Fundamental Aspects

Belief Systems *Spirit*	**7** Violet	consciousness, god, universal awareness, knowing
Thought *Spiritual, Mental*	**6** Indigo	conceptualization, perception, interpretation, imagination, third-eye, claire-voyance
Communication *Mental*	**5** Blue	speaking, listening, claire-audience
Love *Emotional, Mental*	**4** Green	power, peace, forgiveness, acceptance, harmony, understanding, empathy, devotion, claire-sentience
Actualization *Emotional*	**3** Yellow	will, self-esteem, choice, self-expression, confidence, self-determination
Creativity *Emotional, Physical*	**2** Orange	pro-creation, sensuality, desire, co-creation, manifestation
Survival *Physical*	**1** Red	food, shelter, clothing, sex, body comfort

a power-oriented world. Almost all of our personal, social, and planetary choices reflect our projections and attitudes about power. This definition of power through a Third Dimension lens is *my will over your will*. In the shift of consciousness of the collective mind of humanity during this time of prophecy is that we will now define Love as power. We are centering our collective reality base to compassion, empathy, and the virtues that are the mechanisms that show us love by action and deed.

When I look at the Chakra system from this perspective, the new paradigm becomes visceral. Our seventh Chakra has been universally accepted as the highest vibration being the direct connection to the Divine, our observer self, our witness, or in another definition, our Higher Mind. We are now in the Aquarian Age, the end of the Mayan calendar, the essence of the Hopi prophecies, and the biblical apocalypse ready to move forward in our relationship of creating Heaven on Earth. The significance of shifting the hierarchy allows us to see that the evolution of consciousness moves from a linear, male model of power, to one that is neither male nor female, but an integration of both. Love is the omnipresent, ultimate power of the Universe. Love is equanimity. Now is the time of humanarchy!

Each Chakra is intimately connected to the corresponding Chakra above and below the heart. As the center of consciousness and considering Hermetic Law, which is explained in the *Kybalion*, "That which is above, is also below." For example, when we have problems with our communication, we have problems with being able to self-actualize and feel confident. When we have trouble perceiving or have constant negative thinking, we have trouble creating. When we have problems believing, we have trouble surviving.

These Chakra Correspondences can just as easily be seen by positive examples. I thrive in my physical experience with health and happiness the more I am in direct relationship to a higher power. My creativity and passion manifest them more I think about my vision. The more I express and speak my truth, the more confident I am. The more confident I am, the more I am listened to by others.

Primary Chakras

With corresponding relationships to the **Elements** and **Hermetic Law**

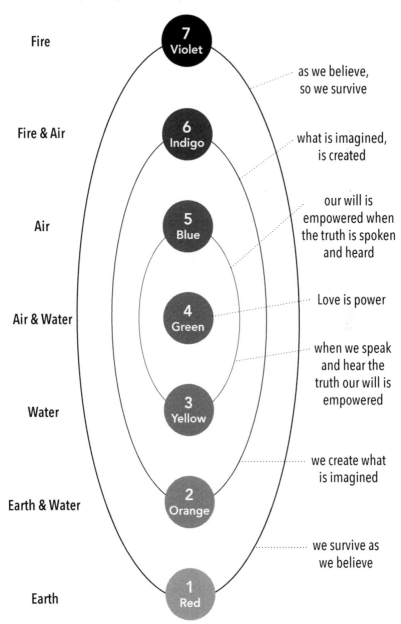

Fire

7
Violet

as we believe,
so we survive

Fire & Air

6
Indigo

what is imagined,
is created

Air

5
Blue

our will is
empowered when
the truth is spoken
and heard

Air & Water

4
Green

Love is power

when we speak
and hear the
truth our will is
empowered

Water

3
Yellow

Earth & Water

2
Orange

we create what
is imagined

Earth

1
Red

we survive as
we believe

From the point of view of the heart center as the source and seat of power, the fourth Chakra is the highest vibration, and the new paradigm emerges. A linear model may not be appropriate in the new paradigm of understanding. When the heart is defined as the center of consciousness, we shift the idea of moving up our spiritual path, to moving in. The higher center Chakras are considered the sixth Chakra, often called the Third Eye, and the seventh Chakra often called the Crown. I propose that the highest center is now the fourth Chakra. The heart is the place where the elements of Heaven-soul and Earth-body, actually meet. Our heart is the residence of true alchemy.

The driving force behind the evolution of life on earth is Creation itself. The human condition moved from primal animal survival instinctual behavior in the environment created by nature, to environments created by us through our ingenuity and shared collective cultural values. Survival of the fittest needs to become an expanded concept to include consciousness not as what separates us from other species, but as what connects us. No life is 'less than' any other form. We are all creations from the earth itself as a species and subject to forces that we do not control. The need for domination to control dominion was the way of Third Dimensional human reality. We still collectively in the zeitgeist define power as my will over your will. What will happen when we define power as ending the illusion of separation and to embrace our ultimate equality from a spiritual perspective? Every one of us at our core is Divine Love. My hope is we will give up killing each other, and other species of life by figure out better way to share the earth.

The human condition is created by the four dimensions in a mash-up. Awareness exists on each of these four dimensions or planes of creation. They function interactively with integration. No matter which dimension we value more such as the mind over my body, or my feelings over my spiritual beliefs, it takes all to be alive. Fire is the element of our souls. In our original state, we are light beings, systems of pure energy. Fire is the spirit within us that manifests as the light in our eyes, our passion, our motivation, our inspiration, our anger, our vitality, and our will to live. Fire is the substance of the personal matrix or our essence. Fire is our aura that radiates through our permeable skin to manifest the energy that can be seen and felt by others. All life forms have this element, or they do not have life.

Air is the element of the mind. It is mana, prana, the breath from which we sustain life. It is everywhere yet it cannot be seen. Air is necessary to fuel fire. It can blend with every other element except earth. Air can cause chaos to earth, tornadoes, hurricanes, high winds or can bring the refreshing breeze on a warm summer's day. We do not see the air molecules, but we perceive and feel the effects of them. We see the tree sway in the breeze, and the wind caresses our skin, but we do not see the wind itself. All life forms need this element in some fashion, or there is not life.

The element of the emotions is water, and it brings to us the qualities of fluidity, flexibility, integration, and adaptability. Water can combine with every other element except fire—it puts out fire. Water like air can cause chaos to earth if there is too much—flooding, or too little—drought. It is also necessary to sustain life for all living creatures. According to The Water Information website, they share these statistics about water in the human body:

1. The human body is more than 60 percent water.

2. Blood is 92 percent water.

3. The brain and muscles are 75 percent water.

4. The bones are about 22 percent water.

All life forms have this element, or there cannot be life.

The fourth element is earth, the element of our bodies and all elements in the Periodic Table. What "matters" is what comes into form. Rocks, plants, animals, are the kingdoms of life that we share this planet, and the building molecules of the planets and heavenly bodies that we have yet to inhabit. Earth in our human condition is the container of our living light. Earth is what we manipulate by our

creativity to bring harmony to our experience. All life forms matter
or there is not life.

The principles of fire and earth could not come into harmonious contact without air and water as their mediums. In other words,
our soul and our body could not function without our minds and
our emotions. The goal is to be balanced with these four planes of
existence or levels of awareness so that we function optimally in our
human form. These elements are integral parts to each other. They
even overlap.

On a plane ride from Denver to Telluride after my brain surgery, I
was on a very, very bumpy ride across the state of Colorado. I love to
fly. However, brain surgery slightly (read with sarcasm) tweaked my
nervous system. I was already an ultra-sensitive, but in that first year,
I was one great big raw nerve. As I learned to live with one ear, classic
brain trauma, a paralyzed face, and balance issues due to the damage
to my vestibular system, less was more. Being tossed around above the
Rockies in a small prop-plane can be difficult without the fragile body
I was living in. I was in panic.

My first method of self-medication is always the same. I pray. I
asked for my guides to help me to calm down. Ani, an Earth Goddess
whom I have met before when hiking in the redwoods near Santa
Cruz, CA at Armstrong state park, came into my vision. She began
to talk to me about the in between connections to the elements.
Her lecture was a very good distraction. Ani gave me the following
examples. Bubbles are the meeting of air and water. Clouds are the
meeting of air and water. Lightning is the meeting of fire and air.
Mud is the meeting of water and earth. Tornados are the meeting of
air, water, and earth.

When I opened my eyes, my seatmate turned to me and asked if I
was o.k. He could tell I was not, so offered compassion and wisdom.
He suggested thinking about riding the airwaves like riding a boat on
a river. The waking dream strikes again! The kind man next to me
continued the healing. Often when I am now in the same position to

support the frightened passenger next to me, I make the same sugges-tion. "Going with the flow" has multidimensional meaning.

In my workshops when we channel the elements I have participants go outside and be with the wind, the land, the sun, and often, my workshop sites are near bodies of water. The messages that are given to my students as they talk with the elements always produce similar epiphanies when they later share these conversations. *"I know that I am not alone." "I now have the understanding of God in all things." "I now know how to take care of myself to be in balance." "I am no longer worried about the earth!" "I feel loved."* The challenge is for to open our awareness in the first place that these living dimensions of conscious-ness exist and have a voice. What do the elements have to say to us? Let us be our own teachers and go and ask!

Amber Elizabeth Gray is a healer and social activist who took my workshop in Jamaica in 1995. The last day we were channeling the elements and snorkeling. Did someone say workshops are work? As Amber was climbing down a very steep rocky cliff, she prayed to the Mother Earth to hold her as she climbed. With her clairaudience, a very calm quiet voice assured her not to worry *"for I am what holds the sea."* The filling of Amber's heart and our entire group as she shared the message that she received is humbling magic. It helps give another perspective of this earth by witnessing the direct relationship of the meeting of both consciousnesses, Amber and Mother Earth herself.

The building blocks for all of the levels of awareness, which again understood as spiritual-fire, mental-air, emotional-water, and physical-earth are the elements on the periodic chart of elements that are the fundamental material ingredients that compose our universe from a scientific perspective. I cannot affirm enough the beauty of this plan. There is no real waste only resistance to the flow of energy as these particles seek to create and recreate. The universe is in constant move-ment bringing these energies together and apart. The seasons teach us the same lesson. We as individuals need to let go. It is the divine plan.

After taking one of my workshops in Chicago, Pat told me about an experience she had with her shampoo. Pat's story brings together the idea of the elements having life in a clear way. In her words, her story is this:

> "About a month or so after taking Sally's weekend workshop, I was getting pretty good at channeling information from items that I was holding (by psychometry). However, so far everything I had been holding had sentimental value to someone. I was wondering if I was to hold something that was just an ordinary everyday sort of object, would I learn something from it. Thinking all of this while taking a shower, I picked up the bottle of shampoo and immediately this aggressive voice comes through, "No one appreciates the life cycle of shampoo. We have a birth-when all the chemicals are mixed together. Our life span is the shelf life. We climax when the shampoo is mixed with water and we burst into bubbles! We are then rinsed away and returned to the earth." After my moment of shock, I thanked the shampoo for sharing with me and thought "Wow! There's no way I would have ever thought of that myself. I must be doing something right." I told this story to a few people and someone asked me "if the conditioner had anything to say!" Of course, with my next shower I asked … a very calm, soothing voice said to me," We are the perfect example of yin and yang. The shampoo is the aggressor with all of its sudsing and cleaning action. The person using the shampoo is also acting with more aggression to be to get a good lather and to clean the scalp. When using conditioner you calm down, you use longer more soothing strokes-exactly the opposite as when shampooing. Even though we are separate entities and whole within ourselves, we are the perfect complement to each other."

Now this story could have gone into the chapter on channeling or the chapter on male and female energy or even the chapter on spirit guides. I put it here for a reason. Life force is in everything. Period.

Earth, Water, Air, and Fire are all alive for within each molecule that composes the element into its unified and identified system to be, is alive. Not only is it alive, but has the memory of every form it has been before. I put it here because it is the Fourth Dimension to know our interconnectedness to everything from unity, instead of from separation.

Love is the standard by which all emotions are gauged. Love is present no matter what we are feeling. Anger, rage, humiliation, shame, doubt, grief, blame, all separate us from the awareness of love, yet, love cannot leave us for it is what we are. Love is available to all of us to receive in our perceptions and experience if we are willing. Love is even greater than the positive emotions, such as joy, happiness, passion, ecstasy, and bliss, for it is omnipresent where these emotions pass. Emotions are simply energy in motion. They are by their very nature, transient.

When we compare the mind to emotions we could observe that it is fixated by its nature. The mind is like a computer. The brain is the mainframe. The system software, which allows the hardware to speak to the software, is composed of our belief systems, values, and language capacities. Then the programs that run on the computer are our innate talents, cultural and personal values, and the ability to interpret our experience to chronicle our personal story that is held in the data or stored in memory. The mind can change, but only through downloading upgrades to the software or getting new programs. Through emotional transformation, we burn out the old belief systems to reprogram the system. We reboot so that we can run more efficiently.

The software programs are our belief systems, which include cultural norms, social customs, mating and courtship behavior, sexual mores, religious traditions and ritual, cosmological context, political systems, and ethical or moral codes of behavior. Not only is the software the ability to perceive experience, it determines how we create and respond to these programs. The software is the framework of how to interpret experience. The mind is a data processing system, albeit an infinitely creative system. The mind is only one-quarter of what creates our wholeness as humans.

Our collective story as humans is a story of innovation, endurance, perseverance, and the capacity to adapt and change as our consciousness and awareness grow. In this time in history, it seems as if we have sped up time. There is a debate in science that global warming is causing the earth to rotate faster on her axis. Humans are rotating faster on ours. What is your axis? How do you find your center? If we want to know peace, it is more likely when we use the internal axis of our heart.

The collective consciousness changes every second regardless of the data moving through the worldwide web of the Internet. The difference now for humanity is we can touch, feel, see and hear this data all around us. It is this environmental change initiating a re-evaluation of the human condition. We are ready to expand again in what we know to be truth as we bridge the inner and the outer worlds, the above and below worlds, the infinite and finite worlds, by the miracle of Love that we are.

Just think about this, when someone asks the question, *"How do you know?"* rarely do they answer, because *"I think it!"* The most common answer is, *"I feel it!"* How does any of us know what is true? At the core of our Being is a fragment of firelight that is love. When we act from that essential fire of ourself, we heal the world. We are revolutionaries of love to transform the human condition to be one of peace. Let's do it moving our understanding of power to where it belongs, our heart.

Chapter 17 Practicum

☒ Using the Chakra chart showing the correspondent relationships, figure out the source of any present pain or issues manifesting physically, emotionally, mentally or spiritually that are connected by the circle to the corresponding chakra. Write about what you learn. Pray and ask for guidance to continue the healing to forgive the pain or conflict. For example, if you are having lower back problems centered near the base of your spine, how is your relationship with God? If you are having issues being heard and understood, what choices are you making and what effects your confidence? If you are confused, what are you doing with your creative energy?

☒ When in a power struggle with a friend, family member or colleague, consciously move your attention to your heart. How does that affect your will and how you express or communicate your side of the conflict? Write about the experience.

☒ Look at videos on YouTube of Dr. Masaru Emoto's work on the living properties of water. His experiments with speaking to water and rice in jars sitting next to each other has been emulated and replicated by many.

☒ Channel the elements in your body asking for guidance of what they need for you to experience a happy, healthy, loving life. Do what they say as long as it brings no harm to any other Being.

Chapter 18

Soulwork

There is a reason that the power of story has always been the medium of teaching about life. It is through story and our ability to project our own feelings onto them, that we end the sense that we are alone. All pain stems from separation and story connects us. Compassion is the result of bridging our isolation, and the story is how we cross the bridge. We have right as witnesses to question the meanings or interpretations of experience, but no right to define them for others. Consciousness is our ability to discover meaning.

Each of us in our human story is living the conditions that will teach us about love. Every interaction and experience is an event for our soul to learn and discover something relevant. The curriculum though varied has one goal—to help us remember who we really are as a light of love. Infinite stories for billions of people are all written with one theme. We are here to do Soulwork. We are here on earth to awaken to our pure creative potential. We are here to work the soul to be a vehicle to express a unique aspect of the Divine. What is often experienced as the absence of love, is happening to show us its presence.

One of the greatest teachers for me early in my practice came in the form of Nancy. Nancy came to see me channel at a lecture at the Red Rose Gallery on Chestnut Street in San Francisco and sat literally at my feet. Moved by what she saw as pure light in my spirit, she came to me for private healing. Nancy had been sexually abused almost daily from the time she was three years old into her teen years. Her story is an incredible one of horrifying proportions. It was an honor that she felt enough safety with me to begin to weave together her fragmented self.

Recovery from trauma often includes denial as a part of the safety latch for the whole being. Abuse, victimization, brutalization, accident trauma, death, and deep wounds of the psyche need denial to keep our beings from acting out our death wish. To split our reality into what we can acknowledge and what we cannot is the essence of denial. Compartmentalizing feelings and the memories that created them becomes a survival technique for any pain no matter the severity. Nancy knew about her abuse when she came to see me, but she did not have specific memories of what happened to her as a child. Her life had reached a point where it was more important to be whole. Nancy had a stable job, her own apartment, and felt secure enough within herself to go deeper into the chaos that was her disowned past.

Bi-weekly we would journey together into her history revealing one vignette after another of her father's rage and sexual betrayal of his innocent daughter. Nancy's small frame and delicate nature had somehow survived these atrocities. The mechanism that allowed this was the splitting of her consciousness from the body awareness and memory. When she had grown strong enough as a person to remember what had happened intellectually, the body memories also began to return.

Nancy had led a life that was founded in her own spirituality and faith. At the time she was working as an art therapist with disturbed adolescents. Our work together, as Nancy describes, fed her "spiritual core" to give her strength to heal the pain in her body. Anemic, anorexic, and without much vitality, she struggled daily to live. Nancy knew that by working with me, her Soulwork—her karma—would be healed not just her body, emotions, and mind.

The memories that we uncovered from her childhood include the betrayal of her mother, father, and family physician. Nancy was the only child and her father was a butcher who owned his own shop in a small eastern American city. In the basement of the store is where he would force his child to have sex with him, often threatening her life with his butcher knives. Once when Nancy was around eight years old, she resisted his sexual advances, so her father threw her down the stairs into the basement. As her small body hit the floor, her hips were broken, and her father took her to the hospital. The reason for the injury, of course, was that she had "fallen" down the stairs but in the regression memory, her body told her the truth.

As the deep grief of this story revealed itself, Nancy became even more enraged at herself that she was not able to stop the abuse. During the two-month hospital stay, rarely did she have any visitors. Her mother was always 'too sick' to come to see her daughter who was incapacitated. Her father was always 'too busy working' to come to see his child. These experiences reinforced the belief within Nancy that she was unlovable, unworthy, and alone. The somatic memories of the anger at herself, her parents, and the world that was so unfair came out of her during our sessions. All I could do as a facilitator was love her with as much patience, kindness, and compassion possible. It was the presence of that love that allowed Nancy to touch these memories, forgive the pain, and begin to weave together the split between her body and her mind.

We continued to go deeper into her memories as her body was ready to reveal to Nancy, her own story. I always allow the body to determine where to what time in their history that the soul needs to heal during a session. Nancy always remembered gaining weight when she was 13, even the detail that it was 140 pounds. She was not a large person; as the 40-year-old adult that came to see me weighing about

110 on her 5'1" frame. In this session, she remembered being pregnant with her father's child. The emotions of this awakening were of horror on every level of her being. We spent most of our session that day with Nancy's tears as she faced her deep sadness of such betrayal from her father to have put his child in this state.

The next session, due to my kinesthetic ultra-sensitivity, I was having contractions in my own uterus all day before Nancy's appointment. I knew where we were going though this is not always the case with my clients. I knew it would be a challenging session and that I was receiving this information to prepare me. During the session that evening, Nancy remembered being kicked in the stomach five months into the pregnancy by her father to abort the baby. It worked and the family doctor delivered the baby with her mother present. Nancy was not allowed to see nor grieve her dead baby. All I could do was hold Nancy and rock her as if she were a child. This comfort and nurturing were essential for her to integrate this memory. In Nancy's life, at 13 there was no such care from her own parents, it was time for her to feel loved. And, Nancy did.

There are many more atrocious stories that I could share with you about Nancy's life, and the lives of many of my clients, and even from my own life. The examples of these two major health crises—broken hips and late-term abortion induced by violence—are dramatic, but the perfect examples to teach of the fragile relationship between the mind and the body. This connection is not absolute. Nancy's mind blocked out an experience of pregnancy; which makes such obvious changes to the body of a woman. The energy that it took to keep these memories at bay, buried within her cells of her hips, arms, legs, stomach, kept Nancy from experiencing a vital, healthy life. Nancy's ability to create her life was disabled from the inside, out.

When Nancy had enough strength to handle the impact of her own story, the memories returned. The anger that Nancy had, in relationship to her mother, had reason and intelligence. It was from the deep betrayal of a mother who denied the abuse, did not protect her child, and offered no loving concern for Nancy's wellbeing. Nancy's mother did not visit her own child in a hospital for two months because of her own childhood abuses. The mother's betrayal of Nancy was also her own wounds which kept her limited in her sense of power, choice, and the ability to be responsible for her child. The ancestral story stopped with Nancy as she had decided as a young woman, that she never wanted to have children. Now she consciously understood why she felt so adamant that she could not handle being a mother.

As Nancy aged, going to college, becoming an Art Therapist, moving across the country to California, she was always aware that her father had sexually abused her. However, she had no idea to what degree until we began her emotional recovery through somatic therapy regressions. How could her family doctor have repeatedly ignored her bruises, cuts, broken bones, and deliver her child, and not tried to help Nancy? It is not for us to know. However, it is our challenge not to let this continue to happen to the children of this world. As incomprehensible as it is, it still happens everywhere every day. This is an example of the collective amnesia we as humans use as a survival tool. This is the denial that all of us carry to some degree to psychologically manage the inequities of the world.

Though Nancy's father had died years before we began our work, the healing included him. Often his spirit was present in the sessions as Nancy remembered the truth of their relationship. He is still responsible for his karma, and somewhere in his eternal life stream, he will create restitution. Nancy's mother lived in her denial and Nancy continued to have a relationship with her until she died. They were not close, but Nancy would not shut the door to communication due to the forgiveness that is in her heart. She now sees her mother as the victim of her own choices and feels compassion for the pain that colored her mother's life. Nancy chose these individuals to work out lifetimes of karmic patterns. She wanted to be able to release as much pain from her Soul before this life ended. Nancy was proactive because she knew that the physical symptoms were a reaction to past experiences. She also knew that forgiveness would set not just her body but her soul free of the pain.

Nancy continues to care for her body and feed her soul. She moved out of the city to be closer to nature as it inspires her to be in a rural environment with a slower pace of life. Nancy is finding the health that she deserves from her body. For many years Nancy believed that her body was angry at her. She owned her soul's anger and now sees the beauty of her body. Though she has never been in a relationship with a man, she no longer judges herself. Nancy has realized the strength and tenacity it took to survive was fueled by the love that she also had inside for the gift and beauty of life itself.

In the many years since we did the work, Nancy and I occasionally speak. She no longer remembers all of the details of what she remembered in our sessions but the essence remains in her soul as the peace she has found with life itself. She will retain what is necessary for her healing journey, and for her continued spiritual path of growth. Why Nancy created such a powerful drama trauma story in this life is her business, not ours. She does know that she is here on the planet to teach about love. Perhaps that is why she gave her permission for me to share her healing story, as this is a story of love and forgiveness. Our opinions and judgments are not appropriate, but our respect is. As we begin to respect the healing that does happen, the love and compassion that is, we will only have more for everyone.

Here is what Nancy wishes to share from her own voice decades later:

> "Sally nurtured my spirit and fed my soul, until I had the strength to move on the next phase of my healing. To date, it has been a process, learning through Somatic work how to re-enter, re-connect, and re-align myself with my body again. The tenacity that I must have had to survive all those years of abuses has served me well in my adulthood. It has enabled me to persevere in the search to find the right ways to heal myself through the deep dark years of depression. I now can say I know the meaning of "joy."

The lessons of love I learned from Nancy have been profound and taught me more about facilitating healing than any book, class, or degree could have. I had to live it. I learned that all I really needed "to do" was to love, unconditionally, them and their unfolding story as much as possible. No matter what intellectual understanding, academic education, tool, technique, process, system, or type of healing modality I knew, love was the only agent to create the space for Nancy to heal herself. By bringing people into an atmosphere of safety, acceptance, and love, they feel secure enough to face their demons, shadow self, persecutors, and pain. This is how Jesus did his work. He was simply just the pure presence of love.

In the 1980's, John Bradshaw's work on championing these inner child parts of ourselves was revolutionary, as it was not just an intellectual understanding, but emotional process. This became an accepted practice today without the necessity of psychoanalysis or talk therapy that produced insight but not necessarily personal transformation. We can help ourselves to release the traumas of the past to liberate and free our energy to create our own health and well-being. We do not have to believe in reincarnation to do past-life work. Addressing even yesterday's traumas can serve us today. If we have not sourced our current frustrations, pain, or fears into our past or present moments, we have missed the opportunity to recapitulate, forgive and liberate ourselves.

Every individual is given the gift of their unique self to perceive and experience life from our own center, viewpoint, and consciousness. We each deserve to be in our full power, not to be willful over others, but to be self-actualized and to express our individuation from All-That-Is. By not making the assumption that current conditions, emotions, physical pain, or symptoms are sourced from the present, we have another tool to bring peace, balance, and wellbeing alive within us.

Emotions are the world of the Fourth Dimension. Height, width, and length are the scientific definitions of the Third dimension, with time the fourth. However, it is thought of as space-time continuum because we can only create experience in a forward direction in linear time. This is true mentally, however, not true emotionally. Think of a sad experience in your life. Can you think of it without not just recalling the memory intellectually, but also recalling emotionally what it felt like in your body, therefore creating a new experience or reinforcement of the old experience in the present?

The emotional state of feeling is alive and does not respond to the memory as if time has passed. Unless the negative charge of the emotion has been neutralized or transformed, no matter what modality of healing it stays alive in us as trauma. Only when our emotional energy that has been processed through expression in some form and integrated into the whole being, can we think of the memory and not be triggered by these latent emotions. If the emotions from the past were not expressed as the soul responded to experience, eventually then the emotions must move, as movement is essential to its very nature. Emotion is energy in motion.

Fear is the primary force of stagnation of emotion. When the energy is blocked it creates depression, repression, denial, and a separation of truth. Eventually, this leads to physical symptoms of drama, disease, and illness. The soul is on earth to learn about love and all of these negative experiences teach love in an outstanding way, often by the sense of its absence. The Dalai Lama was asked the meaning of life by Andrew Harvey the day he received the Nobel Peace prize in 1989. His response, after he roared in laughter, he leaned forward and said with conviction that was absolute, *the relentless pursuit of consciousness!*" I would amend that and say, the relentless pursuit of the consciousness of love. Love is not just a sense in the body, a feeling in our awareness, or a thought in our mind. Love is the essence of Being.

A spiritual teaching is inherent in any physical world lesson that does not have to be as dramatic as Nancy's abuse. There are infinite examples; our car breaks down, the computer crashes, the children are acting out, the sales deal falls through, the stock market or real estate market crashes, we break a leg, we get bumped from the team, our air flight is canceled, a hurricane or tsunami destroys our community. The list is endless and more multifaceted than we can comprehend. All of these real situations trigger emotion, usually frustration, irritation, shame, blame, anger, and rage. There is a reason too that we now have the common vernacular of post-traumatic stress disorder—PTSD. Experiences can and do affect our response to present conditions.

We are now living the cultural post-traumatic stress through the age of global terrorism. Via the media, there is a reinforcement that gives the collective unconscious, which we are all a part of—whether we believe it or not—psychological imprints of vulnerability. This vulnerability is the reminder that we are not completely in control of our own safety and survival. So in the example of Nancy, she lived a life of personal terrorism growing up in her family. The reaction to the terrorism in our world at this time she tempers by living in a rural environment spending a lot of time with nature. By working daily on her inner peace, she gives another message to the collective unconscious of faith over fear.

The *way* we respond to our personal or collective traumas and pain influences our karma. The goal of the conscious soul is to be present in every situation with peace. This does not mean that awake beings do not have feelings or are not reactive in their nature. It is the way of the Fourth Dimension to just not assume that the feelings are totally about the present moment and present conditions. It is the ability to pause, take inventory, and then respond that become the adaptive method of behavior. Feeling the feelings and then letting them go, surrendering them regardless of what time in history they originated, is the action required.

Letting go is the process of forgiveness. Surrendering to the fact that there is perfection, even in pain, is another spin on the evolutionary adaptations in the human condition. To acknowledge both the moments of ecstasy and the moments of pain is living in divine perfection of the imperfection that is life itself. Love helps us to balance the life experience with peace. Feelings, both positive and negative, are meant to be felt or we would not perceive them at all. The tools to handle them in a way that does not perpetuate the pain, are available. Forgiveness and surrender are accessible for anyone at anytime.

The ability to live in the now is possible when we feel our feelings at the moment we have them. When we do not allow this energy to move, we displace it. Sometimes this displacement can last for years if not lifetimes. The energy of emotions is not necessarily held in the mind nor can it be intellectualized. The body can hold it. Just think of this reality, the body is 70% water and 30% minerals. Another way to say it is the sentient human condition is 70% emotional and 30% physical. No wonder we are so driven by our desire to feel good!

Each of our paths to healing is as individual as we are. There is no one right way to heal, yet there are commonalities. We can learn from each other's story. No one has the particular chemistry, karma, ancestral material in DNA, environmental conditions, and body that we do. Somatic healing allows us to awaken even deeper understanding of the 'why' events and circumstances that happen on our journey. Somatic healing was the path that Nancy chose and it gave her body relief from the deep depression that permeated every aspect of her life.

Soulwork is not subject to the spiritual tradition that one practices. It is the relationship our soul has with the individuated personality that we created in this life to learn about love. Somatic healing, shamanic journeys, meditation, self-awareness practices, ritual, and any esoteric learning is about the body/soul connection that we come to earth to literally, work. Pain is the alarm clock timer going off telling us it's time to go to work. Work, however, does not need to be a struggle. When we know that is the task at hand; we can be proactive. I would not be able to live my life without coming back to this question over and over:

How is this experience teaching me about love?

The next question in my problem/solution oriented mind is then a direct quote from *A Course in Miracles*:

"What would love do now?"

When we as a collective are sourcing the answers, we can begin to create a love centered world for our souls to thrive. The answers change our perspective. To reinforce the goal of this chapter I need to reiterate that the memory from unexpressed emotion becomes the life dramas, chronic pain, disease, depression, and illnesses. It is not that I am negating the diagnosis or pain, or life struggles that we experience. I know it is real.

My brain tumor was real. The nerve on my face dying was real. Nancy's broken hip, aborted child, anorexia, and anemia were real. Lynn's miscarriages were real. The wall of energy in Gigi and Tom's marriage was real. Layna and Eli's anger at each other was real. The hurricanes and tsunamis are real. The terrorist acts and wars are real. They are all present to teach our soul about love. The point is that none of it randomly appears nor are we without the power to heal it All.

Chapter 18 Practicum

⛢ For the next week, ask yourself throughout the day with random experiences—neutral, pleasurable, and painful—**How is this teaching me about love?** Write in your journal about the things your soul learned.

⛢ Watch the past life regression video at https://www.intuitiveartsandsciences.com/soulwork-with-sally-aderton.html. This is an opportunity to see how murder, rape, and forgiveness can set free the souls with love. It is mature content so ask your intuition if it is in your highest and best interest to view.

Chapter 19

Life Goes On
All Ways Always

Tom and Gigi, by forgiving each other brought more harmony into their relationship to each other in this lifetime. I cannot say "30-year relationship"; for their relationship of their eternal selves, has endured thousands of years. Thousands of years if we only consider lifetimes as human beings on the earth. It is a mystery how long forever lasts! Feelings of knowing people, both positive and negative, affect whom we associate with in our current life. There is no randomness in the Universe. Therefore, everyone we have in our life is there for a reason. The journey of life is full of the stories of who, what, where, when, how, and the why of these connections.

The carryover of the love and positive feelings for people often allows us to form close bonds with people without a lot of time or shared experiences. All of us have met people that we feel like we know instantly. I attribute this to the veils of time being very thin. It can get us into both successful adventures of this life or challenging ones too. We do not hold the karmic balance scales. It belongs to the great Mystery. It is impossible to know when enough is enough on karmic debts. We must just do the best we can to do the right thing. In this way, we stay free.

The behavior that accompanies the feeling is where we as a culture and individuals must actively use our imagination, innovation, and creativity to come up with healthy systems, choices, and norms. Children are the greatest assets to the future. They are pure potential. Each life comes into the human condition with the intention and the need to exercise the emotional content of their soul, and the responses to the conditions of the moment. The pure potential of a child is the landscape by which new social order and moral codes are created.

The children coming on to the planet now have lived many lifetimes in the human story of evolution. In our historical record, humanity goes back at least 50,000 years. As we have addressed, the universe only knows recycling. Therefore there have been opportunities for souls to participate more than once in the creation of life on Earth. The children coming into our shared consciousness are bringing more enlightened vibrations that match the openings of the collective.

The souls coming to the planet are reflecting the continual opening of the consciousness of what is possible. More and more we hear stories of children speaking about their past lives. We have more and more willingness to share publicly of astral travel, lucid dreaming, near-death or after-life recall, and the unity of the one mind. *Synchronicity*, the Police song from the '80s was the soundtrack as the millennials were being born and raised have the word common in their vocabulary. These metaphysical concepts still produce skepticism, but that too is the human condition. We are here to question and to discover answers.

My desire for truth and passionate quest for knowledge did not begin as an adult. My desire for healing did not begin with my health crisis of my brain tumor. Often it is the result of trauma or personal crisis that we come to seek a greater understanding of the meaning of life. My curiosity of the human condition was innate to the reasons that I as an eternal soul created this lifetime. I chose my parents and them as souls agreed to have me as their child, and my siblings as their sister. I chose my name and my birthday so that my numerology and astrology would support my soul's growth to create the personality and personal cycles of timing for my life's predestined agenda. And, this is true for every one of us through all time. We all come here to learn lessons with the tools to help us along the way to be our unique self. We have the potential to integrate this knowledge into the worldwide human revolution that is occurring on Earth right now.

Embracing this expanded viewpoint, collectively, is necessary for the human condition to survive as a species on Earth. *"We do not save the Earth for our children; we borrow it from them."* This Native American proverb reflects what I hope to impart. We will die, we will be born again, and this never ending story can change from conflict centered power to love centered power. The choices we are making today, affect the experiences possible on earth for future generations starting with our own.

It is not the goal of the soul to stay in the same form again and again. The goal of the soul is to be a unique divine eternal participant in the unfolding creation of infinite possibility. As all of it, earth, water, air, and fire are recycled. We are recycled too. Acknowledging the soul's timelessness, our path life influences, and our ultra-sensitivity are ways to have a different outcome than perpetuating our shared historical recorded. Let's write another story about resurrection.

So far, I have given examples from more adults than kids about expanding their consciousness of what is. Kids have an even greater ability to perceive beyond the apparent. Our collective fear, accepted educational tracks, and social conventions condition them away from what they intuitively know. This is the time for the revolution, as children are less willing to shut down their light, their consciousness. The ultra-sensitivity on the rise is another reason ADD, and ADHD is so prevalent today. Yes, the manipulation of our chemistry by food, drugs, and environment create the dis-ease. These kids have so much awareness and intelligence; they are off the charts. These kids are demanding that we step up to the challenge to learn how to provide for them. They do not fit a mold, and that is their gift to us all. They are demanding we pay attention to the uniqueness of each soul.

Culturally our education system exercises more of our left and not the right hemispheres of our brains. Inner knowing, ultra sensitivity, intuition, meditation, and spiritual development, not just intellectual development will help heal us all. Daniel Goleman's work on Emotional Intelligence is already decades old. It, however, is still not a part of our standard education and development to be good citizens of the world. Past Life Healing is another tool that we have to learn how to cope with the relationships that are inevitable in life. For three decades I have watched my clients create better lives for themselves, their families, and for us all by diving deep into the great mystery of eternal life. The more we take advantage of the consciousness tools that exist, the more consciousness we all get to benefit from.

One of my teenage clients realized that the anger at her father was there when she came into the womb. By moving this, she became a less surly in her relationship with him. Another child at eight was having trouble in her second-grade class because of past life recall as an American soldier in Vietnam, and this was confusing her. She had such strong memories she would forget who she was in this life, which made it difficult to pay attention in school. Nancy, whom you met in the last chapter, remembered past life influences in her relationships with her mother, father, and family doctor. In addition to releasing the traumas of the current lifetime, this helped additionally in the forgiveness of these souls from their experiences together in the past.

Gigi was very pregnant with their son when she and Tom did work to heal their marriage. Here is what Gigi shared about our work when we spoke in 2015:

During our first session, I think around 1988, you described our first child, who is now 25 years old and very much as you described her. A pianist, singer, actress, artist, very sensitive, psychic, and funny. It was during my pregnancy with our son in 1993 that I had an incredibly strong message to do the regression work with you. I have always felt that that strong message came from Jackson himself because he wanted us to clear that up before his birth. Another interesting thing is that before that regression I could not turn my back on Tom—obviously because he had shot me in the back. I was uncomfortable lying in our bed and sleeping on my side with my back to him. I thought it was very weird, but it went away after that session. Another clear memory I have of being the young, Native American man in that life is teaching the young boy, now my son, how to carve wood, making tools and wonderful things. He was so good at it, and I enjoyed being able to pass these skills on to a young, white person. I thought sharing some of our Native American skills was the right thing to do.

That baby in her tummy wanted them to address this wall and their collective issues before he arrived into their arms. He was coming to be the son of the Tom-Irish settler and Gigi-Native American but as a millennial in the 21st century America. Past lives are first triggered by people. It was time for Gigi and Tom to heal this latent emotion and the catalyst was this soul stimulating the karma/chemistry to heal. The pain of this wall was no longer tolerable and affecting their happiness as a couple. The past life regression was preventative medicine too. It liberated the negative belief systems to set a healthier psychological stage for them to raise their son with more acceptance and less fear which had been present before when they were all together in different roles. We take turns, play different roles and co-create these never ending stories.

While doing Reiki on a five-year-old, he began to describe our past life together when I was his mother in a Native American tribe. I was there in his hometown of Telluride, Colorado to speak at a spiritual festival on the actual land of the past life he was remembering. There is not one system that is the best system to help us retrieve past life material or information or stories which are soul memory. We do not even have to believe in past lives for us to access it. And, it is possible with our developed intuition to perceive not just our soul history, but those of others. There are many practitioners now who embrace past life work, and even Dr. OZ has done shows on the topic. The most public voice for this is Dr. Brian Weiss, the famous American Psychiatrist who wrote the classic book, *Many Lives Many Masters* nearly 30 years ago.

Past life memories are triggered in our waking lives by people we encounter first. Then next by places, then things. After that is is all the senses sight, sound, touch, smells, and taste. How many times have you smelled an aroma that reminds you of your childhood? When was the last time you heard a song that triggered thoughts of days gone by? These are past life memories. The potential to have recall coming into our awareness is—All the Time! This is one of the reasons we have such challenges to keep our awareness on the present moment. Past life awareness is triggered into our consciousness for a reason. Even remembering joyful times of childhood, our first love, a great vacation serves our process of day-to-day living. Always, I find the information helps us to understand the present and give us solutions to current issues. Past life memories, or stories, are not the reasons or justifications for doing any harm to others or ourselves in the present or the future. This expanded consciousness is here on earth now to help resolve the ongoing cycle of violence with humankind's inhumanity to itself.

I arrived in Telluride, Colorado in 1993 to speak at the annual *Steps to Awareness Festival*, not knowing that almost everyone in the festival I had hurt in a past life. Was this a karmic trap? Absolutely! I had to address my past actions and forgive myself, or I would not be able to finish the first draft of *Energy in Motion* and continue teaching modern metaphysics. Telluride was full of memories for me triggered by the people—the Kolar family who was hosting me, the organizers of the event, the attendees, and the land itself.

Immediately, I began to facilitate the healing that was present, first with the family hosting me. After all, in the waking dream, I was there to teach about *steps to awareness*. Waking up the first morning in Telluride, the 5-year-old Grayson, had pink-eye, so I was helping him by doing energy healing. With my hands laid on his eyes, he began to talk about seeing himself dancing around a fire as a young Indian brave. He could see the tribe around him, his father and mother in this life, and myself were all there in his vision also as Native Americans. Grayson was so thrilled by his vision he jumped up off the couch and ran to his bedroom. He came out with his fake leopard rug thrown over his head and shoulders. Grayson danced around the living room in a circle for us to demonstrate his vision. Grayson also described his boots, which looked like his dog Tracker's, an Alaskan malamute, feet. The innocent instant recall was stored in his eyes and manifested as pink eye.

There was no randomness that Grayson's emotional body welcomed the disease of the pink eye into his auric field and therefore his body when I was coming to visit. Though Grayson did not go through all of the steps to forgiveness consciously, his soul allowed the opportunity of my hands to stimulate his memory and then to dance out the joy instead of pain created a spontaneous healing of grace. The pink-eye cleared very quickly, and he began to spend even more time outside, adventuring, feeling safe to do so. They were in a new community, and this was a part of Grayson's releasing some of the anxiety of the move, which was manifesting in some of his behavior of the present.

The next person to need healing was Grayson's Mom. Donna, who invited me to stay with them, had organized local sessions and promoted me to the Steps to Awareness Committee. Donna wanted to address several issues she was having while I was in town. She was having difficulty letting go of her college-aged son Garrett, difficulties in her marriage fully accepting the move from Boulder, and difficulties finding fulfillment with her work on earth. It was a trifecta of growth opportunities for her.

Donna saw in her regression a piercing ceremony for her son as he prepared for battle. Garrett was the son in that life also. Though we can manifest in infinite ways with the matrix of social order, they had reincarnated again with Donna as Mother and Garrett as the son. In the regression, Donna knew intuitively that her son would not return, he did too. This ability to have intuitive knowing in that life did not help her nor bring her comfort. She also remembered being the wife of the Native American chief, living in the valley of Telluride, and feeling limited in her creativity due to the duties of the chief's wife.

So this memory incorporated all of the difficulties of her present moment, her son going away to college, living in Telluride, and feeling limited due to her husband's job precipitating moving the family to another side of the state. This is the infinite wisdom of past life work. Our souls know where the healing and forgiveness need to happen for our highest good in the present time. Well, the story gets really, really interesting as Donna is the wife of the Chief Marshall. They moved to Telluride because of her husband's career advancement opportunity and Donna left a career as a neonatal nurse that she loved. Her husband of that life is her husband of this life Jim!

I was feeling a lot of Donna's emotions not just due to my relationship with her as a facilitator in her process, but because I too was a part of that lifetime. Grayson's pink eye first brought this life to all of our conscious awareness. I was his mother in that same tribal life in Telluride. It was not random that not just Donna, but myself had past material up for healing. My career at the time was going well, but I was single and not happy about it. As a facilitator of past lives, we are not always so intimately connected to another's memories. Remember, people around us first, then places first awaken past lives and, no connection is random, ever! Every person we meet, we have known somehow before.

During Donna's regression, she additionally saw that her feelings of resentment toward her husband were in regards to her younger sister.

In that lifetime, since her and her sister's parents were no longer alive, when her sister's husband died, the chief determined that she came to live in their teepee as his second wife. As Donna remembered this, I was triggered not just by empathy for her sadness, and anger, but a deep and profound grief. I was Donna's sister in that past life! She then forgave me for the role I played in her unhappiness. By releasing the grief over the loss of her son, the resentment toward her husband, and the sadness of being in Telluride, she set herself free. Donna liberated herself to use more of her creative energy to be the seer, healer, and teacher she is in this lifetime.

A few weeks later, I was returning to Telluride after working in Boulder. Telluride had captured my heart, and I canceled my work in Portland, OR, to return to this, now sacred to me, beautiful valley. Coincidentally, Jim was teaching in Fort Collins, near Boulder. Jim offered to bring me back to Telluride with him as our timing was in perfect sync. I had some trepidation about spending 6 hours in the car with Jim. He too had been a client and done private sessions, but it would be the first time we had spent more than an hour alone.

Donna had done a session with me in Denver in 1991. The next time I came to Denver to work, she brought her husband Jim, her daughter Dez, and her son Garrett. Grayson was just four at the time. At that time, Jim still worked as a detective for the Boulder police department. Jim credits some of the work we did together, with preparing him to take on the role of Chief Marshall. Though my friendships were growing with his wife and children, Jim and I had not spent much time together.

We chatted as we drove across the state of Colorado and the time went quite quickly. About an hour from Telluride, Jim ask me, "Sally, what about our past lives? Have we known each other before?" As sessions are confidential, neither Donna nor I had talked about what had been revealed. Grayson's dancing, of course, we all watched together in amazement and joy though, at the time, we had not realized each of our roles in his life as a young Native American male.

When Jim asked me about our past life connection, though there have been many, the Native American life was current in our collective consciousness, so that was what was present in the car. I told Jim generalities of our story remembered by Donna when we were living the tribal life in Telluride but not the specific forgiveness of the anger, resentments, and fears she had in that life. I shared the matrix of our relationships but not the karma or pain associated with the roles we played in each other's drama.

There are consequences though to stimulating the past life material in our consciousness. If there are latent emotional energy, unexpressed feelings from the past, they too besides the memory recall, will awaken. I knew by talking about it, and because Jim was willing to do this work, he would be facing his issues in a session while I continued to stay in his home with Donna, their teepee of this life!

Though I had feelings of love when Grayson called me his Mother, and Donna her sister, the feelings I had toward Jim at this moment were not positive but full of resentment and anger. A wave of sexual energy coursed through my body. I told Jim only that we were "one big happy family" and did not mention my body's reaction to his question nor the negative feeling that came with it. My trepidation to ride with Jim across the state took on new meaning.

Each of us is responsible for our karma. I knew that I would have to deal soon with the pain of that lifetime for myself. I was feeling shame, anger, and deep, deep grief. For me, processing myself, with these tools that I share with others is second nature. The analogy I use is this: if I have something like aspirin in my medicine cabinet, and I have a headache, why would I not use the aspirin? Past life processing for me is just like taking aspirin for a headache. I had all of these feelings that were ready to go stimulated by my current karma trifecta: who I was with—the Kolar family, where I was—Telluride, Colorado, and what was happening in my current life—being upset that I was not married with a child.

The next day, Donna had wanted to take me on a walk across the valley floor to some rock outcropping to the west of the town. My emotions were already out of balance from the car ride with Jim the day before, and I was still feeling very sad. In the morning, talking with Donna, I began to share with her that my forgiveness work, needed to happen that day. I was obviously emotional. Even Tracker, the dog, walked over and put his paw on my foot as if to hold my hand. He had stayed very near to me since arriving back in Telluride as if I had a large, furry, guardian angel. Though I felt safe in their home, I was not feeling safe within myself.

As we walked toward the rocks, I started to cry and began having visions of the Indian summer encampment. As Telluride is at 9,000 feet, this tribe would go there for the summers and would return to lower elevations before the snow began to fall, and temperatures dropped accordingly. During Donna's regression, she had seen that I was her sister, so I knew the context of the story. What I did not know were the repressed feelings that were mirrored with my frustration of not having a significant other in my life at the time. I had knowledge of the story from Donna's perspective but had not forgiven my part in the karmic drama. My work is to teach others how easy this material is to access, so I insisted that Donna regresses me right there on the rocks. As I was crying, and clearly in pain, she acquiesced.

Donna did not have to 'guide me' into the memory. It was already active in my conscious awareness. Donna sat with me to help me feel safe and loved as I faced the traumas of that incarnation. I remembered losing my husband whom I loved very much in that life. He had been killed when thrown from a horse that he had captured for me. Our love of that life was full and fun. He treated me with great respect and honor. He had died before he knew that I was carrying his son. The child in my memory of that life was Grayson in this life.

The mystery that is this web of eternal life goes so very deep, and broad, and high that to understand and remember every detail is not the point. Just think of all of the thoughts, conversations, activities, experiences, feelings that we can have in just a day. Multiply that by the number of years of life. Then take that number and multiply it by the number of lives we have led as human beings. Suddenly the wisdom of why we forget is apparent. We would not be able to function in the present at all. It is vast, complex, and we are not supposed to know it all from the human perspective.

One of the most amazing things I have witnessed over and over is that our conscious self can go to the moment in all time that is most essential to heal for what is present in our life today. The energy with Jim did not get triggered for me until we were returning to Telluride. We had ample opportunities as we had known each other for three years, done multiple sessions in person or on the phone, and I had already stayed at his home in Telluride for a week before going to Denver and Boulder to work. There is deep and clear wisdom in each of our unfolding lives. It is why we do not know everything. We are not supposed to!

The divine timing of Jim asking the question that awakened sexual energy and anger was not specific to healing just our karma but included a man I had met at the festival. The energy came up to help me heal and understand some of the magical experiences. It also came to illuminate some of the quandaries I had found myself experiencing in the weeks I had been in Colorado. There was a lot going on. It did not have to do with any chemistry with Jim to invite infidelity. I knew better than that. There had been some interactions with people that did not make sense to me until after I did my regression on the life as Donna's sister and Grayson's son.

Love, sexual energy, and attraction can, and does, carry over from lifetime to lifetime. This causes confusion and is one of the clear reasons that fidelity can be a challenge. Remember, chemistry is karma. I am not negating the physical sensations or reactions in the body. I am not negating the feelings that are visceral and real. I am asking us all to question if they are from this moment or another before acting or reacting on this feedback arrangement of the soul and the body. Our emotions communicate the reaction of a soul in a body. The mind interprets that feeling. We *assume* the mind is observing from an objective viewpoint. Rarely is that the case.

The chemistry between people, including sexual chemistry, might be real but might not be appropriate to actualize in the present incarnation. To use past life regression as a tool can be helpful to stay faithful to our intimate partners if that is the agreement between the souls. The investigation of chemistry, karma, is also important when in relationships that are unrequited, unidirectional, or obsessive. It is true that the issues could be from this life, and it can also be true that the energy comes from other times. What is important is what we do with the energy, not that it exists.

At The Steps to Awareness Festival, which had been the 'reason' I was in Telluride, to begin with, I met a man. This man was single, attractive, spiritual, and there was definite chemistry between us. During the regression in the meadow, I saw this man as my husband of that life and the father of my unborn child. One of the reasons I returned to the valley instead of continuing to Portland as planned, really only one of them, was to see if there was any potential for a relationship. Little did I know making the decision to change my course forward, would teach me so much about past life influences.

As I reflect and update this vignette of my life written just months after it happened, I recognize how that decision to not go to Portland, but return to Telluride was important for my destiny. It is only in hindsight that we can see how we got to where we are. We do not get to where we are if we have not been where we have been. And, again, Buddha's wisdom resounds in my consciousness *"When one is truly ready for something, it puts in its appearance."* I was ready to know more about my intimate connection to everyone wherever I traveled. I was establishing a relationship with the Kolar family that would continue to unfold with magic, laughter, grace and love to this day.

Grayson and I, on the last day of the festival, met the man on the street after my last lecture and began to chat. There was an immediate connection between them, and they were playful and affectionate. Later Grayson even called him his 'best friend' though there is 30 years difference in their ages. The energy between them had confused me at the moment, but during the regression in the meadow, it all began to make sense.

Grayson was coming back into that Native American lifetime as our son whom my husband did not know existed as my husband died before I could tell him. In the life before incarnating as our son, Grayson's soul had previously been my husband's best friend. Grayson as the friend had died in battle the year before. So, the memory of being best friends, the kid Grayson felt when they met in front of the Sheridan Opera House. In the present, on the street in Telluride, they acted as if they still were those men though now one of them was just a little boy!

The horse that my husband had captured was one of Tracker's past lives. This explained some of Tracker's attentiveness to me and the obvious love that was present between us. This continues the topic about the infinite ways our souls manifest. We are not limited to human forms. It was so very present and evident in Tracker's behavior that we loved each other. I have been allergic to dogs in this life, and that relationship with Tracker began to shift my allergies as I healed the deep pain of the Native woman who lost her love, her freedom, and her power.

In the innumerable regressions by that point in my life, I had not yet felt such immobilizing grief from a past life. I cried like I had never cried before, the sorrow was so great. This too was a part of my healing process as there was a belief locked into that grief that I was not to ever show it. Donna, as my sister in that life, had not allowed it. My forgiveness of her was even more powerful for now in her presence. I was able to heal not just the loss of my love, but the loss of my ability to heal myself through grieving.

During the regression, I also addressed the sexual energy and anger that came up on the road while riding with Jim across the state of Colorado. The basis of our sexual connection in that life had been about power and control. I had manipulated him sexually, withholding love, enjoyment, and affection. He had not been the mate of my choice, so I punished him for it with uncensored resentment, hostility, and spite. The residual for Jim was reflected in feeling manipulated by women. As I forgave this loss of love, the belief that I was not able to grieve, and my anger at Jim, it shifted him as well.

The healing opportunities from this life did not stop with Grayson, Donna, Jim and me. Desiree, their then 20-year-old daughter, was also a part of this Native American life too. Dez lived in Arizona, and several weeks before on the phone we had done a regression for her about a Native American life. She 'happened' to be in Telluride visiting when I returned, so was on the walk in the valley with us that morning. Donna began to have strong cramps in her body on the right side of her stomached. She asked me to find out what was going on. I challenged her to figure it out herself. I suggested she ask the pain what it wanted to tell her, and who did it belong to. Remember, just two weeks earlier Donna had embraced even more of who she came to this life to be as an intuitive healer. Here life was presenting her with the opportunity to learn even more about her intuitive skills.

Donna knew almost immediately this pain was Desiree's and not her own. So together Donna and I worked with Dez on the trail to continue the healing. Dez and I had started but apparently had not finished during our phone session. The choice then allowed Dez to go deeper into her karma to forgive the unresolved emotional energy with her parents because she decided to visit while I was also there. We are connected by so much more than the apparent. There is a reason for everything. Forgiveness can bring peace to every level of the body, physical—pink-eye and stomach cramps, emotional—anger and grief, mental—thinking that everything is at the moment we are in when it does not make sense, and spiritual—that we can touch the infinite and eternal love that is.

Jim had awakened to this memory of this lifetime before us all and had not told anyone. He had attended and Inipi ceremony, a sweat lodge, and then walking by those same rocks, had spontaneous past life recall. He describes the memory "that was just there for him in his mind." Jim's healing came from both the mental awareness, the intuitive flash of the memory of the valley floor as a Native Indian encampment and the emotional process of his regression session more than a month later. All of us from that drama story had come together then to help us help ourselves with the current life dramas that were going on.

The man, who I was attracted to from the festival, did not want to participate consciously in the healing. That is the right of his soul and will as he has his path of awakening his consciousness. Our evolution is our own. Nor did he want to date me but the initial attraction was there for us both. Chemistry is never a one-way street. However, it might feel different on the other side though the molecules are moving for both. For Donna and Jim's family, it brought more love and acceptance into their home. This is the reward always for facing our pain and forgiving it. We just get to have more love in us, and therefore, around us. As we are healing ourselves, we are healing everything our lives encounter.

Grace can move our pain in an instant. Medicine heals our pain. Therapy heals our pain. Education heals our pain. Art heals our pain. Music heals our pain. Adventure heals our pain. Religion heals our pain. Family heals our pain. Friendships heal our pain. Travel heals our pain. Forgiveness heals our pain. And, conversely, all of these things can also create pain. The choice is ours to make. The choice determines our karma, and our karma determines our choices. What is important is that we have power with all of it when we engage with courage. There is a greater truth that is being revealed as we awaken to more consciousness of the energies that move with us through time.

The honesty required to be true to one's heart is the challenge of the human condition. This is true though civilizations, languages, technologies have come and gone. The ethical, consciousness and moral dilemmas have not changed. We must look for the love in us and all around us. We must also recognize that we are interconnected with physical experience to others through our compassion and empathy. On every level physical, emotional, mental and spiritual we are connected in our human condition. This is why it is necessary to self-assess, self-reflect, and become self-actualized. Awareness is our responsibility as a part of the whole. They and them, are us. It is that simple—and that complex.

Donna was feeling Desiree's pain. Gigi was feeling Tom's fear. Layna was feeling Eli's anger. I was feeling Nancy's contractions. Not only can we feel, see, hear, and know another's reality in the present, we can also sense their pasts and futures too. This is not only for special people, psychic people, spiritual people.... I mean every one of us has the power in our Being to end separation from all life in all time! The collective challenge is to be able to open to this reality with kindness and love, and not manipulation and fear. If we choose the first, we have the capacity to continue to work toward the potentiality of Heaven on Earth. If we choose the latter, we will extinguish our species. Which do we really want? We get to choose.

Chapter 19 Practicum

⌘ Past-life material is always present. Sit face-to-face or screen-to-screen if using video chat with someone willing to explore deeper the relationship between you. It is not necessary to have obvious conflict but know that something negative might arise. Be in agreement that you will resolve whatever story you remember. Use the 5-Steps of Forgiveness as a scripted guideline for your healing.

⌘ Notice which side of their face calls your attention and look deeply into the eye on that side of the face. Take turns looking into each other. Look with both eyes to see how you have known them in a past life. Enter the eye as if it were a portal to another scene, setting, or place. Allow your imagination to be totally free. The face may shapeshift, and you will see how they looked, male or female, and the age that is most appropriate for this exercise. Find out why you have come back together in this lifetime and what is the unresolved emotional energy. Stay with the process until you can only see love in each other.

Chapter 20

Again? I Thought I Was Done With That!

No matter how many times I tell others and remind myself that our destination is the journey, we still want to get someplace. Forward is the only direction that we go. The human condition is to embrace and not fear the only eventuality that is certain—we will not always be the human being we are in this moment. We can learn to enjoy the mystery journey toward the end. We will be gone, so how do we make it good along the way?

We live in a mysterious, vast, expanding Universe with no top, or bottom or sides that humanity has yet found. This divine abyss is pure potential. In this abyss, we have the gift of free will. The perfection of the abyss is that we can engage our self with it to create. What we create does not come just out of necessity. What we create comes from this divine potential. This mysterious creative force is God.

Though my brain surgery was now 19 years ago, nearly every day,

I am still witnessing the evolution of my broken face, challenges with my balance, and have difficulty to hear being 50% deaf. There are some days when there is a pain on my face. I celebrate these days because they mean that another branch of the nerve has awakened into function again. There is no reward for me or reality that I am recovered. The experience of my brain surgery changed my life, forever. Recovery is not a place for me. Recovery is the way I choose to actively capitalize on the myriad of ways to heal available to me. My karma is to release the sorrow of what was lost and to celebrate the gifts that were given.

When we have a baby, we cannot go back. When we get married, we cannot go back. When we graduate from college, we cannot go back. When we have a loved one die, we cannot go back. When we get divorced, we cannot go back. The Earth always spins in the same direction. We do not have the option to go back. Forward is the only direction we can go and learn about love is all there is to do. So pain becomes the impetus if we embrace it to move our consciousness forward or pain can impede us. Free will lets us choose.

Though we cannot recreate the past, what we have is the option to look with a constantly evolving perspective. We have the option to see through new eyes, hearts, and minds every day. As we move forward, we as perpetual motion machines of consciousness, have the capacity to find new information, perspective, and truth. The Christian teaching of being 'reborn' is fundamentally the same concept. We have the ability through our free will to choose, to begin again.

After decades of working with the Kolar family, we just expect that when we get together, we will be visiting a past life drama story to heal each other and ourselves. It happened again in the spring of 2013 when I was in Colorado to work. Over the years we have remembered numerous lifetimes together. The Native American life, shared in the last chapter was followed by one as Tibetan monks, which was followed by a life with a Celtic King and his court. All of them remembered timely to the personal growth all of us were experiencing simultaneously no matter where we were residing, or what jobs we were doing or our current state of health.

These experiences are one of the reasons I love these people so much—we have fun together—healing! Instead of fearing these healing opportunities, we watch, we learn, we forgive, and we grow together by recovering the content of these lives. Always, the drama story accurately reflects each of our individual issues or life lessons that we are working with at the moment. Nothing is random, ever. And, it is not up to us to decide that we are done with nothing to learn from each other. We cannot see the end of our soul's connections to each other. What we do get to see is the willingness we all have to go with whatever karmic material shows up. The Universe always conspires, so it does. I cannot say my karma is finished with these souls because I am not arrogant enough to think I know. It will end when it does, in the meantime, we just keep supporting each other to be free, face our conflicts with love, and carry on.

This last healing journey together started with Donna making reservations for a dinner party. We were to celebrate Jim's birthday with friends. It was also a chance for me to meet Garrett, his partner Shannon, and their two beautiful boys. Dez was not supposed to be in town so Donna figured she would not come because, in the course of organizing people, she realized we would be going for Indian cuisine. As Dez does not like it, it was an opportunity to take advantage of her convenient absence. Grayson was coming, but his girlfriend was not able to join us due to her work schedule.

Donna, as the plans came together, began having a vision of being a 17-year-old female with silk garments dancing and doing specific mudras with her hands. She just laughed and made a reservation at Taj Mahal, an Indian restaurant in a location easy to get to for all of us. Dez though was now in town, her work trip canceled. She would still not come because she does not like curry and coriander the main spices used in Indian food. Donna surmised this as her daughter's aversion to 'doing the work' that this life would bring up for Dez.

Donna did not judge her daughter as right or wrong. She just noticed the resistance.

At dinner, there was a lot of chaos as there were two small children, a busy restaurant at 6 pm on Friday, and the emotions of the Indian life were already activated. I sat next to friends of Donna and Jim that I had slightly known for multiple decades as well. The wife I had only done a session for once and had never felt warm and fuzzy feelings around her. Her husband, it was the first time we were meeting in this life. We had quite a lively conversation as he grew up in San Francisco, the place I leave my heart always. During dinner, no obvious karmic story lines revealed themselves. I knew that I would be spending more time with the Kolars, so I figured when it was truly ready, the truth would reveal itself about what we needed to heal.

The next day, I did sessions during the day. It was Saturday night, my last night in Colorado, and I wanted to go out and play. I had arrived in Colorado the week before and done sessions every day. Donna and Jim, always committed to work on their love story, had planned to do a session at 7:30 pm. They wanted to wait to confirm until Donna was done with her 12-shift as an ER nurse at the Boulder hospital. Though the possibility was huge that they would cancel, I still felt obligated to be available until it was confirmed either way. We already knew we were going to address her past life as a beautiful Indian who danced in saris. It would just have to wait one more day.

At about 7:40 pm I got the word via text that they were not coming. In anticipation of this possibility, I had a plan ready for my single-on-the-loose Self. I had already gotten onto my Flixster App on my phone to search out the local movies, schedules, and location options nearby. As most of the movies were starting around the 7 pm hour, the choices were few. However, I was ready and immediately jumped in the car and headed to the Boedecker Theater. My Maps App said it would be 11 minutes and there was a documentary that I wanted to see starting at 8 pm. I would be in perfect time with extra to park and purchase popcorn.

Feeling quite pleased with myself, I pulled up in front of a building that did not look like a theater at all. Spontaneously, I was at *The Dairy Center for the Arts*. My heart was really happy that I had 'randomly' found such a cool place to visit on my last night in town. I marched up the steps and walked up to the counter to purchase my ticket to see *Sound City*, a documentary about a recording studio in Los Angeles. One of my clear motives was a not-so-hidden agenda. If there were single men in Boulder, looking for a place to be on a Saturday night like me, culturally or artistically or musically inclined, and not wanting to be in a bar ... they could be at this show!?

As I asked the man at the ticket counter for the 8 pm show, the theater doors opened up, and out came all of these people. Many of them were single men looking culturally, artistically or musically inclined! I turned just in time to see them as they were leaving the building. The man behind the counter said, "Do you want a ticket to the 8:30 show of *Rasa Yatra*?" I told him I was there to see *Sound City*. He said, "That show is just getting out."

Explaining to him that I had been 'mislead' by my Flixster App, he shrugged and told me that rarely, if ever, did they have the right time. He then recommended the next show, which was an epic visual documentary about a spiritual journey to the center of India and Hinduism. I laughed and bought the ticket to *Rasa Yatra, A Pilgrimage Into The Heart of India*. Donna was right. We were going to India for our collective healing!

While waiting the half hour for the film to start, I wandered around smiling at the amazing art and absorbed the feeling of the magic of the moment. Art Galleries and Cultural Centers are always soul food for me. I created the hashtag #artislovecomealive for a good reason— it is! My Master's Program was a pro in Creation Spirituality. The supporting philosophy is that every creative act is a direct pathway to the Divine. Here I randomly ended up in one of my 'churches' going to a movie about India. I could not wait to tell Donna the next morning about the movie and scene I found myself in. She, Dez and Jim was giving me a ride up the mountain to catch my plane from Vail. We would have ample time in the car to investigate this past life story.

During the movie, I asked myself, *"What was my role in this life and where was the memory in my body?"* Immediately, I felt my heart open up to deep grief, my chest became heavy, and a feeling of my breasts full of milk ready to feed a child. The Universe and I had a laugh . . . I am at *The Dairy Center*! The overwhelm however was too much for this moment. I pushed these feeling aside. I was just too tired. It was my 'night off, ' and I settled back to enjoy the incredible cinematography of the landscapes of the Himalayas, the beauty of the rituals, and the melodic sounds of devotional chanting as the soundtrack. My spiritual journey was well on the way. *"The focus of the film is the power of the unrelenting moving still,"* the review said. The paradox of consciousness was revealing itself there in the dark, reminded me that I never have a 'night off.' Who was I kidding?

The next day I was not completely ready when the Kolars arrived. My fatigue from all the energy of the trip and the feeling that I was not ready to go back to California were influencing my ability to get organized and packed. They arrived to fetch me a bit earlier than we planned as the weather had changed again. Another snowstorm was dumping wet snow in upper elevations, and we needed to drive through it to get me to the airport. There was some anxiety in the car for all of us as an undercurrent, but all of us were in a celebratory mood.

It was Jim's birthday, and we were off on an adventure up the mountains. When I am with my dear friends the Kolars, there is always a lot of laughter when we are together. As we turned onto Hwy 6, to drive through a scenic canyon to reach I-70, I wished Jim a happy birthday from the back seat. I asked him if he wanted a past life regression as his birthday gift. Donna is always game. Dez wanted to know if it was safe. I knew there was nothing else to do but go there. Jim laughed and said, "Why not!"

Healing sessions do not begin when we enter the door of a therapist's office or when a video chat or phone call begins. Workshops do not begin when we take our seat in the meeting room or sit down to the computer for the webinar. When we make the decision to do something, it begins. My favorite quote is an amalgamation of the wisdom of Goethe but written in *"The Scottish Himalayan Expedition"* by William Hutchison Murray:

> *"Concerning all acts of initiative (and creation), there is one elementary truth, the ignorance of which kills countless ideas and splendid plans: that the moment one definitely commits oneself, then Providence moves too. All sorts of things occur to help one that would never otherwise have occurred. A whole stream of events issues from the decision, raising in one's favour all manner of unforeseen incidents and meetings and material assistance, which no man could have dreamt would have come his way. I learned a deep respect for one of Goethe's couplets:*
>
> *Whatever you can do or dream you can, begin it.*
>
> *Boldness has genius, power, and magic in it!"*

Of course, even now as I write this text, it is not random for this quote to have popped into my head to share. Hutchison wrote this when describing his journey to the Himalayan landscape. Though Donna and Jim had planned to do a couple's session with me the night before but had canceled, it was clear that the healing work of this past life would address some of the tension between them currently operating in their marriage. I do not believe that marriage is a destination but a journey as well. I believe that committed couples must fall in love everyday. The session had started when they decided to do the work though the actual healing had not happened in the privacy of my office the night before. It was apparently happening instead in the car. The higher we climbed, the slower we drove due to the conditions of the slippery, snowy, unplowed roads.

We all began to ask ourselves, *"Who were we?" "How did we know and relate to each other?" "Where were we going in the Himalayan Mountains?" "Why were we together?" "What feelings did we have in our bodies or emotions?"* The story unfolded with both laughter and tears. It was not like a hypnotic regression as we were actively using our imaginations and together remembering the story of the past.

Pretty quickly, Dez and I identified ourselves as twin younger siblings to Donna. We all felt a royal heritage, and with the help of Wikipedia, my 3G connection, and my smartphone, I read about the early families of Dharmsala. When sharing this information, Jim's back began to bother him, and his right leg began to hurt. Donna began to cry. She felt nauseous and cramping in her stomach, suddenly remembering being pregnant with Jim's child.

Donna and Jim's intimate connection in that lifetime were between people of different castes and forbidden. Jim, our driver in the moment up to the mountains, was a Sherpa! We were running away to the other side of the mountains to meet our grandmother who supported their love. Dez and I were coming to support our sister. Personal agenda was to also get away from our father. I did not like our father . . . at all! The father of that life was the girlfriend of Donna's who had been at dinner Friday evening and her husband, a Eunuch in the community, had helped us escape. Dez, our brother, was coming because he felt obligated not because he wanted to.

As we merged from Hwy 6 on to I-70, the snow was falling heavier, and the emotions in the car were getting heavier too. Donna began to cry more, and I encouraged her to tell Jim how much she loved him. It was clear that Jim, with a spear thrown into his back. Donna and Jim due to circumstance live across the state from each other which is difficult for them both. This arrangement is not because they do not love each other. It is because their professional needs, personal needs, and family needs are in both Telluride and Boulder. Jim shed a few tears as he took in the sincerity of Donna's proclamation.

Dez then realized that she had abandoned us and gone back to Dharamsala. She began to have visions of a beautiful woman who he realized he loved. This longing is reflective of Dez's love life. She felt she has been waiting a long time to be loved. As she worked with the energy of that past life as this young man, she realized she could change the belief regarding the longing for love. This is the point of doing Soulwork. We can move the latent emotions that hold the mental constructs in place and fuels behavior that perpetuates it as our truth. There was a feeling in me that Dez could now find her love of this life. She is beautiful, fun, loving, and kind. It is her turn for sure.

Meanwhile, as everyone else was recalling the memories, I had my awakenings to my story of that life. I remembered that Donna had died in childbirth and I was left alone with her baby. I felt responsible for keeping us alive and keep going forward instead of following my brother back to Dharamsala. I felt guilty because I had failed. Though I was able to keep Donna and Jim's love child alive with my milk for a short while, I killed us both anyway. The terrain was treacherous, and I fell hitting my head with my dying thoughts of my stupidity.

On Wednesday evening four days before the drive up the mountain, a buzzing had started on my right cranium moving from the back and down a nerve line on the right side of my face. I had a cranial sacral session for myself already in my schedule for Thursday afternoon so I figured it was my body getting ready for that session with Lynn Abraham. Yes, this is the same Lynn that I met in 1995 to help her heal herself to be a Mother. While in Boulder, I was staying in her home with her beautiful Chance Boys.

Little did I realize Thursday, it was also where my body stored some of the trauma memory of this Indian lifetime. Though it did not come into my consciousness during the session on the therapist's table, that buzzing in my cranium was directly related to this India life. The belief system attached to memory in my cranium was of my self-loathing which did not become clear until we were driving up the mountain. It was time for me to heal both of these negative images of myself. The memory in my breasts, triggered by the movie Saturday night, was the grief that I lost not just my child but Donna's.

In this current incarnation, Donna and Jim had been pregnant with Dez when they were married. Garrett had followed quickly. When Dez and Garrett were nearing their teens, Donna had wanted to consciously conceive a child. They loved their children that had shown up without planning, but Donna wanted to have another love child that was planned. Donna's desire to have another child became a challenging issue in their marriage as Jim did not want another baby.

After Donna had a vision on a hike in the Flatirons above Boulder of a handsome young man, she convincing Jim that it was necessary to have another child for their marriage to continue. Grayson arrived at the Kolar family welcomed and wanted. The child that was unexpected in this Indian past life to the princess and the Sherpa, now in this lifetime in the 21st century is the expected child, Grayson. Our souls do not always incarnate into the same circle of life. However, clearly, there are deep and profound soul agreements with the Kolar clan. The story of the Indian princess and the Sherpa who ran away to the Himalayas to be free to love each other, continues. I feel fortunate that I too am a part of these soul agreements and true love.

Grayson had come to me for a private healing session on Friday before our dinner at Taj Mahal. He was feeling stuck, angry, and frustrated with his employment situation. Grayson felt disconnected from his essential artistic self. I rarely worry, it is a waste of time, but I found myself deeply concerned for his welfare and happiness. Grayson feels like one of my kids in this life. His mother says my influence with Grayson from a very early age, helped Grayson to become the man he is today. Donna thinks of me as Grayson's other mother. Dez too has this role, as she was 13 when he was born. Grayson's love of this life is a very confident woman. It is not surprising with Donna, Dez, and me as his role models! It was no surprise to us all in the car when Donna said, *"Grayson is the baby!"*

By the time we had cleared the Eisenhower tunnel, most of the healing had happened. As we moved toward our destination of the Eagle airport, there was an internal calming for each of us. Dez and I though decidedly needed to use the toilet. It was not an option to continue all the way to the airport, another 40 minutes away, so we pulled off in Vail. Eliminating water from our body as tears, sweat, or pee are all ways to let go the emotions that are attached to it. I had not cried much in the car, nor had Dez. We continued to talk about this Indian life but not with the intensity we had on the way to the Vail Valley.

Donna reminded Jim about a time when they began dating in this life as college students in Michigan. There was one date when she had to pull him out of a snow bank. Jim's leg was broken, he was on crutches, and he had fallen into a deep well in the snow. The past had recreated itself only differently. During the following Christmas, they were engaged and shortly after that, they became pregnant with Dez. Now 40 years later they remembered a life with a surprise pregnancy, and a broken leg, as we drove through the splendor of the snowy, beautiful Rocky Mountains. Amazing!

It was hard for me to leave the comfort of such good friends that day once we arrived at the Eagle airport. I know the karmic connection is not over, nor will it end, or can it ever be. The life of our soul is eternal. Relationships are already an opportunity for growth. When past life material is a tool, it can help make sense of underlying feelings or evident ones. It is never a justification for bad behavior or retaliation. We as humans do not hold God's balance scale. However, it can help us to let go of limiting beliefs about others and ourselves. The freedom that comes from this forgiveness is the ultimate goal of the soul. We all long for the freedom to just Be.

In the context of done, I have realized I am still not over the loss of my first love Stu to cancer so young. Waves of grief still come up with memories of things we did together. Sometimes those memories bring a smile, sometimes tears, and sometimes both. When his father passed away, I cried the whole day I got the news. Later, I posted on Facebook sentiment about their family, the community we were raised in, and how the experience of knowing them was so significant to who I am today. Often it is only with the loss of someone, that we can go to even deeper levels of healing and forgiveness. This is a common experience I witness with my clients. The permanent change with death allows another layer of their consciousness to evolve through the grief and opens more love to the karmic lessons the relationship facilitated.

There is no one right way to heal. And, we do not have anyone randomly in our life. Every one of us is connected to all of us. The intimacy of witnessing and participating in the exchange of energy with another is the basis for our karmic dance. From my participation in past life work, repeatedly witnessing the liberation of behaviors, attitudes, understanding, judgments, and issues, I can only support and encourage its use. Why not? When we know, something is valuable for others and ourselves, sharing it is the ultimate gift for us all. For our ripple in the pond of love and forgiveness creates waves that touch and serve the whole world. The colloquialism—*time heals all wounds*—is true. We just do not know how much time, for infinity has no end.

Chapter 20 Practicum

⛢ What personal issue—conflict with your spouse or partner, conflict with Mother or Father, conflict with a boss or co-worker, conflict with your behavior—do you define as completed, finished, over and done? Dig a bit deeper into your memory. What else can be forgiven? Can you view the conflict as a waking dream and interpret the dream as a lesson for your spiritual growth? Write in your journal any Ah-Ha's that come. Make amends if you can forgive and make a difference in this life.

⛢ Who in this life do you think that you "karma is done" and that you have learned or experienced everything that God had in mind for you? If they are alive, write them a letter and thank them for all they taught you about life, yourself, and love. Burn it if you do not have the courage to send it.

⛢ If you are willing to risk the fear of more rejection—the truth is you or they have already rejected each other—send the letter.

Chapter 21

Living Life At-Large

Home is the most fundamental aspects of the Human Condition. We are animals that need nests and community to survive. I do believe *"Home is where the heart is!"* Where ever we are, the center of our power is with us. The heart is where we begin, where we end, and the compass for us to follow as we move forward. Several times over my journey as Sally Aderton to the now, I had a personal workshop specifically on being home. Without a permanent address except for a PO Box and my personal belongings in storage, there was no home other than my body. For this colloquialism, once again I must say, I am a believer! In this chapter, I share more of my life lessons to give tools and wisdom of how I return back to myself and my heart.

In 1993 I specifically embarked on a chapter of my life story labeling myself, *The Wandering Mystic*. It was a conscious choice though precipitated by an eviction in San Francisco. My roommate and I were not emancipated from the apartment we shared due to a negative action on our part. It was a loving act as the owner wanted to inhabit the space with her new partner and had the right under rent control to do so. Her decision to evict us with five months notice allowed both my roommate and myself to plan our next experience with a lot of lead-time.

The landlord's 'no,' became a chance for my soul to have a 'yes'! When I asked myself just moments after the news what I wanted next, I knew immediately. My healing practice had now become national, and it was growing. With trips to New York, Denver, and a trip being planned for Florida I wanted to be at-large and follow the Mystery. So, I did. When it was time to land, I made a decision where I wanted to live, created workshops and session to manifest the money for a house to rent, and landed magically in Santa Cruz in November of 1994.

By January of 1997, my work trips that year had me swirling the globe. I was going to New Zealand, twice to Europe, trips planned nationally to New York, Chicago, Colorado. It made no sense to me to keep paying rent to house my possessions, not me. The time had come again for me to have home be on the road. I put my belongings in storage, and I traveled. By the late winter, now engaged to be married I wanted to take my computer and a few belongings to Telluride. My fiancé and I were hoping to live in both Telluride and Zurich. I was following my heart as my compass. So, I prayed for someone to do the drive with me. One of my clients David Kennedy had been feeling called to visit a Reservation on a spiritual pilgrimage went with me. David had followed his heart to San Francisco from the east coast. His 'plan' was not working to create a home and felt adrift though grateful to be learning and discovering spiritual pursuits:

> So it's been said life is the people you meet along the way. One of the best road trips in my current journal dates back to 1998, the early part of the year. I'm camping out on the edge of the Mission District in San Francisco and looking to hitch a ride to the Zuni reservation down in New Mexico— gotta' do some ceremony, maybe hang out with the locals for awhile. I, by happenstance, am on the phone with my

longstanding confidant Sally Aderton; my gal Sal, and it's a truly epic story. Have you never heard that famous Eagle's tune? Winslow AZ is on that path, and a flatbed truck is all I'm looking for. Brilliant plan Einstein. Sally in her wisdom went out of her way, got me to Gallup. This guy made his way to Zuni Corn Mountain without a hitch.

My infinite wisdom, nor my heart as a friend could leave David on a long lonesome highway east of Sedona waiting for a flatbed truck to hitch a ride to Gallup. When negotiating our life's journey, getting off the ego's plan is always a part of the Divine plan. David and I both were listening to our intuition and acting accordingly. We just had to go. The road ahead would give us the reasons and the answers to call with our soul to adventure into the unknown. For David, it was a vision quest. For me, I thought it would be to create my family.

It would be six years later, post brain surgery and graduate school before I unpacked those boxes that were waiting patiently in Santa Cruz for me. Writing this chapter, I realized the **Sally Swirl** is a spinning of all the wisdom in this book into one perfect narrative. In the first—*Evolution*, we addressed the need for humans to step up or forward or back to our intuition to survive. Living without a home of mine own, put my nervous system on constant alert for a safe place. Where I find that safety is in the heart of my faith, my self-love, and the hearts of those who truly love me. Without the intuition and the trust of my intimate relationship with the Great Mystery, I have survived and thrived.

In the second section—*Revolution*, we expanded our perception to include the spirit guides and the living consciousness in all forms to end the illusion that we are ever alone. Daily I am trusting beyond the apparent to help me manage the resources that I have to keep the show on the road. I am continuing inviting a dialog with the Divine *"What is the best use of this moment to serve love?"* If I can quiet the noise in my head that fear creates, I hear clearly directions, tasks to do, and guidance to get through the expectations of others or myself. As my perception extends beyond the apparent, I am constantly listening to the clues from my environment in the waking dream, listening to the messages that come in the sleeping dream, and being mindful of who comes into my daily life as my God/dess reflection.

Here in this last section—*The Human Condition*, we have learned a new way to understand eternal life, karma, and how forgiveness sets us free. The miracle that allows me to return to the love that I am is letting go. I am in a constant state of being born again by forgiving my past, my pain, my expectations, my judgments, my self-crimination, and my story . . . or current version of my story. The human condition is our personal stories that become the collective story of the culture of the time. Cultures come and go. I believe that the culture of consumerism and righteous secular mentality is on its way to being a story of our past. I believe that the culture of connectionism and the celebration of diversification are being born every day as the new world order. I know this because I am living this new story.

Before my surgery in 1998, I was living self-sufficient with no debt. I lived marginally without savings. Yet, I was able to travel and teach where ever the wind blew me. After my surgery, I had a lot of debt and a lot of healing to do. I chose to work with my friends at their real estate company because of the emotional security, the free creative license to be inventive with their people and services, and economic benefits of consistent revenue, they provided. It was an inspiring time. Above my desk I made a sign that read *The Creation Station*. My job at the company was to innovate, working on the business instead of in the business, by recruiting, marketing, and management.

The beginning of the decade I call the Double-Os was the dot-gone era. It was the first crash leading to the Internet re-evolution. Businesses went online to never return to just 'brick and mortar.' In 2001 I came out of my graduate program with an MA but still not able to care for myself physically. I'm an Ultra-sensitive who had their head cracked open willingly. Now I thought of myself as an Uber-Ultra-sensitive! Though I never stopped doing healing sessions, or teaching, it was not how I sustained my life. Student loans, disability, trades for services and a place to live, a borrowed car, and lots of love of my family and friends kept me going.

Though fortunate to have my now vintage sallyaderton.com website created, and confidence built by achieving an academic goal, I did not have the chutzpah nor energy to re-create my business the way it was BBS. It was clear that I needed another revenue source. At the end of January 2002, within two days of telling that to my dear friend I needed to make more money, I had a part-time job. It was a blessed gift to return to a work environment with people I loved. Put in charge of one French intern 'to do a little marketing' I spun the task into an International Internship program mentoring hundreds of young people. My friend Zoya said, "Since Sally could no longer go to the world, she brought the world to the corner of Van Ness Avenue and Lombard Streets in San Francisco!"

The first year was pretty tough. I was still doing my acupuncture, working to revitalize my healing practice, and learning to take care of myself. I finally had my apartment and unpacked those boxes packed in 1997! My schedule was Monday, Wednesday, and Friday and by 5 in the evening, I did not want to talk. Speaking through the paralyzes made my face tired. The noise of the office kept my nervous system on high alert. The functioning ear over compensated my deaf ear. Nearly every evening by the time I was home, I would cry with exhaustion. On Tuesdays and Thursdays I slept, to be able to get through the next day. I was still in recovery even though the surgery was four years behind me. I still 'faced' it every day in some way.

In March of 2003, I felt the need to perhaps take on one more day at the office. Money was still tight, and my practice was not rebounding. The opportunity came about for me to go to work full time instead. Though that would cure my financial needs, it meant putting even less energy toward my practice, my life's calling. Instead of reacting to a snap decision, I spent the weekend praying if it was the right thing to do. The message from my guides was very clear. One of the partners in the business was dying of cancer. I was told that I was to take the job to help the remaining owners transition his death and *only to do it for five years.*

By 2008, when my guidance was to leave the business, the land-scape for me had changed literally and physically, and our economy was changing rapidly. I had moved to San Diego to build our office there in 2005. I was in a committed relationship for the first time since the BS which ended in another crash and burn. This was a deeper level of depression than I had ever experienced even immediately after the surgery. I was so depressed that even my therapist at the time threw his hands up and said, *"Sally there is nothing more I can do for you unless you go on anti-depressants!"* My own pattern of rejection from a man, combined with living now separate from my friends and family in the San Francisco Bay Area, the sense of isolation began a spiral that went out of control; I listened to him and paid the consequences. We suffer when we do not listen to our intuition.

As Healers our responsibility to our word is beyond any measure. People come to us for compassionate care. My therapist's proclama-tion was not to my benefit and with my pattern of 'being the good girl' it created issues I had no idea would bring even more new shame into my self-concept. In my vulnerable state, I listen and acted against my own wisdom and also of my spirit guides to take pharmaceuticals. This began another kind of recovery that to this day convinces me that we are innocent to what we do. Forgiveness of him, the drugs, and myself, was my only option to stay alive ... and of course, to stay committed to the responsibility of healing myself.

During the depression in the year after the brain surgery, my doctor had wanted to prescribe anti-depressants. I had adamantly refused. It seemed natural to me that I would be sad, angry and fright-ened that my face was paralyzed, I was deaf in one ear, and my fiancé ended our engagement with an email, and my publisher canceled my contract. My belief is we are here to learn to deal with our emotions when we have them. Storing them away was what created the tumor in my head in the first place. However, I was not the same person in 2006 that refused the drugs in 1999. Nor was I who told the doctor at Stanford no to surgery to hotwire my facial nerve because it would never function. We evolve and who I was at that moment listened to the authority outside, instead of inside.

That choice made me be one of the people the commercials for all of them disclaim: *"If taking these drugs makes you feel suicidal, please see your doctor immediately!"* In all the years of experiencing depression, I was never suicidal. Once I got on the drugs, within weeks, I stopped eating, sleeping, and became agoraphobic. None of my tools for self-care worked. It was like the mechanics in my consciousness to receive the love that I know is holding the planets in the sky, just stopped. The color went out of the world, and all I could see was gray. For the first time as a Healer, I finally understood the people who came to see me who had no faith. It was like living in a flat world having no idea that I could stand perpendicular to it. I no longer wanted to stay on Earth. I wanted to go and I had no free will do decide anything else.

The very same doctor who insisted I needed the drugs to get out of the depression hospitalized me for my suicidal condition. To write about this is necessary. It took me four more years to know the drugs I took produced a manic-depressive or bipolar diagnosis. The shame of mental illness in our culture is even more of a stigma than physical illnesses or disease. After the hospitalization in 2006, I would go on and off the drugs, which is also not a good idea. They are called drugs for a reason. Our bodies are 24 hours 7 days a week chemistry labs producing the vehicle for our soul to learn about love. My chemistry lab was not creating peace but manifesting another war inside of my being. This one I almost did not win, not just once, but three times.

By 2008 the financial world began to collapse with every industry affected especially real estate. Though my guidance was clear that it was time to go, I did not. I was afraid and listened to my fear, and the false sense of security I had, with *a Job*. What I did not understand about that time was how my chemistry lab was reviving up my behavior with more and more anger. By the end of 2009, I was a bitch on wheels. I was trying to keep moving in the perfect storm of the market collapsing, the company suffering too with the real estate market in shambles, the owners having to deal with my confrontational erratic behavior, plus my fear of not being able to control all three was brutal for everyone. It is only in retrospect that I understand how debilitating that storm was for me to learn about coming home to myself.

On November 1, 2009 I was asked to leave, fired is another word or it, from a salaried job. There will be many stories as we look back on that decade of destruction of the American middle-class way of life. Millions of Americans lost their homes, jobs, and understanding of what security means. Greed is a mighty force, and I believe, love is mightier. In this case, it was not helpful to know I was not alone. In truth, there are still millions of people like myself who have still not recovered from the trauma of the recession. When I crashed again this time, the suicidal tendencies were even worse. I could feel an unwinding in my brain, physically, and nothing would stop it.

It is specifically because of this experience of feeling the physical changes in my brain that I challenge the metaphysical teachings that we are what we think. Changing my thoughts from negative to positive was not the simple solution to the degradation I felt. Daily affirmations, prayer, meditation, therapy, personal rituals did not just reprogram my brain. I had to change my biology to stay alive. Mortified, here I was again feeling the desire to leave my life as Sally Aderton. This was happening with greater intensity as I lost my place to live, my home at the same time.

We are integrated systems: physical, emotional, mental and spiritual. If you change one, you affect them all. The physical loss of my face and hearing produced a new emotional climate inside on how I felt about myself, and outside of how others treated me. The spiritual experience of hearing and seeing my guides allows me an expanded mental construct of what is real. But the physical feeling of my mind unwinding forced another level of faith. When I look back, I see how love kept me from taking action to harm myself. I could not believe it was happening again, but it was with force, speed, and vengeance greater than the first time. And, it was love that kept me alive.

Our Angels are all around us all the time, out of forms, or in them.

Because of the therapist, acupuncturist, chiropractor, support from my family and friends, and my spiritual reality I did not end my life. One friend stepped in when my roommate asked me to move and found me a couch to sleep on. The shame of this desire to end my life was again forcing me to go even deeper into self-loathing. Once again I was not sleeping, not eating, isolating, and the mind chatter every day to myself at all. My possessions went into storage and I was a mess.

As I dropped further and further down to the point of a plan and preparation to end my life, the quiet voice inside said, *"Live one more day Sally, just one more. That is all you need to do."* The very next day, I walked into my Angel acupuncturist who took one look at me and said: *"I am NOT going to let you do it!"* It was the moment the spiral was able to turn around. Here was my Earth Angel literally saving me because her intuition told her exactly what was happening for my soul and she took immediate action. I had not said one word to her about what was happening inside. She had not even read my pulses or looked at my tongue to analyze my wellness. She just knew. On this day another miracle manifested by the courage to love, trust her intuition and serve the healing for another. Her actions got me to the right doctor who diagnosed the manic-depressive condition and prescribed drugs to balance my brain chemistry.

Where was my intuition? Where were my Spirit Guides? Why could I not heal myself? Why was this happening? Where do I go? How do I get there? What am I supposed to do? The questions went on and on. Thank God I listened to the quiet, still, voice that told me *to live just one more day*. There is a very, very good reason that after a century this is the tenant and the wisdom of Alcoholics Anonymous to recover from any addiction. It is also the spiritual truth. We can only live one day at a time.

My Healer became then right cocktail of drugs which brought my emotional equilibrium back. The persistent care of my friends who called me everyday telling me to get up, get dressed, fix food, go for a walk, and do one thing for someone else kept me going. Where the drugs were my enemy, they now became my ally. This is the paradox of life. My enemy, the antidepressant prescribed 2006, was known to stimulate a bi-polar condition if there was epilepsy in your family history. My mother's brother had debilitating epilepsy and lived as a dependent and invalid his entire life. The drug that became my ally was invented to help people with epilepsy. I learned months later, when in research trials, it was shown to help people with mood disorders.

There is no one right way to get to God nor is there one right way to heal nor is there one way to virtually anything but higher mathematics. Each of us are on earth to live out our karma, destiny and life purpose to teach us about love. Though I know spiritually and intellectually that regrets are a prison, I punished myself for years incarcerating my soul again due to shame. To liberate me from the profound regret of the decision to take an antidepressant at the advice of that therapist took years.

From April of 2010 until February of 2016 I lived in no house or apartment that I could call mine. This independently karmically designed personal growth workshop to integrate another level of walking-my-talk, I called *Living Life At-Large*. Though it was not my intention to share this part of my journey nor my brain surgery here in this book, it is clear I must. The spiritual lessons that have been mine are too universal to omit out of my shame. As I have already shared, shame is one of my personal growth opportunities. Though I healed much of my pain in this life, I am not done learning or I would be gone from the earth. My task is to keep learning to love others, the world, and myself as Sally Aderton, or I would lay this character and costume down. I am not 'there' yet or I would not be here. And, I am super duper uber glad I am here!

When I was asked while Living Life At-Large, "Where do you live?" my most common answer was: *Where I am!* That actually is everyone's truth all the time. Some of the other ways I described my situation were: *rent-free, mortgage-free, without residence, couch surfer, house sitter, and welcomed guest.* All of these were and are euphemisms for *homeless.* Without fail, often with not much notice, I was provided accommodations. This epoch was even more challenging for my self-love than any life lesson before including all the losses after my brain tumor. The fact I have maintained any self esteem, let alone my sanity, is just an outright miracle. The simple reason that I have survived is that I am truly loved by my family, friends, and clients. Remember the axiom I suggested at the beginning of the book: **To be loved, be loving!** It is Truth. It is not sympathy, guilt or obligation that has opened many homes to shelter me; it is my open heart being met by another.

Slowly, as my brain chemistry began to balance again, I was sleeping on a friend's futon now back in the San Francisco Bay Area. On unemployment, I was able to pay my bills. Opportunities began to present themselves for me to house-sit, so I began to float from place to place. My mantra at that time was: **Just do what you can, to the best that you can.** Accepting what had happened was not an instantaneous healing. A dear friend challenged my self-recrimination about taking drugs and sadness that prognosis was it would be for the rest of my life. She said very eloquently: *"Would I love you less if you had to take insulin to balance your blood sugar?"*

Over time, I began to feel like I was 'supposed to' go without my home. We clever humans have the capacity for justifying pretty much anything. Over and over, friends or clients say to me, *"Sally, I cannot live like you do!"* I felt both ends of the polarity. I had pride in my ability to adapt, go without, be free from the responsibility of caring for stuff, and not be dependent on structure or consistency as my safety. However, I felt also the self-hatred that I had not been able to establish again consistent income and a home of my own. I continued to tell myself every day *"This is changing and I am too!"* I tell myself this still today because it is true. I am in a perpetual state of evolving and transforming no matter what it looks like to others. I am energy in motion.

In retrospect, Living Life At-Large was a magical time too. The light and the dark are always together. Which polarity we put our attention on creates the lens determining how we interpret what we see. I was accepted into a state funded program in its final phase before it was canceled for adults to learn computer skills. Learning basic HTML, CSS, and some Photoshop gave me new confidence. I sold several properties, traveled to Europe to see clients, spent five months in one stretch in Chicago with my family, and house sat in Monterey for 13 months. All these vignettes were stages to bring people, experiences, and knowledge I am so grateful now to have in my story. Through all of the uncertainty of what was to be and the question to find a solution to my problem to create financial stability, the certainty, the constant, the dependable was always the same. Family, friends and clients love me, unconditionally. I also find something of true value to appreciate about life on earth everyday.

Though I have never thought of myself as a victim, there have been many that call me that. I do not step away from friends in pain. However, there were many that could not handle my emotional and physical storms. They stepped away like after my brain surgery no longer wanting to witness or participate in my pain. They gracefully or dramatically stepped out of participating in life with me. People come and go. Lifetimes come and go. Civilizations come and go. The pain is holding on to what was when it would never come again. The spiritual lesson was crystal clear: **I am to learn to love myself no matter what.**

Patterns of behavior present themselves based on the conditioning in both our conscious and our unconscious minds. The wisdom of Buddha regarding divine timing reminded me that I must not be 'ready.' My home and financial stability were not appearing in my path. I had just to keep on keeping on. It was ahead of me, so I had to go on one more day to find it. The trauma of the mental illness in combination with losing my job seemed harder to heal than the trauma of the brain tumor. It was also clear to me that these traumas were directly related. And, all of it is just a story to teach me about love for me to share with others. And, it still hurts.

Though I have often said to God: *REALLY this is enough!* The shame was being cleared to liberate my light. It is the light that attracts abundance and prosperity. I do not need more than enough, I need just enough to care responsibly and participate in the economic system, as it exists currently. Writing about my shame is not to dump toxic waste on the world but to open up my blocks to being free.

There were incredible spiritual and material blessings along the way forward. Never have I gone without a place to sleep where I am welcome. My compassion for people who do not have a loving community and home to shelter them has grown light years. Just like I 'thought' I knew compassion for people with disabilities before my brain surgery, I 'thought' I had compassion for mental illness and homelessness. My knowledge of social media went into orbit with such a desire to be heard, to be seen, to shout out to the world that I existed. My healing work continued to bring insight, spiritual growth, peace and healing to others. I started using my creativity to help other businesses get seen and heard too. But there has still been something disabled within myself to receive consistent income and feel safety that is associated with a place of my own.

With the all of my experience and wisdom always ringing in my awareness I feel I should know better, do better, be better. Should-ing on ourself does not love our self. Nor is it love to add guilt, regret, anger, and the biggest voice of all FEAR to the chorus of self-flagellation. When we pray for help and listen for guidance, it will always come. We just do not know how. We do not have to figure out our toils alone. There are billions of people to talk with. We just have to be willing to bridge out of our pain by asking or extend a hand to someone else who is in pain to ease suffering.

Every day I am more aware that all of us must continue to find our survival safety in our hearts, first, before having it in our physical power, our emotional balance, and our mental acuity. We must find our safety and our self-worth not by comparison to others. We do not hold the balance scale for the Universe. We do hold power to love and that is all we need. Instead of being worried or afraid for others in distress, pray that we find our way. Instead of judging someone, take the time to listen to them. Perhaps their story has a pearl of wisdom for us all.

By 2014 I was keenly aware of what was keeping me faithful to keep on, keeping on. At a dinner party with friends the hostess asked what were the lessons I was learning, how was I surviving and insisted that I write this chapter. Effortlessly, I shared the four tasks that had begun to do every day to stay connected to the Divine. They have become what I believe will keep us all working toward a peace filled world by encouraging gratitude and individual creativity. They are not complicated nor are they meant to be:

1. I find something nature has created and appreciated it with awe. When we praise silently or a loud, that energy is given back to the earth.

2. I find something that a person has created and celebrate their creation with awe. The energy of honor will come back to them somehow. I will share it on social media if I can to keep moving that awe in the world. My hope is to be able to thank them personally or publicly. A compliment is most effective if it is shared.

3. I bring something into being that has not been before. I create something myself from my passion for creation itself: writing, photography, making jewelry, cooking, gardening or designing marketing materials for others.

4. I tell people I love them … and mean it!

The love that we are sustains our living. We are challenged now to find our right livelihood in alignment with our individuated soul purpose. When we hold our self-value, others see it and respond to that light they see and feel emanating from us. If I am staying true to in my talent, my skills, and my creative drive to serve, opportunities to participate keep coming my way. When we keep believing that if we are taking action in the direction of our dreams, combined with being in service, we are not victims.

Life to me is an inside job. I manifest daily gratitude and celebration for what is inside of me—the light of love—and what is outside of me—the beauty of my family, friends, and the world. I want to pay my bills too. I am not talking about a lifestyle. I am talking about the essentials. Can you imagine life just without a phone, let alone a home? From the wisdom in my Chakra Chart of the circular connections, the solution to the pain of living without my home was in my root or first chakra and the solution could be sourced from my crown or seventh chakra.

The basic human needs of food, shelter, clothing, and sex described by Abraham Maslow will be transformed the more I engage in my spiritual growth. So here I was a pilgrim of progress toward a deeper understanding of life on Earth as a soul reflected in the material challenges of being without residence. I was in good company—the Buddha, Neil Donald Walsh, Eckart Tolle—and countless more. I was learning to love myself no matter what, where ever I was, whom ever I was with, how ever I was able, when I was homeless. I did not have external values of success. I was learning to answer the question why we are alive. I was learning even more about love itself.

There would have been no way I could have imaged that seven years later now in 2017, I would be living as I do in Descanso, California. The waking dream strikes again! Descanso in Spanish means "to rest," and it is here that I have come home to myself ready to go out to the world with an even stronger voice championing the new paradigm. I realized after the third time that my soul started down that slippery slope of the brain unwinding due to the chemistry. I needed to return to the scene of my crime against myself to change the pattern of being homeless. I had not ever accepted the diagnosis nor integrated the shame that I did it to myself by not listening. We pay for our mistakes, and I was making sure I punished myself. The sad part is it punished others around me too.

Living Life At-Large ended after I got it I had to go back to the scene of my crime against myself. What forced me to change my behavior was once again, listening to someone else tell me how to heal myself against my intuition. If we want the conditions of our lives to change, we have to change our behavior. I was still running away from what had happened in San Diego.

I was seeing a powerful energy healer whom I love deeply still. However, they challenged me to get off the drugs that were keeping my chemistry balanced. I wanted to please them, so I did. It began to happen again—not eating, not sleeping, not being able to figure out what to wear and the spinning energy I could feel in my brain. However, this time was different. The third time was the charm! I got pissed off, royally! I was NOT going there again. So I changed my pattern and committed to a place where I did not want to be but needed to be, to get free. I got back on the drugs and pulled a geographic.

When I returned to San Diego in June of 2015, once again, I was inspired to finish *Energy in Motion*. I contacted more of my clients from decades past for testimonials, focused on work, began to rebuild my business in earnest, and faced my anger to heal myself. David Kennedy sent an offering as a testimonial instead of the road trip story. Of our numerous sessions together, he had chosen the road trip story because it was a pivot point on his path toward his wholeness. Both stories found themselves here in this chapter because it is where they belong. They are about coming home to our self.

It was during our last conversation that you stated, "sometimes you have to return to the scene of the crime." You actually said it twice, and I took that tidbit in, but as is often the case, there's an incubation period, and it was a couple/ few months later that those words you spoke resonated again and struck the 'Aha!' bell within me. More than one time your words to me have done that, and it been an enduring draw between us. I'm not privy to the details of your San Diego professional craft and livelihood, and your reasons for returning there; I can only speak to my homecoming of sorts back here at the lake on the East coast. It's been seventeen years already since I returned to the scene of my original wounding, and at the time it was the last place on Earth I would have chosen to inhabit. But as they say, the sound that you hear while busy making plans is that of God's laugh-

*ter. After our last conversation, I realized that my return here
was essential for my further healing and completion—very
much a cyclic process of unconscious redemption, as odd as
that sounds. Your words to me Sally brought forth and into
the light the understanding that David has completed all
his reasons for being back at the lake, and is, therefore, free
to move on anywhere at all—or simply stay put for awhile
longer, at peace with one's self and all one's relations.*

After his personal vision quest to New Mexico, David's intuition
sent him back east again to his childhood home. Sometimes we have
to go where we least desire and expect to learn the lessons of love
that are appropriate for that chapter of our life. Within nine months
of returning to my crime scene—the last place on earth that I would
have chosen to inhabit—I was living on a beautiful property that I
sold to my friends. We are living together because it serves all of us
to have a home that is welcoming and a retreat. Though I still live
'rent-free,' it is without a doubt my home and my possessions are once
again are liberated from storage after six years.

By choosing to say 'yes' to the invitation, I have healed more of my
story around shame. It is o.k. for me to have a home, live in comfort,
and be the art of love come alive. We are vulnerable to this world,
and it is love that keeps us safe. It is also true it is not forever for me
to have this address as my home. I am still on my journey forward
working on my soul's life priorities. My man and family are still before
me, and I am on my way there. I will arrive to that chapter when I
am truly ready. I am not attached to arriving—to love, safety, healthy,
recovery—somewhere in the future. I am at home within myself to
the best of my ability, today.

Another reinforcement for me that life is the journey came by doing
soulwork sessions with my clients no matter what my immediate
personal circumstances were. During all those years without external
stability, I was still doing what ever work I could—spiritual teaching, weddings, managing a financial company's marketing, coaching

and assisting my small business clients to promote themselves, and volunteer work with non-profits. In fact I found being able to make a powerful, beneficial and supportive difference in others lives even in our own darkest moments is possible. *Even in pain* we can still be in service to others. Helping someone else often is the best way to get out of our own way.

This lifetime so has flown by with amazing grace and tremendous grief. My philosophy and tagline have been unchanged since starting my healing practice. I must continue to walk the integrity of my talk. By sharing the survival skills I have learned, it will impart survival skills to help us all as we move into the unseen future for us all. Brene Brown became an Internet sensation with her TED talk on vulnerability given in June of 2010. This talk has had 29,171,438 Total views million at the time of this writing in April of 2017. There is a reason that we are drawn to this commonality of sensitivity. The Human Condition includes the capacity to be wounded and to be healed physically, emotionally, mentally or spiritually. It is not for sympathy I share my story. It is the empowerment and raw courage of the Truth that has the power to set me free and inspire you to do the same; then we are all free.

To be another example of living humbly reminds me that I am the change I want to see in the post-technological acculturated world. The external value system of bigger, better, more, glutton, greed, are not virtues that precipitate what is authentic and true. We are all the light of love, and there is something bigger unfolding. To define ourselves by what we have or what we do does not necessitate a peaceful world. This value system perpetuates hierarchy in how each soul performs in the theater of our waking dream. When we change the soul story of others being more important or valuable to us all, we can write a new story in the zeitgeist.

We are all living life at-large metaphorically. If all the material world is transitory, let us turn our attention to what is not, the light within. Let us look for the light in others. Can we see it in the eyes of everyone we come into contact with? Can we see it in the wind, the

clouds, the music, the bees, the trees, the lakes, the snow, the computers, the art, the movies, the cell phones, the governments, the books,
the bears, the beach? For God/dess the Great Mystery is everywhere,
always. We do not have to be humbled by forces greater than human's
inhumanity to each other, the power of the dollar, and our individual
egos. We can embrace those forces and live free to Be. We decide what
we value. It is an inside job. My hope is that this chapter's practicum
will help you be more love in the world. My prayer is that we learn to
value ourselves and learn to love our self no matter what. When we
do, we have the capacity to love others and the world no matter what.
Imagine that!

Chapter 21 Practicum

- ⌑ Find something nature has created and appreciate it with awe praising silently or out loud, so the energy is given back to the earth.

- ⌑ Find something that a person has created and celebrate their creation with awe. The energy of honor will come back to them somehow. Share it on social media if you can to keep moving its awe in the world. Try to thank them personally or publicly as compliments are most effective if they are shared.

- ⌑ Bring something into being that has not been before. Create some-thing yourself from your passions and interests.

- ⌑ Tell people you love them and mean it!

- ⌑ NOTE: Additional insight to these exercises—there is no right way to do or create these tasks accept hear with your heart and act accord-ingly. These daily personal rituals are shared to help you come home to love, to yourself, and to share that love with the world.

Chapter 22

The Thing Called Love

So what is this thing called love? Love is the cosmic glue. To be in love is to transcend separation and to be in unity. We out of habit or conditioning limit the definition to and attachment to a special intimate relationship, family and friends, and often, idea, fantasy, hope, place or expression of awe. I believe we can be in love as a constant state of being. Love is not a destination. It is the way.

One sunny spring day I was in Union Square in San Francisco meeting someone I was hoping to collaborate on a project with. It was a beautiful day with flowers, people, and magic in the air. We were approached several times by homeless men for donations. One of the men asked us, "Are you in love?" Though we had just met for the first time not 30 minutes before, immediately both of us turned to look at each other. We grinned like Cheshire cats, turned back to him, and said in unison, "Yes! Of course, we are!" So we were promptly serenaded with a R & B love song. How fun to savor the magical feeling of together making a memory that would forever bind our souls. We both were in love with life itself, our individual selves, and honestly with each other for the contributions we both make to bring more love to the world. This is how it can be for us all, all the time. This is heaven on earth.

Real love has the quality of freedom, not attachment, and reverence for that connection. True love is the opportunity for the highest spiritual teaching. When we commit to another human being to be in the intimacy of partnership, the dynamics change. We take on the journey of love that is one of the most profound paths to Divine consciousness or All-that-is. Because we are perpetual motion machines of consciousness, we have to fall in-love every day, again and again. It is like healing or recovery, being in a committed love relationship is not a place. True love is a promise. It is the way.

To be in love is to be in the recognition of the God presence of our self or of another. This state comes through our interactions and ourself actions with the world. If we have chosen an abusive family, friends, or partnership, we are learning through the negative polarity. In the absence of the love, is its presence of what we long for and know can be present. There was a reason our soul were attracted to these other souls. We can experience love through forgiveness, and we do not need to negate that though pain may have been present, we still loved them anyway.

Respecting the "in love" state of being, there are, however, other mechanisms at work that draw us into the experience. We each are universes with patterns that we reflect into the world. Those patterns bounce off of other universes, and sometimes it is a "hit, " and sometimes it is a "miss." During a healing massage with my friend Brian Silva years before we walked into my brain surgery together, I was talking about my current infatuation. Brian's comment was very simple, profound, and cut right through my denial about my current "dream date." He said laughingly, *It sounds like you have matching luggage!*

Our personal emotional "baggage" are the unconscious patterns that help create the chemistry that we feel toward a potential partner.

The karma with chemistry will unfold with the lessons that we have attracted to us to learn from on our spiritual journey. The energetic exchange is not just an instinctual biological urge to merge. These energies are the belief systems, soul recognition, and the potential for learning from each other that is present. We created and manifested this connection conduit of chemistry out of our presence energetically responding to the other.

In another chapter, I emphasized that we chose our partners. In Harville Henrick's book *Keeping the Love You Find*, he said that we are subject to these energetic patterns and therefore, cannot deny them. He is absolutely right. Our belief systems are how we create our lives, so there is a sense that we are powerless to those belief systems. But when we awake to them, take responsibility for them, we have the power to change those beliefs. We also possess the capacity to transform. We can own our power to reprogram the belief systems to then actualize a different experience. We can change, learn new ways, and move us out of the patterns that do not make us happy.

This psychological and energetic information is important to consider when talking about soul mates. In my experience of decades of helping couples in their relationships, there is no randomness to healing stories they find themselves. Individuals come into human form to be in relationships with another or many, particular souls. Our souls have lessons to learn with each other. We have specific work to accomplish together. We also know each other from past lives. Destiny brings us inevitably together. These relationships and marriages are not necessarily happily-ever-after stories.

Souls are incarnating with a particular agenda, reflected in the patterns we came with from past lives, cultural messages, and the patterns created from our childhood. The way the agenda is manifested is by free will and our choice to participate. God's gift to us is the choice, how we choose then is reflected back to the universe. I do not believe in twin flames, or that there is only one soul in all of the Universe who we are destined to love. My experience is that we do not know how infinite love is. What then is the benefit to give it only one face, one vibration, one radiant stream of eternal light?

My Swiss Fiancé was the perfect soul mate for me in that moment of my life and his. When our relationship began to dissemble, and I had to return to the United States to work, I was already spinning. I felt lost, without direction. The diagnosis of my brain tumor became the focus I was missing. Even though it was a threat to my life, in the reality of the moment, it gave my life purpose. We did love each other, and we still do. It just was not our destiny to be together co-creating our dreams in this life. By doing the work of forgiveness, I was able to open my heart to love again. Though I have yet to commit to a relationship, I have already had three more broken hearts. I will keep breaking mine till it is big enough to hold a sustainable relationship.

In December of 2011, I saw my Swiss Fiancé for the very first time since he took me on his motorcycle to the Zurich airport June 30th, 1998. Our engagement completely ended just three weeks ABS-after brain surgery then became a villain in my story. By 2004, we exchanged a few emails. My pain was beginning to soften and was starting to date again. I learned he had married, had children, and hoped that I could forgive him for the pain of our relationship. When I went to Europe in 2011, I knew that it was time for us to meet face to face. I could not have been more right.

We spent a wonderful afternoon together in Zurich. During that time, I was reminded of the man I fell in love with. He was chivalrous, funny, and talked with such pride and enthusiasm about his family. He had made our dream, the one we talked about together creating—a farm, a family, and a healing practice—all come true without me. At the end of our time together, I asked him what he regretted the most. He looked me right in the eye, and with tears in his, he said, *"All of it. All of the hurt I caused for us both."*

At that moment, I felt vindicated, and I know he did too. I felt released from the villain with his face that lived in my head, and the villain I created of myself for falling in love with him in the first place. When I think of him now, I feel only love between us. I do not want an intimate relationship with him. What I did want was to resolve this pain in my heart. I know it is a part of setting myself free to love again. There was an opportunity for both of us to heal, so we did.

Any couple is comprised of soul mates. We all have karma between us. When we sense the potential mate is The One, they are. They are the one for that moment in time. We are in a co-creative process with God for the future. There are probable realities, which co-exist with destiny. This is similar to the nurture verse nature debate when both human conditions are true. The mating game changes when we add karma. To take a spiritual connection and make it into a legal contract, it changes the energy field created between us. It brings an esoteric agreement and creates a physical life form born in the agreement. True of all contracts. They are spiritual agreements that manifest life into form.

In the state of marriage, we make a public promise to love, comfort and care for one another until death when we then part. The spiritual marriage happens before the physical repeating of the vows, and often the spiritual marriage ends before our bodies cease to function. In the privilege of being an officiant for marriages, I have had first-hand experience with the karmic contracts between souls. Just like our individual lives come with an agenda, so do our marriage contracts.

The third life form that is created when souls marry has its priorities, karmic healing, and agenda to manifest more than just love on earth. When we take something that is esoteric and writes it down, we bring alive form. I can channel the spirit of the life of a marriage. This life does not look like one side of the partnership. It is the responsibility for both sides. Therefore, this life has its story, karmic patterns, and destiny.

Marriage begins in the etheric and spiritual realms of being. Souls come to a place in their personal evolution where a marriage with another will serve their growth. Matched by another soul via destiny and fate brings the opportunity for two people's paths cross. We meet someone either new to us, or we meet again someone whom we have known through school, or work, or play; neither of us is the same person we were before. However, it is free will that determines if we take the chance to play with the chemistry.

The marriage life then comes into our mental awareness. We begin to think about someone. Imagine—I magnetize to action—doing activities, being with this person, talking to them, and how it could unfold. We think, then create opportunities to do what we imagine. We wonder about each other. "What are they doing? Where are they now? Who are they with? When will I see them again?"

As we are in the manifesting, our emotional awareness becomes engaged. We are filled with hope, desire, joy, sorrow, enthusiasm, anger, guilt, and all of the myriad ways that our interactions can create a response. We feel incomplete without their presence in our life story. This feeling is reciprocated. The feeling of wholeness, the ending of the original sin of separateness, is alive and well and living in our consciousness.

This process then becomes physical. We move in and live together. We sleep together. We eat together. We have sex together. We walk our walk together. We negotiate the trials, tribulations, and titillations of life together. We label ourselves such. We are introduced to others as a couple. We fill in forms, share bank accounts, tax returns, and operate in the world as a duo.

Now in our collective experience, the institution of marriage is calling for revolution. More than half of all marriages end in divorce. It would save immense amounts of grief if we evolved our institution of marriage with our understanding of eternal life. Acknowledging and adapting it to the reality of the continuum of life, instead of expecting a marriage to live until our bodies die, but until the death of the soul agreement, we become proactive instead of reactive. Why are we adhering to a standard that is obviously not working, then carrying the shame of failure?

One way to understand the divorce rate is to look at the spiritual function it serves. The life journey is a series of lessons designed to help one know the self and God. So when one enters the sacred union of marriage, they promise to support the life journey of their partner.

When a marriage fails, it is the soul of the one or both of the partners saying they feel complete with the lessons learned with that person and would like to learn in a new way. The statement comes across *"I'm not in love with you anymore."* In other words, *"I don't see God or the Goddess in you anymore."*

It is maybe more appropriate to see marriage as a team sport; the team is created to get accomplished what you could not accomplish alone. This goes for homosexual, transgender, bi-sexual or lesbian commitments. So the team has its individual agenda. I believe that marriage is an entity with a life of its own. The purpose of the entity might be to have children, see the world, learn about one's addictions, found a company, build a house, support someone through a mid-life crisis, or to get us to move to another location that would be best to accomplish our personal agenda. The reasons are unique to the individuals and the karma that brought them together. It might not be the most romantic view of marriage, but it is practical, and, it is real. When the function is complete, many times the marriage ends. It doesn't always stop. The spiritual partners often recommit to the marriage and it, the marriage, evolves.

These thoughts on marriage can bring some solace to those who have come through a divorce. They can also sound trite compared to the ideas of romance, passion, and intimacy. I am not saying being "in love" is not the best reason to partner. Those feelings are how we know what will be for our highest good. We just cannot guarantee those feelings will always last.

By the couple recognizing that they are both responsible for the creation of the intimacy, it can be recreated again and again. It takes devotion, which is the highest commitment on the planet earth. Devotion is the willingness to completely give yourself over to the devoted. This does not mean giving your power. It means giving without measure. It means giving without the need for reward or outcome. If both partners are devoted to each other, there would be no scarcity of love. In the giving, we do receive. When loving another, love comes through us. Thus we are being loved.

Developing a level of non-attachment, even in a marriage, honors the individual journey and our spiritual truth. The most evolved state of human relating is friendship on the planet right now for it provides us with the unconditional love that is the basis for this bond of fellowship. To see each other as "free ends," independent and yet open to sharing space, time and presence. To have friendship in a marriage allows the partnership to evolve as each of the partners grow in their process and with the life of the marriage. It is the best possible way to ensure that the expectation of staying together can be not just endured but enjoyed.

"Until death do us part" is the ideal and it is best to live with the ideal as a goal and as a hope. To find the solutions to unhappiness within a marriage is the best possible scenario for it is the karmic arena for the process. When there are problems in a marriage, is impossible to lay blame on only one of the partners. When we are responsible for our choices and creations, and there are always sources for help when we are in pain. If the hope is not met by experience, we can choose again.

I am not saying that relationships or marriage are disposable. I want to help bring some peace of mind to all of us who have been through relationships that did not work. The negative residues are a part of our individual karma, and the goal of the soul is not to have lingering pain. Remember also the collective belief systems, which emerge out of our individual thoughts. The fear of loving and commitment is becoming the wave that perpetuates separation. We can reverse the tide to unity with our conscious awakening. Love is forever. Marriage comes and goes.

Sexuality is a very easy karmic energy connection to retain. It is important when discussing a marriage that we address fidelity. The highest level of psychic bonding occurs when two people are intimate on a physical, sexual level. Our awareness does not always extend this far. When we enter the state of ecstasy with someone, we open up the universal energy to take us into orgasmic states. The experience of an orgasm is only of total surrender of awareness. The energy exchanged charges the emotional system and creates an opening to each other's "stuff," their emotional baggage. One of the benefits of fidelity is we can then continue to process this in our daily interaction.

Fidelity is also a risk. The risk that we might miss something special, fun, adventurous, or playful. The challenge is to bring these qualities into the sacred bond. Sexual exploration is important in acknowledging our whole being. It is the honoring of self which fidelity offers. To commit in this way to another is one way that we can communicate the value of another emotional universe. For those who do not see sexual activity as emotional, it is just not possible. We live in all four dimensions all of the time.

When we make the marriage commitment, fidelity becomes the opportunity to go further in intimacy than we have yet gone. Picking up other's "stuff" is easy to do. Sexual contact just increases the free exchange of energy. Sexual energy, spiritual energy, and creative energy are the same vibration. They are energy that is the part of God within us. To be intimate is knowing God with some other person. I suggest before following the body's impulse and readiness for sexual contact, we ask our self, *"Do I want this person to touch the God/dess within me?"*

Marriage is now an institution in the culture that must be grounded in the Fourth Dimension for survival. All the aspects, physical, emotional, mental and spiritual are growing through the commitment. This interaction, however, does not always come with clarity. Marriage was necessary to ensure the survival of the family, the community, and the human species. Now the survival of the institution of marriage itself is challenged. We have the opportunity to change our assumptions about its service to the world. Marriages have not gone away as an institution that serves love. The blessed news is they are opening up to all love regardless of the body the soul resides.

When we see that marriage can ensure a greater connection to the divine, that marriage can help us more readily feel the love that is possible. We begin to realize the function of having a true partner. It is spiritual growth to be here on earth, and the purpose of life is to know love. Marriage becomes one of the most effective ways to know this love. For me, I would go as far to say that we learn more about spiritual growth through a committed relationship that we do from reading a book, attending a lecture, and the rituals of organized religion. **In a committed relationship, we have to live love**.

As perpetual motion machines, as a consciousness evolving without end, we must integrate a new understanding of what we are getting into with the pledge of love and commitment to a partner. Often I hear in couple's counseling sessions, *"He is trying to change me!"* or *"Why won't she change?"* Well, it is an illusion to think that we will not change. It is one of the constants of this universe. The challenge is to fall in love again and again as each goes through their transformations.

Marriages are successful when we fall in love every day. Work under the assumption that you must fall in love every day. Never assume that the state of being "in love" is a destination. Also, don't assume that you will not change because of your partner. We change anyway! With or without marriage and partnership, change is the natural state of being. When we love ourselves, it is easier. When we don't love ourselves, we cannot assume that it is our partner's job to give us what we cannot give ourselves. In unconditional love, we give it regardless of the ideas of reciprocity.

The greatest benefit to marriage today is the ability to grow as spiritual partners. To become better human beings by the devotion, we show each other. When our partners ask us to change behaviors that are unkind to ourselves and others, they are acting from their integrity. By our devotion, we must then look at our willingness to make changes for the person that we love. I challenge us to question why we wouldn't want to please our partner? In true love, the desire to please is our empowerment, and thus the empowerment of the relationship.

We are in the process of redefining and understanding the commitment of marriage. The failure of so many marriages has forced this evaluation. The pain of separation reminds us of the pain of separating from God as we come into life on earth. Let us not confuse what we are grieving. Let us not confuse what issues are being healed by the confrontation to be in Truth with our partners. Let us celebrate the willingness to serve in the most profound way of knowing love on this earth. The courage to create marriages that work for our changing world becomes simple when we change the expectation of partners to be best friends.

In the decades of counseling couples, I have found there are four specific qualities that create successful marriages. Without anyone of these items, it is like the life force of the marriage does not thrive. They are: **shared values, shared vision, shared passion, and shared play**. It is these four pillars that create the stability for a life that is without a body, but lives between each partner's hearts, to be fulfilling. Switching metaphors to the vision of a pillar, when two or more of the pillars are not strong, the platform or stage of the theater called marriage, cannot stand strong and stable.

Sharing values is essential as these are the basis of what choices we make on how be create the theater of our lives. Values are how we determine what we do with our time, our resources, and what we are willing to do/take action toward. If it is important, we bring our attention to it. When something is important to both partners, then it creates a platform for shared experiences. Values can be physical, emotional, mental or spiritual but not necessarily on all levels of human being.

Marriage is the consecration of promise to create a life together. This is the **Shared Vision** that can be for the life of the marriage or the lives of the people in the marriage. Marriage is co-creating a dream again on any level physical-a home, a baby, a business, travel; emotional-safety, companionship, friendship, self-worth; mental-personal development, problem-solving, understanding the world, expansion of knowledge interpersonal or intrapersonal; or spiritual as a sense of the meaning of life itself.

Without the chemistry to attract each other in the lower chakras, it is hard to match in the upper chakras. The spark of delight, the intrigue of discovery, and the exploration of the senses allows for again a sacred place to share with another that is special and unique. **Shared Passion** gives the vitality to do the work necessary to build the vision from the shared values. Sexual pleasure is not the only aspect of intimacy that is shared a passion of which I speak. It is the passion for life itself.

The final pillar is **Shared Play**. The joy of life is what allows us to endure the pain of life. The play does not mean the abandonment of responsibility. The play is how we co-create so that it is fun. The play is also those moments when we must step away from the work of life. Bodies, careers, education, healing, commitment to a vision can all be overwhelming in their need for care. The play opens up possibility and possibility is the essence of the Great Mystery, the Abyss, of the Divine. Each of these four pillars holds steady so that each can dance in harmony, weaving the intimacy of their sacred union.

If you are married or in a relationship, you would like to take to another level of commitment and reading this material, ask yourself if you have those four pillars as the foundation of your relationship with your partner. Are they truly your Beloved? Are you love with them? If you are single, perhaps these pillars can be guideposts to know if you are in a relationship that can be a successful marriage.

John Lennon said it best, *"All we need is love."* When we love ourself for the unique, divine, original person we have come to earth to be; we create from that energy instead of from lack and need. Love create like itself in infinite forms. Our growth opportunity is not to limit the design or manifestations on how we can give and receive what we already own. Our job is to be the love we wish to see in the world. Let's do it and see what happens!

Chapter 22 Practicum

☐ Make a list of the four pillars—**Shared Vision, Shared Values, Shared Passion and Shared Play** and define them for you. Ask your partner to do the same. Schedule a Date Night to compare your lists.

☐ If you are dating, use them as inquiry when getting to know the person.

☐ If you are single, remember them when the chemistry sparks and you have those feelings like this might be "The One!"

Conclusion

*T*hroughout this book, I have desired to show how we as human beings can expand our potential, our reality, and our existence as conscious individuals that are a part of a greater working universe. Now is the time on the planet that we can gather our strength and courage to embrace the future in love, with love for love. It is love that is the essence of us all. By uniting in love, we can begin to mend the rifts of illusion found in separation.

The mechanism that will create this new vision of wholeness is first recognizing we are spirits with bodies, not bodies with spirits. How the spirit seeks transformation is through movement and change toward it's greater good. By consciously knowing that every action and thought that we generate do not happen in isolation, then we are responsible for what happens in society. In the law of cause and effect, both positive and negative, we can move beyond the polarity experience into peace.

Each of us is the artist creating with our body, our emotion, our mind and our spirit the world of self. The complexity and simplicity of human existence live in the same breath. Peace is the state of knowing this truth and opening our will to the next moment, the next breath. Surrendering the struggle and embracing the love that is, will let us be reborn into ourselves eternally.

The Bible says in Matthew 5:5, " *the meek shall inherit the earth.*" The meek are not the weak; they are the ultra-sensitive, the empathic, and the ones who live by compassion. It is possible to use the age of technology to create the age of peace. Bringing virtues to technology, instead of greed and power, will bring abundance to all instead of just a few. There is more than enough of everything to share on this planet. It is the management, of the resources that are our problem. There is not lack of material support for life. I see there is a lack of value-based decisions to share those resources.

This desire to hold on, to protect, to not share or create a sustainable economy is fear in its purest form. When we insist on staying in the scarcity, the universe will obligingly prove to us we are right. We keep poverty and deprivation our experience based on our belief. It is time for us to learn how to share again like we did in kindergarten. There is more than enough for everyone so let us stop rewarding those who take more than they need.

Allowing the present to be restricted by the past or the future can keep us from expressing the power of the moment. Creativity lives in the moment. It is. When we are holding on to the way things were or expecting the way things should be, we bring our attention away from what is. Keeping our attention in the present moment brings our living consciousness to the point of creation. Would, should, and could I believe need to be eliminated from our collective vocabulary!

Let us acknowledge we have evolved to a new form of human. We can choose to celebrate our ultra-sensitivity and intuition, practice it, educate and encourage this potential, and use it for our survival. We have the power to revolutionize human experience by an expanded awareness. The choice is ours to engage with the mystery and possibilities of what is perceivable beyond the apparent. By honoring all life, including our own, we share the abundant resources for thriving instead of surviving. Forgiveness will set us all free. By harboring the emotions of the past, we perpetuate the behavior that is detrimental, habitually responding to conditions that were painful for ourselves, others, and our ancestors. It is time to let go of what got us to here, enjoy being here, and open to the infinite journey ahead.

By accepting our reality to include what is esoteric, we bring the light home. Using the tools that I have described in this text, combined with our willingness, we can have the freedom that is possible. What we do with the freedom, only God can know now. For it lies in the future which is under construction. The ultimate plan is not for us to know except that love is the goal, the answer, the question, the way, and the reality base that will give us heaven on earth. Realizing we have eternal life the destination is not so relevant. We have forever to get there so why bother wondering when we will have peace on earth. Abraham Lincoln said, *"The best thing about the future is that it only comes one day at a time."* Embracing this day knowing it and us will never come again is our opportunity to focus on the now. It is where we have a choice to engage with creation. Now at this moment is where the magic of life lives to create miracles for us all.

There is no doubt in my mind that if we continue with the patterns of behavior, and the value and belief systems that are currently accepted, we will destroy not just human life but all life on earth. Would we jump out of a plane without a parachute? The greed, fear, nuclear technology, and narcissism are pushing us out of the plane. Love is our parachute. Please do not see me as a fatalist. I am a realistic idealist. I am an optimistic pessimist. I am a believer that we have a choice. I am a part of a movement, voice, a chorus; we know it is our time not to ask, or expect, for others to change the world. I am living true to the principles I have shared. I am inviting you to do it with me. We are the ones we have waited for.

From the beginning of my conscious knowledge that I was here to be a Spiritual Teacher and Healer, I have never worried about humans destroying the Earth. It is much more realistic we will destroy ourselves. It is totally possible for humanity also to make the planet uninhabitable for any of the species that are now our neighbors and cohabiters. It is hilarious to me that the scientific community considers the human species at the top of the food chain. The scale they use is complexity but is that truly the top? I do not see other life forms capable of opening a hole in the ozone, depleting our source of oxygen-trees by deforestation, nor have the capacity to bomb and obliterate all that has been created. I suggest simplicity at the top instead. Love is simple, peaceful and will endure no matter what.

The earth herself will continue to spin around the sun. This will happen until the ever-expanding Universe begins to implode. Science nor mysticism does not know what, or when, or where, or why, or how that will happen. This possible eventuality does not matter to me anyway. What is my concern is a linear value system for the human condition, is not sustainable. We cannot continue to take, without giving back. It is not natural. We have this information intellectually. The moment is now to get it emotionally. The human condition on earth is tenuous. We have an infinite power at our disposal. We have love. Let's use it now while we can.

We do not know where or when we will meet someone again. "*No man ever steps in the same river twice, for it's not the same river and he's not the same man,*" said Heraclitus, the Greek philosopher around 500 BCE. This human condition has not changed. Recognize that we are flowing with the cosmic forces by the power of our choices. And we will never be here again. We will respond to these choices depending on our relationship to the river. Let us choose wisely and know that our choice does make a difference for we are creating the river. It is not creating us.

Each of us is a part of the greatness of all Being. What gift did you come here to give? Oscar Wilde said, "*Be yourself, everyone else is taken.*" We are here to be our best self. No one else can do that for us. It is our job, period. When we look at the way of earth's creation to this point has manifested, there is not one leaf, tree, forest, snowflake, animal, nor person that is the same as another ... ever! In *The Universe Story* by Thomas Berry and Brian Swimme, my favorite book from my graduate program, they present a creation myth to us with what we know from science. What a beautiful concept, science and art, the theologian and a mathematical cosmologist, together wrote a story that can help us understand our experience of life on earth out of the unity of the mystic and mundane instead of separation.

In their book, Berry and Swimme take us on a journey through all known scientific record and evidence of the evolution of life on earth. There are only three consistencies in all time. Three, yes, only three in, oh about 3.8 billion years! The majority of this text was written before I read the *Universe Story*. Berry and Swimme's work from their expert perspectives, substantiate what I believe. These consistencies are mirrored in my thesis on the human dance of eternity.

What these brilliant men presented as hard scientific fact, through the lens of the simple, relatable language of the story, collaborated what I know to be true. My truth is decades of evidence knowing people from the inside out. I have witnessed and experienced as a healer true miracles that follow Berry and Swimme's findings:

1. Change it is guaranteed.

2. Everything that is created, has the knowledge of why it is created within itself. The intention is already there.

3. The potential lies within us, not external to us to create heaven on earth. Autopoiesis is the term they use to explain that every level of creation, from subatomic quarks to macrocosmic star systems, can organize itself. My example to help clients understand this principle is that a cloud knows how to gather itself to be a cloud, and to rain when it is too full of water. There is not a switch external to the cloud to do this. It just knows it is time and rains.

When we integrate Berry and Swimme into the wisdom of energy in motion, the parallels are apparent. We already know why we exist. Not only do we know, not one of us is here to exist exactly like any another person. The ability for us to organize the management of the resources and building blocks of life is already within humanity. There is hope, intention, and vision for a better world within us all. It is that bright spark of light that is the essence of our soul and the source of God within us. When that light goes out of the body, it is the body that dies, not that light. That light cannot dim, but it can recreate itself again, and again. That light is love.

Each of us on the planet Earth can experience deep emotional pain. I hope my perspective on why and what we can do about it will revolutionize your experience. The time is now for us to handle our pain responsibly. We as individuals are what are creating the collective experience. Our emotions are the key to peace, which is beyond the state of feeling. Peace is a way of being.

When we look at the world today and think of future generations, we must question what we are creating which they will inherit. We see very real, very inhuman, and moral problems. We can also see the converse of the negative in compassionate care, the rise of mindfulness and spiritual growth, and the desire for many to rise to the challenge of creating change for us all. With the advent of the Internet and electronic technology connecting all of us in real time, the global consciousness is now, not later.

Changing the way we relate to one another effectively as individuals, and as world cultures are necessary in the creation of a better world. Not only is it vital to our existence as a species on the planet, but vital to every other life form as well. The collection of stories and ideas shared throughout the book were meant to stimulate thought to encourage us to question our beliefs and to move us out of passivity into the active creation of a peace filled world for us all. We deserve it and have the power to make it real, not just a hope or vision or dream or goal.

To image a peace filled world is possible, but I believe beyond our capabilities at this point without a shift in human evolution; for the world that could be created is without many of the attributes that are a part of our shared assumed reality. We must evolve into a new human for us to be in a new experience of this world. What would be new is proactively creating from love rather than reacting to the world from fear. From this consciousness, of reality based in, and created from, love, a new sensational experience will be the norm. It is only through a new value system, can a new paradigm be born.

The human condition seeks peace even if we do not fully understand it, or how to create it. The assumption is that peace is an experience contrary to war, conflict, stress, fear, poverty, anger, and separation. I believe it is beyond duality. I sense that we are ignorant of what a peaceful world is, and what it looks like. The possibilities of a utopian human world experience cannot be seen through the paradigm that most of the human species take as truth. We are immersed physically, emotionally, mentally and spiritually in the paradigm of good and evil. It is time to let it go.

It may seem simplistic. It is. The new way of being the harmony of control and chaos, the east and the west, the good and the bad, men and women, imprisonment and freedom, and anyway we split our reality in half. It is the fusion of duality into one path that is all paths, which will become the identified truth. Love, experienced by the unity of consciousness is the path to the creation of experiencing heaven on Earth.

Energy in Motion is written as a testament to a growing awareness of the Universal Mind. The structure, the principles outlined, and well over half of the text in this book was written between 1993 and 1995. At that time I was inspired to write down what I was teaching to my clients and students. I wanted to chronicle some of the magical and miraculous experiences of my clients and myself. I am so glad I did as they are even more relevant today. Each of these people, teachings, experiences and the steps I have walked to this moment have created the voice of faith and conviction with which I write.

This book is meant to challenge the reader to question my words, think about what I say, and wonder about all of our potentials. This book is meant to challenge fundamental belief systems and concepts of what you assume to be true. I could be absolutely wrong with what I propose as theory. However, there is no option to deny what is my experience and interpretation of those experiences. You cannot also deny what is true for my clients who willingly shared their stories here. In turn, I cannot deny your experiences. I invite us to listen with our hearts, and not our heads, for reality lies somewhere in between us and everyone else. Not one of us can exist without the other, and that is the miracle.

Respect for all life begins with respecting our own. We are a magical, incredible, cosmic gift that will never manifest in this form again. We are all a part of a divine plan that includes not knowing the details, nor the destination of that plan. The Lakota Indian language the word that is most close to translating as "God" is Wakan Tanka or "Great Mystery, " and so it is. We can though embrace this Mystery even if we do not understand it to co-create a peace-filled place to call home. Trust of the Great Mystery and our relationship to it allows us to be in peace.

We can celebrate moving into the trust of ourselves, the trust of the Great Mystery. I believe as we heal ourselves, we heal the world. As we tend to our pain, it is easier for others to deal with theirs. There is an unconscious permission that happens when we witness another waking up or becoming more aware. The medium of compassion that creates this to happen is unconditional love. Love is our original source, and, it is to love that we must return for our survival. I am referring to the living consciousness that is the source of all. God is love no matter what religion we practice.

The principles to form the bridge of love into a more compassionate, balanced, and joy-filled world are not new to humanity. What is new is the awareness that we are the creators of experience and the powerful masters of our destiny. Each of us is responsible for all of us and our creations, our communities, our children, our dreams, our challenges, our healing, our relationships, and our attitudes toward life. In unity, there is no separation. There is no one to blame for any ill. We are all creators of pain and therefore have the power to heal it too.

We are not victims to change we must change, to survive. Evolution of our bodies has not magically stopped because we have become conscious of ourselves. The growth of technology and science has been the determining measurement to human progress. Evolution can also embrace awareness as its tangible gauge of growth. Here lies the simple truth: We must adapt to the expanded perceptions of consciousness and live the value of our spirituality, to survive.

The definition of evolution is the capacity to adapt for survival. We already possess the potential to bring consciousness to the inevitable change and it is our destiny to use it. History shows us that landforms, cultures, languages, technology, fads, and species come and go. Humans are not exempt from this process of creation on Earth. Just because we are self-aware, does not give us a ticket or hall pass or a promise of resistance to evolutionary change. It never stops. The 'it' here does not just change it **transforms**. Why do we think that safety is found when stability is present? Why do we aspire homeostasis when it is not real? Why is conformity what we wage war to create? The answers to these questions begin to awaken new possibilities from which peace can be created for us all.

In the first section, *Evolution—Intuition in Everyday Life*, I discussed the power of our intuition as the way human beings can be successful as an evolving species. I believe it is the power of our sensitivity, not our force, which is the key to the next leap of experience for humans on earth. I described various kinds of sensitivity and how it manifests. I gave examples from my life, and from those of my clients, to illustrate my interpretation of the power of intuition. It is a power that every human possesses. It is not a learned intellectual endeavor but our instinct and animal nature. Here the wisdom is by celebrating that we are animals, instead of separating us from every other life form on earth, we heal the myth that we are ever alone. Remember I said: *all pain begins with separation*. The more we heal this illusion, the more love we will each make feel, have and will create from, instead of from pain.

The next section, *Revolution—Perceiving Beyond the Apparent*, I shared astounding ways that eternal spirit of consciousness manifests. All life forms originate from the Great Mystery or God. We are arrogant to think that human beings are the most evolved species on Earth. The revolution I am speaking of is not between factions of people with different values. The revolution is ending the war of separation of ourselves from God, ourselves from all life forms, but even more, ourselves from Eternal Life without forms. I talked about Spirit Guides and their teachings about life on earth. Channeling, to be a medium or pathway of communication, is one tool that is valuable. We all have the power, as it is where we begin, to touch the Divine. To fine tune and exercise our perceptions, we benefit in multiple ways. I hoped to inspire us to look beyond the apparent and open up the awareness of our innate connection to the Divine in all, which again ends the origin of all pain, separation. In sharing stories of the dialogue between the Great Mystery, Spirit Guides, other living species, and people I illustrated how practical an expanded awareness could help with the mundane. The revolution of awareness is not just mystical it is practical!

In the last section, we addressed *The Human Condition—Healing the Fourth Dimension* from the perspective of the natural order of the Universe, recycling. I see as a path of co-creation from an eternal perspective of human existence on earth. In The Human Condition—Healing the Fourth Dimension, I offered a modern definition of karma, how I perceive the Fourth Dimension, a process of how to actually forgive ourselves and others to be free from emotional pain, and examples of how consciousness of our eternal life can help us in the present, be present. I also shared how I learned to love myself no matter what.

A Course in Miracles states, "*There is nothing to fear.*" The adage says, "*There is nothing to fear, but fear itself.*" When we move beyond fear, we are free. Freedom allows us to feel our potential and personal power. Self-empowerment is the goal of what I offer as the journey for all of us. Freedom is innate in the essence of each and every life form on earth. Freedom is how we will change the world. Gandhi said, "*We must be the change we wish to see in the world.*" Let us choose to be free. I propose that as we liberate ourselves from limiting beliefs, from expectations of conformity, and from past pain, we will create heaven right here on earth. There is no place to go. We have already arrived.

In conclusion, I leave you hopefully with a desire to dive deep into your soul's legacy and your self-awareness. I hope you are encouraged to learn more about who you are as the absolutely unique, never to be experienced again, soul with a body, on the earth in this 21st century.

I hope you will forgive the transgressions of your life, your past, and forgive others for their transgressions against you. I hope we can collectively forgive our ancestors; for their decisions and values have created the societies that we have inherited. I hope that we actively engage in transforming the human condition so that peace can manifest within us, through us, and among us. I dream that the legacy we leave for our children and their ancestors be a civilization created by the presence of love, instead of by its absence.

We have the power, it is love, to have a peaceful world now. My life has been like no others I know. As high as I have been in joy, is as deep as I have gone in sorrow. The delight in the Great Mystery unfolding always keeps me curious, interested and engaged in co-creation. We are all healers for each other. My 'tagline' since 1986 is *"As we heal ourselves, we heal the world."* My intention was to share my healing journey thus far that it can be inspirational to heal your own. When awakening the love we are, we make the world better for everyone. I do have hope that we will choose wisely. I hope we will step into Fourth Dimensional reality and embrace our unity. We all deserve to live in love, with love, for love. More important though than this entitlement is the knowledge that we possess right now, the power to create it. Let's just do it!

The miracle is life, and I celebrate it all, the good and the bad. I will end these thoughts on *Energy In Motion* with the quote from another wise person who understood we are all on a path to somewhere. This cowgirl and cowboy communicated my truth perfectly. As Dale Evans and Roy Rogers so brilliantly wrote and sang, "Happy trails to you, until we meet again." I have no doubt; we will.

Benediction

We began our journey with a poem channeled in 1992. So until we meet again, here is another poem to serenade you on your way forward. It was wordsmithed for my graduate program October 11, 1999. The assignment was to answer the question *"Who Am I?"* and is my answer given as a farewell to you. I think it is the answer for us all.

Who am I?

I am the stars that shine in the night
I am the moon that recycles the sun's light

I am the wound the wonder the tears and the pain
I am the healing the awe the reward and the rain

I am the prose and the word the tree and the book
I am the breath that brings them to song

I am the love that I have had all along

I am the dream and the movie and the play
I am the courage to face each new day

I am the will and the want and the desire
I am the passion that fuels all fire

I am the sea and it is the sum of me
I am you and the promise of we
I am the love that is that can be

I am the depths and the heights and the center
I am the moment that connects forever

I am the peace and the war and the bridge and the river
I am the receiver and I am the giver

I am stillness and calm and darkness and the advent of ideas
I am the rainbow the sparkle the clouds and the sun
I am your heart and mine that beats as one

I am the who the what the why the how and the when
I am the beginning the middle and the end.

And so it is! And so it shall be done! Amen! Alleluia! Shanti! Right-On! Shalom! Salaam! Namaste! May All Blessings Be!

Appendix I

Sally Aderton's 30-Day Simple Meditation Mantras

Instructions: *Set a time frame and focus your attention on breathing in and out with awareness these simple concepts, affirmations, prayers or mantras. I recommend 20 minutes before getting out of bed. Periodically through the day a 5-minute meditation can help bring peace when in fear, anxious, bored, or any other negative emotion. Also, meditate if you are obsessively thinking of others in an unkind or fearful way-it's not helpful for either of you. Just breathe!*

Mediation Practice Day #1 Mantra
>Breathe in with thought:
>>I am.
>Breathe out with thought:
>>Possibility.

Keep doing it until it shifts to something else or return to it if you drift.

Mediation Practice Day #2 Mantra
>Breathe in with thought:
>>Breathe in peace.
>Breathe out with thought:
>>Breathe out joy.

Keep doing it until it shifts to something else or return to it if you drift.

Mediation Practice Day #3 Mantra

>Breathe in with thought:
>
>>Peace begins with me.
>
>Breathe out with thought:
>
>>Now I am.

Keep doing it until it shifts to something else or return to it if you drift.

Mediation Practice Day #4 Mantra

>Breathe in with thought:
>
>>I am the Light.
>
>Breathe out with thought:
>
>>I illuminate the dark.

Keep doing it until it shifts to something else or return to it if you drift.

Mediation Practice Day #5 Mantra

>Breathe in with thought:
>
>>I am __ name a person you love __.
>
>Breathe out with thought:
>
>>We are love.

Keep doing it until it shifts to something else or return to it if you drift.

Mediation Practice Day #6 Mantra

>Breathe in with thought:
>
>>I am as infinity created me.
>
>Breathe out with thought:
>
>>I am _____.

Example: real, a child of God, unique, perfect, love, creative, a dancer, a Mom

Keep doing it until it shifts to something else or return to it if you drift.

Mediation Practice Day #7 Mantra

Breathe in with thought:

I am Love.

Breathe out with thought:

Love creates _____.

Example: kindness, joy, wisdom, family, friendship, opportunity, me
Keep doing it until it shifts to something else or return to it if you drift.

Mediation Practice Day #8 Mantra

Breathe in with thought:

_____ healing

Example: body, emotion, mind, soul, relationship, financial, heart

Breathe out with thought:

Begins with _____.

Example: choice, now, me, freedom, faith, a decision, courage, action
Keep doing it until it shifts to something else or return to it if you drift.

Mediation Practice Day #9 Mantra

Breathe in with thought:

I embrace _____.

Example: change, courage, faith, forgiveness, love, partnership, honesty

Breathe out with thought:

I release _____.

Example: doubt, judgment, fear, control, chaos, laziness, hopelessness
Keep doing it until it shifts to something else or return to it if you drift.

Mediation Practice Day #10 Mantra

Breathe in with thought:

I am Truth.

Breathe out with thought:

Justice is _____.

Example: real, possible, free, honor, willingness, joy
Keep doing it until it shifts to something else or return to it if you drift.

Mediation Practice Day #11 Mantra

Breathe in with thought:

Today I create _____.

Example: wellness, joy, my future, love, wonder, my dreams

Breathe out with thought:

Thanks be to _____.

Example: Love, The Universe, God, Goddess, The Mystery, All-That-Is
Keep doing it until it shifts to something else or return to it if you drift.

Meditation Practice Day #12 Mantra

Breathe in with thought:

Grace lights _____.

Example: the path, my way, truth, happiness, innovation, peace

Breathe out with thought:

_____ is heaven here.

Example: the path, my way, truth, happiness, innovation, peace
Keep doing it until it shifts to something else or return to it if you drift.

Meditation Practice Day #13 Mantra

Breathe in with thought:

I __ verb __ with __ virtue __.

Example: I run with grace. I drive with peace. I think with humor.

Breathe out with thought:

I create heaven here.

Keep doing it until it shifts to something else or return to it if you drift

Meditation Practice Day #14 Mantra

Breathe in with thought:

Love is __ *noun*___.

Example: Love is a dog. Love is a tree. Love is the sky. Love is my Dad.

Breathe out with thought:

__ *Noun*__ is Love.

Example: A dog is love. A tree is love. The sky is love. Dad is love.

Keep doing it until it shifts to something else or return to it if you drift.

Meditation Practice Day #15 Mantra

Breathe in:

A color of light—Visualize the color, using words only if necessary.

Breathe out:

A rainbow—Visualize the rainbow using words only if necessary.

Keep doing it until it shifts to something else or return to it if you drift.

Meditation Practice Day #16 Mantra

Breathe in:

I am __ *element*__.

Example: earth, water, air, and fire

Breathe out:

We are One.

Keep doing it until it shifts to something else or return to it if you drift.

Meditation Practice Day #17 Mantra

Breathe in:

A smile—Visualize/feel a smile using words only if necessary.

Breathe out:

Love light—Visualize/feel Love light using words only if necessary.

Keep doing it until it shifts to something else or return to it if you drift.

Meditation Practice Day #18 Mantra

    Breathe in:

        I am connected.

    Breathe out:

        Love fuels my way.

Keep doing it until it shifts to something else or return to it if you drift.

Meditation Practice Day #19 Mantra

    Breathe in:

        I embrace _____ *a feeling, virtue, or character trait* _____.

Example: beauty, happy, presence, patience, solvent, satisfied, complete

    Breathe out:

        I am __ *your name* __.

Keep doing it until it shifts to something else or return to it if you drift.

Meditation Practice Day #20 Mantra

    Breathe in:

        An Ocean—Visualize/feel the ocean, use words only if necessary to start.

    Breathe out:

        I flow in Being.

Keep doing it until it shifts to something else or return to it if you drift.

Meditation Practice Day #21 Mantra

    Breathe in:

        Today is holy.

    Breathe out:

        Holy is now.

Keep doing it until it shifts to something else or return to it if you drift.

Meditation Practice Day #22 Mantra

Breathe in:

> I embrace the future.

Breathe out:

> I forgive the past.

Keep doing it until it shifts to something else or return to it if you drift.

Meditation Practice Day #23 Mantra

Breathe in:

> The Land—Visualize/feel a landscape, use words only if necessary to start.

Breathe out:

> I'm grounded in Love.

Keep doing it until it shifts to something else or return to it if you drift.

Meditation Practice Day #24 Mantra

Breathe in:

> When is.

Breathe out:

> Now.

Keep doing it until it shifts to something else or return to it if you drift.

Meditation Practice Day #25 Mantra

Breathe in:

> _____ make(s) me happy.

Example: Dancing, clouds, bling, kisses, snowflakes, kayaks, dolphins, travel

Breathe out:

> Happiness is mine.

Keep doing it until it shifts to something else or return to it if you drift.

Meditation Practice Day #25 Mantra

Breathe in:

The Stars—Visualize the night sky, use words only
if necessary to start.

Breathe out:

I am starshine.

Keep doing it until it shifts to something else or return to it if you drift.

Meditation Practice Day #26 Mantra

Breathe in:

Keep it simple.

Breathe out:

My vision is clear.

Keep doing it until it shifts to something else or return to it if you drift.

Meditation Practice Day #27 Mantra

Breathe in:

I am a Mystery.

Breathe out:

Discovery is my power.

Keep doing it until it shifts to something else or return to it if you drift.

Meditation Practice Day #28 Mantra

Breathe in:

___ A person, place, or thing ___ deserves love.

Example: alcoholics, anger, poverty, the Mississippi, my Mom, the Ozone

Breathe out:

They/it has mine.

Keep doing it until it shifts to something else or return to it if you drift.

Meditation Practice Day #29 Mantra

    Breathe in:

        The Sky—Visualize/feel wind, use words only if necessary to start.

    Breathe out:

        The wind is my friend.

Keep doing it until it shifts to something else or return to it if you drift.

Meditation Practice Day #30 Mantra

    Breathe in:

        I am __ *your name* __.

    Breathe out:

        Love is my way.

Keep doing it until it shifts to something else or return to it if you drift.

Appendix II

Sally Aderton's 5 Steps to Forgiveness Process

The key to peace in our bodies, emotions, minds, and souls is the ability to forgive. The definition of forgiveness is to "give over, let go." The process is surrender. All of us as human beings are taught by our culture that by holding on, we can control our lives, the lives of others, and our creations. The opposite is truth. It is by letting go that we move into faith. Faith allows us to end our separateness and merge with something greater than ourselves.

Life is a co-creation with God. It is by this ability to touch the eternal we can then know peace. Peace abides in the state of balance, grace, and harmony that is love. The basis of all healing is ending separation. By embracing the pain with love we merge and unify ourselves. To heal means to be in balance with the wholeness of love that we truly are.

STEP 1: Ownership

If we do not claim our issues and concerns, we cannot let them go. The definition gives us the power to develop a relationship to the situations that cause pain. The more specific we can be in the definition of a situation, the more clear the healing. If we do not own it, we do not have the control to give it away. In this relationship to our own issues, we do have control! We must own our pain.

STEP 2: Empathy

In order to let go of blame, guilt, regret, anger, or fear we must know the perspective that created separation from ourselves, and whatever we are forgiving. This is true for individuals, aspects of ourselves, groups, and whomever we project the responsibility of moving us out of our personal power and peace. We must see from their eyes the situation to bridge the separation. This ends the illusion of separation and compassion occurs. Write down before you begin this process of empathy 10–12 stepping-stones, turning points, experiences, or conditions that helped evolve the person, situation, or yourself. This will help to see the world through their viewpoint.

STEP 3: Release

Letting go, forgiving, releasing not only the belief but also the product of conflict, emotion, is necessary to re-pattern our behavior. Energy from our spirits, which manifests in form through emotions, creates the response toward experience. The essential nature of energy is movement. Forgiveness is only possible when the energy is released and transformed. The best way to release the energy is by tears. It is the nature stress reducer for the body.

However, any creative action can also help to let the energy go. Talking, writing, painting, drawing, dancing, singing, sweating are all different ways to shift the vibrations that manifest in us as anger, sadness, grief, depression, shame, guilt, regret, blame, and fear. We have to let go in the physical because the energy is in our body. If we do not, we create disease and illness from the repressed feelings

STEP 4: Understanding

We are not victims to any experience in the greater truth. Keeping ourselves, and others, accountable for our actions holds the truth in the process of being able to let go of what inhibits us from being free. Learning and service are the basis for the human condition. Every situation can be reduced to how it helped us learn about love and how it served the greater mysterious Universe. Wisdom comes from being able to understand that everything serves us in some way. Finding out how it serves makes it easier, again, to let go.

STEP 5: Change

The final step in forgiveness is change. We must change our energy, our attitude, our understanding, and our behavior and move on. In the eternal truth, our spirits are energy, which is constantly seeking freedom. Forgiveness allows us to be free. The balance of movement and stillness, therefore healing, is possible when we change. The change must happen physically, emotionally, mentally, and spiritually to be complete. Moving with the circles of dark to light, chaos to control, pain to love, is the circle of life. This is the change of every moment of our living experience. Change and love are the only constant states in the Universe.

Forgiveness brings us into the eternal truth where there is peace for our freedom-seeking spirits. In each moment we must surrender the past for the future. By forgiving ourselves, and those whom we hold accountable, for our pain we can move into infinite possibility. Joy abides in this place of freedom. Let us give others, and our self, liberation so more love comes flooding back in with all the pain we release. Love that we are and that we deserve to be.

*To help learn the **Steps to Forgiveness**, please follow the written script of questions as a guide. I know that we do have the power within to heal our life from anything. Let's just do it!*

STEP 1: Ownership—I am:

_____

_____

_____

_____

STEP 2: Empathy—I feel you:

_____

_____

_____

_____

STEP 3: Release—I let go of:

_____

_____

_____

_____

STEP 4: Understanding—This happened in my life story to teach me:

_____

_____

_____

_____

STEP 5: Change—I now believe:

_____

_____

_____

_____

About the Author

Sally Aderton perspective on healing has come from a life-long pursuit of knowledge, her passion for Creation, the quest for her health and wellness, and staying true to herself to be who she came to the planet to be. Sally received a Bachelor of Science from Northern Illinois University in Anthropology with minors in Sociology and Woman's studies in 1983. She received a Masters of Liberal Arts from Naropa University in Creation Spirituality in 2001. Her thesis, *Forgiveness: A Path to Peace*, was based on over a decade of experience helping clients heal the pain in their lives by a process she designed. Between those degrees, she earned what she jokingly calls her 'PhD in Healing' surviving an Acoustic Neuroma brain tumor.

Sally credits her Methodist minister, James Scorgie as her first spiritual teacher. For her confirmation into the church in 1975, Rev. Scorgie used Microcosm, a self-awareness workshop in a book to teach the class about who they as individuals were in the context of the world. Sally taught her first self-awareness workshop in Chicago at 18-years-old in 1979 at the Annual State Student Council Convention, *You Where it All Begins*. Sally started her business Intuitive Arts & Sciences in 1985. Always she is relentless in the quest for discovering her mystic path.

Sally has counseled and taught worldwide from the beginning of her business. In 1990 she was a guest speaker at The 2nd World Congress of Healers for Peace in Hamilton, New Zealand. Sally's been interviewed on countless radio shows even hosting her own in 1990, *Midnight Magic* on KEST in San Francisco, California. Sally is a Universal Life Church Minister and officiates weddings, baby or home or business blessings, and End of Life Celebrations. Sally's Spiritual Direction Coaching Programs offer an opportunity to do ongoing personal growth work from the inside, out. Sally has been a guest lecturer on consciousness and self-awareness for corporations, organizations, schools and universities including Webster University in Geneva, Switzerland.

In addition to her healing practice, Sally is a Licensed California Realtor. She offers business marketing consulting services helping organizations with authentic creative panache. Sally lives in California, a Mecca for innovation, and is the land that calls her soul home.

Made in the USA
San Bernardino, CA
23 May 2017